THE BRIGAND.

BLANCHE DE BEAULIEU

DON CARLOS.
THE BRIGAND, *Frontispiece*.

THE BRIGAND,

A ROMANCE OF THE REIGN OF DON CARLOS.

TO WHICH IS ADDED

BLANCHE DE BEAULIEU,

A STORY OF THE FRENCH REVOLUTION.

BY

ALEXANDRE DUMAS.

Fredonia Books
Amsterdam, The Netherlands

The Brigand: A Romance of the Reing of Don
Carlos

And:
Blanche de Beaulieu: A Story of the French
Revolution

by
Alexandre Dumas

ISBN: 1-58963-702-X

Reprinted from the 1902 edition

Fredonia Books
Amsterdam, The Netherlands
http://www.fredoniabooks.com

INTRODUCTORY NOTE.

THE BRIGAND.

In the tale before us, now translated for the first time, we are carried back to a period somewhat anterior to that dealt with in any other of the author's historical romances included in this edition. The great Emperor Charles V., whom we have seen in "Ascanio," in the prime of life and the plenitude of power, passing through the dominions of his powerful rival, Francis I., whom he had but lately held in prison in Madrid, — the French king having fallen into his hands after the battle of Pavia, — and whom we have seen again in the "Page of the Duke of Savoy," in the decline of life, laying aside his sceptre and resigning his vast dominions to his son Philip, preparatory to entering upon the life of monastic seclusion and retirement of which our own historian, Prescott, has given us so faithful and vivid a picture, — the same Charles is here presented to us at the outset of his career, when the vast projects which he subsequently went so far toward realizing were just beginning to take shape in his mind. The portrait herein put before us of the man for whom "a long train of fortunate events had opened the way to the inheritance of more extensive dominions than any European monarch since Charlemagne had possessed," is remarkably true to life; and if, as we well may do, we consider him the central character of the narrative, the "Brigand" is fairly entitled to a place in the class of works to which the illustrious romancist owes his greatest fame.

It should be remembered that Philip the Fair had never been King of Arragon, as Ferdinand the Catholic outlived him many years. Upon the death of Isabella, Ferdinand resigned the title of King of Castile, and Philip and Joanna were proclaimed sovereigns of that kingdom; on the death of Philip, Ferdinand became regent of Castile on account of the incapacity of Joanna; and it was not until the death of Ferdinand in 1516 that Charles, then sixteen years of age, became the undisputed heir to both kingdoms: to Arragon by virtue of Ferdinand's will, and to Castile by virtue of the continued incapacity of Joanna, — although, as a matter of form, he was proclaimed king by the Cortes of Castile in conjunction with his mother, it being provided that her name should be placed first in all public acts, and that if she should at any time recover her reason, the sole authority should be vested in her.

The disaffection of the Spanish nobles to their Flemish-born king was the most prominent feature of all the early part of his reign, no less after than before his election to the imperial throne. "Notwithstanding the obsequiousness of the Cortes to

the will of the king," says the historian Robertson,
— speaking of a period immediately subsequent to
Charles's first arrival in Spain and to the death of
Ximenes, who had acted as regent since Ferdinand's death, — " the most violent symptoms of dis-
satisfaction with his government began to break out
in the kingdom. Chièvres had acquired over the
mind of the young monarch the ascendant not only
of a tutor but of a parent. Charles seemed to have
no sentiments but those which his minister inspired, and scarcely uttered a word but what he
put into his mouth. He was constantly surrounded by Flemings; no person got access to him
without their permission, nor was any admitted to
audience but in their presence. As he spoke the
Spanish language very imperfectly, his answers were
always extremely short, and often delivered with
hesitation. From all these circumstances, many of
the Spaniards were led to believe that he was a
prince of a slow and narrow genius. Some pretended
to discover a strong resemblance between him and
his mother, and began to whisper that his capacity
for government would never be far superior to hers;
and though they who had the best opportunity of
judging concerning his character maintained that,
notwithstanding such unpromising appearances, he
possessed a large fund of knowledge as well as of
sagacity, yet all agreed in condemning his partial-
ity toward the Flemings and his attachment to his
favorites as unreasonable and immoderate."

Upon leaving Castile and journeying into Arragon, where he had not thus far been acknowledged

as king, Charles found even more disaffection and opposition, and only after a long hard struggle did he succeed in persuading the Cortes to confer upon him the title of king in conjunction with his mother.

The constant preoccupation of Charles during the interval between the death of the Emperor Maximilian and his receipt of the news of his own election to succeed him, was taken by Victor Hugo as the *motif* of the sublime monologue in the fourth act of "Hernani," supposed to be spoken at the tomb of Charlemagne at Aix-la-Chapelle, and beginning:

> " Charlemagne, pardon ! ces voûtes solitaires
> Ne devraient répéter que paroles austères." [1]

There, as here, we find a parallel drawn between the emperor and the pope : —

> " Quand ils sortent, tous deux égaux, du sanctuaire,
> L'un dans sa pourpre, et l'autre avec son blanc suaire,
> L'univers ébloui contemple avec terreur
> Ces deux moitiés de Dieu, le pape et l'empereur.
> — L'empereur ! l'empereur ! être empereur ! — O rage,
> Ne pas l'être ! et sentir son cœur plein de courage !" [2]

The king was at Barcelona when he was informed of Maximilian's death, — " an event," says Robertson, " which interested him much more than

---

[1] "Forgive me, Charlemagne. These solitary vaults should echo none but words of gravest import."

[2] " When they come forth, equal in majesty, one in his purple robe, the other in his white *sudario*, the dazzled world gazes with awe at these two halves of God, the pope and emperor. The emperor ! the emperor ! oh ! to be emperor ! O God ! to fail ! and yet to feel one's heart aflame with courage !"

the murmurs of the Castilians or the scruples of the Cortes of Catalonia." There, too, — not at Granada, — the intelligence of his election reached him, having been brought in nine days from Frankfort to Barcelona. "He received the account" (of his election), says Robertson, "with the joy natural to a young and aspiring mind on an accession of power and dignity which raised him so far above the other princes of Europe. Then it was that those vast prospects which allured him during his whole administration began to open, and from this era we may date the formation, and are able to trace the gradual progress, of a grand system of enterprising ambition, which renders the history of his reign so worthy of attention."

The madness of Joanna was doubtless due in large measure to the effect upon her of her husband's gallant propensities, but it does not appear that there is any historical foundation for the episode of Queen Topaz and her child, nor that Philip died by poison. He is said to have died of a fever in his twenty-eighth year.

The obstacles that Columbus was obliged to overcome before he succeeded in obtaining the privileges he desired from Ferdinand and Isabella are interestingly sketched anew; and the purely fictitious part of the narrative — the sequence of events from the rupture between the father of Don Inigo and Mercedes and its fortuitous influence upon the prospects of Columbus, the instinctive lack of sympathy between Don Fernand and his putative father and its effect upon Fernand's career, the determina-

tion of Don Carlos to banish brigandage from
Spain, and the controlling influence wielded by the
gypsy — is ingeniously worked out and interwoven
with those portions for which there is historical
warrant.

BLANCHE DE BEAULIEU.

THIS episode of the first uprising in La Vendée, and
incidentally of the Reign of Terror as it existed under the auspices of Carrier at Nantes, has not before
been translated. It is included with other brief
sketches in a volume entitled " Souvenirs d'Antony,"
in the authorized French edition of the works of
Dumas. The present publishers have thought it
well to include it in their series, for two reasons:
first, because of the intense interest and strength
of the story itself; second, because it is closely
connected with the events described in some of the
volumes heretofore published, and is expressly referred to by the author in that connection. In " La
Comtesse de Charny " (vol. iii. page 376 of this edition) he says : —

" Our readers are already aware that this is
an historical work we are writing rather than a
romance. We shall never probably recur again to
this great epoch, to which are related two stories
already published, ' Blanche de Beaulieu ' and the
' Chevalier de Maison-Rouge,' " etc.

There is no nobler and more pathetic figure of
the French revolutionary era than that of young

Marceau, whose republicanism, as Dumas says, was so pure that his name protected his family no less than himself from any shadow of suspicion, and who, at the same time, was absolutely free, not only from participation in but from sympathy with the excesses and horrors which have done so much to blind the most impartial observers to the wonderful results achieved by the French Revolution. He was born at Chartres in 1769, and first enlisted in 1785; he distinguished himself greatly in the Ardennes in 1792, and was made general of division in the following year, when he commanded in La Vendée; he turned defeat into victory at Fleurus in 1794, and took Coblentz in the same year and Königstein in 1796. He was mortally wounded in a reconnoissance at Altenkirchen in Rhenish Prussia, in September, 1796, and died three days later.

The various outbreaks of civil discord in La Vendée and Bretagne throughout the revolutionary period in 1793, 1796, and 1799, have occupied the attention of the greatest of French writers: Victor Hugo in "Ninety-three," Balzac in "The Chouans," and Dumas himself in "The Companions of Jehu" and "The Whites and the Blues." The sketch translated in the following pages describes an episode in the first Vendean war, which might very well have happened at that time and in those regions, under the auspices of the justly execrated Carrier, than whom no more detestable figure has ever soiled the pages of history. It is made doubly interesting by the assignment of the leading rôle to an historical character so justly revered as Marceau, and to the casual appearance of the elder Dumas, for whom his son seems to have had a feeling of profound veneration, surpassing filial affection. The author's memoirs tell with pride and satisfaction of the firm, unyielding stand taken by his father, the general, in opposition to the "representatives of the people," in the same La Vendée, at a period when such opposition was more than likely to lead to the guillotine. His report as to the condition of affairs in the Army of the West was the cause of his transfer to the Army of the Alps at about the time when the action of this story is supposed to take place. The last part of the general's life was darkened by a serious misunderstanding with Berthier, and through him with Napoléon, and when he died, in 1807, he no longer held a commission in the army. His bold stand in behalf of more humane measures in dealing with the Vendean insurgents won for him the name of *Monsieur l'Humanité.* Says the author in his "Mémoires": "Deny my right to the name of Davy de la Pailleterie, if you will, messieurs, but you cannot deny that I am the son of a man who was called *Horatius Cocles* before the enemy and *Monsieur l'Humanité* before the scaffold."

The brief scene at the Odéon, rechristened "Théâtre de la Nation," is one of the most graphic and interesting among the many that we owe to the gifted pen of the author of the "Three Musketeers." Danton and the Dantonists were soon to fall. Danton was guillotined April 15, 1794, and only three months later, on July 28, the Incorruptible himself, the representative on earth of the Supreme Being, and worshipped by Catherine Theot as the Messiah, followed him to the scaffold, and the Reign of Terror was at an end. Whether Robespierre's motives were purely selfish, or whether his ambition was a noble and honorable one, based upon a virtuous, single-hearted desire to deserve well of his country, is a question that can never be settled; but he is the one figure who, more than Marat, Mirabeau, or Danton, represents the French Revolution in the eyes of the vast majority of mankind.

THE BRIGAND

THE BRIGAND

LIST OF CHARACTERS.

Period, 1492-1519.

———◆———

Don Carlos, King of Spain, afterwards Emperor Charles V.

Philip the Fair,
Joanna the Mad, } his father and mother.

Pope Leo X.

Ferdinand, King of Arragon.

Isabella, Queen of Castile.

Beatrice, Marchioness of Moya, her friend.

Christopher Columbus.

Archbishop Don Ferdinand de Talavera.

Don Luis de Saint-Angel,
Don Alonzo de Quintanilla, } partisans of Columbus.

Don Inigo Velasco de Haro, grand justiciary of Andalusia.

Doña Flor, his daughter.

Don Ramiro d'Avila, in love with Doña Flor.

Don Ruiz de Torrillas.

Doña Mercedes, his wife.

Don Fernand, her son, the Salteador (chief of a band of brigands).

Cardinal Adrian, of Utrecht, tutor to
    Don Carlos,
Count of Chièvres, his minister,
Count of Lachan,
Count of Porcian,
Lord of Furnes,
Lord of Beaurain,
Amersdorff,
Lord Duke of Bavaria,
} of the Flemish suite of Don Carlos.

GINESTA, a gypsy, natural daughter of Philip the Fair
TOPAZ, a gypsy queen, her mother.
BEATRICE, Fernand's nurse.
VICENTE, a brigand.
HOST OF THE MOORISH KING INN.
GIL,
AMAPOLA, } his servants.

CONTENTS.

THE BRIGAND.

THE BRIGAND.

—•—

I.

THE SIERRA NEVADA.

AMONG all the mountain chains which traverse Spain in every direction, from Bilbao to Gibraltar and from Alicante to Cape Finisterre, the most poetic, beyond controversy, both by reason of its picturesque aspect and its historic souvenirs, is the Sierra Nevada, which is a continuation of the Sierra de Guaro, being separated from it only by the lovely valley through which flows one of the feeders of the little river Orgiva, which empties into the sea between Almunecar and Motril.

There, even in our day, everything is still Arabian: manners, costumes, names of towns, monuments, landscapes; and that, too, although the Moors abandoned the kingdom of the Almohades two centuries and a half ago.

This region, which came into their hands through the treachery of Count Julian, was the chosen land of the sons of the Prophet. Situated between Africa and Europe, Andalusia is, so to speak, an intermediate country which shares the beauties of the one and the wealth of the other, without their melancholy and rigid features: there is the luxuriant vegetation of the Metidja watered by the cool waters of the Pyrenees; the scorching heat of

1

Tunis and the harsh climate of Russia are alike unknown.   Hail, Andalusia! sister of Sicily, rival of the
Fortunate Islands!

Live, love, and die as joyously as if ye were at Naples,
ye who have the good fortune to dwell in Seville, Granada,
or Malaga!

I have seen at Tunis Moors who showed me the keys
of their houses in Granada.   They inherited them from
their fathers, and expected to bequeath them to their
children.

And if their children ever return to the city of Aben-
el-Hamar, they will find there the street and the house
in which they dwelt, but little changed in the two hundred and forty-four years that have elapsed between 1610
and 1854, except that the wealthy population of five
hundred thousand souls has been reduced to eighty thousand; so that, in all probability, the hereditary key will
open the door either of an empty house or of one of which
their indolent successors have not even taken the trouble
to change the lock.

In truth, nothing Spanish has flourished on that soil,
whose natural products are the palm, the cactus, and the
aloe, — nothing, not even the palace which the devout
Charles V. began to build in order not to inhabit the
abode of the emirs and caliphs, and which, being dominated by the Alhambra, never succeeded, under the
mocking glance of its rival, in rising higher than a single
floor.

Embracing all those marvels of an art and a civilization
which its present inhabitants will never attain, the kingdom of Granada, the last remnant and last example of the
Arab empire in Spain, stretched along the shores of the
Mediterranean, from Tarifa to Almazarron — that is to say,
about a hundred and twenty-five leagues, — and extended

into the interior from Motril to Jaën; that is to say, from thirty-five to forty leagues.

The Sierra de Guaro and the Sierra Nevada cut it about two-thirds of its length.

From the summit of Mulahacen, the highest peak, the eye ranged over the whole territory, from end to end.

To the south the Mediterranean, a vast sheet of blue, stretching from Almunecar to Algiers; to the north the *vega* of Granada, — an immense green carpet stretching from Huelma to the *venta* of Cardeñas.

And, to the east and west, the endless chain of snow-covered peaks, each of which seems like the suddenly frozen wave of an ocean rising in revolt against the sky.

Lastly, upon a lower level, to the right and left of that sea of ice, a double ocean of mountains falling away gradually to hills, covered near the top with powdery lichens, then with reddish heather, then with dark fir-trees, then with green oaks, then with yellowish cork-trees, then with trees of all sorts mingling their different shades of color, but with open spaces between carpeted with low-growing shrubs, the arbutus, mastic, and myrtle.

To-day three roads, one starting from Motril, another from Velez-Malaga, and the third from Malaga, cross the snow-capped Sierra, and lead from the coast to Granada, the first by way of Joyena, the second by Alcaacin, the third by Colmenar.

But at the time when this narrative opens, — that is to say in the early days of June, 1519, — those roads did not exist, or rather were represented only by paths, faintly marked, which the feet of the *arrieros* and their mules alone traversed with insolent security. These paths, rarely perceptible on level ground, wound through gorges and over mountain-tops with alternations of ascent and descent which seemed to be provided for the express purpose of trying the patience of travellers. From time to time the narrow thoroughfare wound about some perpendicular cliff, red and hot like a gigantic Egyptian pylon, and at such times the traveller and his indifferent steed were literally suspended over the chasm into which his frightened eyes gazed. The steeper the path, the hotter the rock became, and the greater the risk that the foot of man or beast would slip on that smooth granite, which the steps of many caravans, by wearing away its asperities, had finally made as polished and slippery as marble.

To be sure, when you had once passed that eagle's nest called the Alhama, the road became less difficult, and descended gradually — assuming that you came from Malaga and were going to Granada — to the valley of Joyena; but in that case, what might be called a physical danger was succeeded by a danger which was none the less present to the imagination because it remained invisible up to the moment when it became imminent: as soon as the two sides of the path became practicable and afforded hiding-places in the thick underbrush, the aforesaid two sides of the path bristled with crosses bearing ominous inscriptions.

Those crosses marked the graves of travellers assassinated by the numerous bands of brigands who, in those days of civil discord, particularly infested the sierras of Cordova and Granada; that is to say, the Sierra Morena and Sierra Nevada.

The inscriptions upon the crosses left no doubt as to the manner of death of those who rested in their shadow. While crossing those same Sierras three centuries after the travellers whom we propose in a few moments to introduce to our readers, we saw crosses similar to those we describe, and we copied these inscriptions from their

fateful cross-bars, — inscriptions ill-calculated to reassure
those who might read them: —

HERE
A TRAVELLER WAS ASSASSINATED.
PRAY GOD FOR HIS SOUL!

HERE
THE SON AND THE FATHER WERE ASSASSINATED.
THEY REST IN THE SAME GRAVE.
GOD HAVE MERCY ON THEIR SOULS!

But the most common inscription is this: —

AQUI MATARON UN HOMBRE.

Which means simply: A man was killed here.

This mortuary hedge, as it were, extended for a league
and a half, or two leagues; that is to say, all the way
across the valley; then the path crossed a little stream
which, skirting the village of Cacin, empties into the
Xenil, and entered the second part of the Sierra. This
second part, it should be said, was much less rough and
difficult of passage than the first. The path wandered
about in a vast forest of pines; but it had left behind
the narrow defiles and perpendicular cliffs. You felt
that you had reached more temperate regions; and after
travelling about a league and a half among the sinuosities
of a wooded mountain, you espied at last a sort of paradise to which you descended down a gentle slope, over a
carpet of turf dotted with the sweet-smelling broom
plant with its yellow flowers and the arbutus with red
berries like strawberries, but with a slightly coarse flavor
that reminds one of the taste of the banana rather than
of the luscious fruit it resembles.

Upon reaching that point in his journey, the pilgrim
might well heave a sigh of satisfaction; for it seemed

that, having got so far, he was delivered thenceforth from the twofold danger he had escaped: of being crushed by rolling over some precipice, and of being assassinated by some ill-disposed brigand.

On the left-hand side of the path, about a fourth of a league away, could be seen a small building, having something of the appearance of an inn and of a fortress, and gleaming white in the sunlight as if its walls were of chalk.

It had a terrace with a crenellated parapet and an oaken door with iron bars and spikes.

Above the door was painted the bust of a man with a swarthy face, black beard, and turbaned head, holding a sceptre in his hand.

This inscription was carved beneath the painting:

El Rey Moro.[1]

Although there was nothing to indicate that this Moorish king, under whose auspices the inn was conducted, was the last sovereign of that race who reigned in Granada, it was none the less evident to every man who was not wholly unversed in the noble art of painting, that the artist intended to represent the son of Zoraya, Abu-Abdallah, surnamed Al-Zaquir, whom Florian took for one of the principal characters in his play of " Gonzalvo of Cordova" under the name of Boabdil.

Our haste to follow the example of all travellers and to put our horse at a gallop in order to reach the inn, has led us to neglect to glance, in passing, at a person, who, although she seems at first sight to be of humble station, is none the less deserving of a particular description.

To be sure, the person in question was hidden by the shade of an old oak and by the inequalities of the ground.

---

[1] The King of the Moors.

She was a girl of some sixteen to eighteen years, who, in certain respects, seemed to belong to some Moorish tribe, although in others she was entitled to claim a place in the great European family; the fruit probably of a union of the two races, she formed an intermediate link which presented a curious commingling of the ardent, magical charm of the woman of the South with the sweet, soft beauty of the virgin of the North. Her hair, which was so intensely black that it had the bluish sheen of the raven's wing, fell about her neck, forming a frame for a face of regular outline and of matchless dignity. Great eyes as blue as periwinkles, shaded by lashes and eyebrows of the color of the hair; a milk-white complexion; lips as red as cherries; teeth to put pearls to shame; a neck whose every undulation was as graceful and supple as the swan's; arms rather long but of perfect shape; a figure as flexible as that of the reed reflected in the lake, or the palm-tree swaying gently in the breeze in the oasis; feet whose diminutive size and perfect form were hidden by no covering, — such were the physical characteristics of the individual to whom we take the liberty to draw the reader's attention.

As for her costume, barbaric in its oddity, it consisted first of a wreath of Virginia creeper taken from the trellis of the little house we have already described, its green leaves and purple flowers harmonizing admirably with her jet black hair. Her neck was embellished with a chain composed of flat rings of the thickness of a gold philip, linked together, and giving forth yellow rays that seemed like tongues of flame. Her dress, of a strange cut, was made of one of the striped silk stuffs with alternate dull and bright stripes, which were then woven in Granada, and are still manufactured in Algiers, Tunis, and Smyrna. The waist was encircled by a Seville girdle with gold fringe, such as is worn in our day by the elegant *majo*, who goes forth to serenade his mistress with his guitar under his arm. If the dress and the belt had been new, they would perhaps have offended the eye with the somewhat too pronounced tones of the brilliant colors that Arabs and Spaniards love; but the wear and tear of long usage had made of the costume a charming *ensemble*, which would have rejoiced the eye of Titian at the time, and, later, would have made Paul Veronese's heart leap for joy.

The strangest thing about the girl — although this anomaly is more common in Spain than elsewhere, and was more common there at the time of which we write than at any other time — the strangest thing about the girl, we repeat, was the contrast between the splendor of her costume and the humble nature of her occupation. Seated on a large stone, at the foot of one of the funereal crosses of which we have spoken, in the shade of an enormous green oak, dabbling her feet in a brook whose gleaming water covered them as with a veil of silver, she was spinning with distaff and spindle.

Close beside her, clinging to the rocks and browsing on the bitter clover, as Virgil hath it, was a goat, a restless adventurous creature, the usual property of him who has nothing.

And, as she turned the spindle with her left hand, drew the thread with her right hand, and looked down at her feet, around which the water bubbled and whispered, the girl sang beneath her breath a sort of popular refrain, which, instead of being the expression of her thoughts, seemed simply to serve as an accompaniment to the voice which murmured at the bottom of her heart, and which no one heard.

From time to time, not to call her to her side, but rather

as if to say a kind word to her, the songstress ceased
singing and working, and called her goat by the Arabian
word which designates her species; and whenever the
goat heard the word *Maza*, she shook her head rebel-
liously, making her little silver bell tinkle, and returned
to her browsing.

These are the words the spinner sang, to a slow,
monotonous air, whose dominant notes we have heard
on the plains of Tangier and in the mountains of
Kabylie.

It was the *romancero* known in Spain as the "Ballad
of King Don Fernand."

> "O Granada, my beloved!
> Thou with the golden girdle,
> Be my wife, be mine forever!
> Take for thy dowry, in Castile,
> Three convents with their cells,
> Three strongholds with their dungeons,
> Three cities with their towers.
>
> "Search, in thy jealous humor,
> This lovely casket, Andalusia,
> Which the Lord hath bestowed on me.
> If in thy fickle mood,
> Giralda doth thy fancy move,
> We will e'en steal Giralda
> From malcontent Seville.
>
> "And what Seville may say,
> And what Castile may say,
> Now, or a hundred years hence,
> It matters not, Granada!
> So let the wind fly hence with it!
> Open thy gates to me, Granada;
> I am King Don Fernand!"

At that moment she raised her head to call her goat; but she had hardly pronounced the word *Maza*, before her voice died away and her eyes became fixed on the most distant point of the road coming from Alhama.

A young man appeared on the horizon, galloping as fast as his Andalusian horse could carry him down the slope of the mountain, intersected by broad · bands of shadow or sunlight according as the trees were many or few.

The girl looked at him for a moment, then returned to her work; and as she continued to spin more absent-mindedly than before, as if, although no longer looking at him, she were listening to his approach, she went on with the fourth stanza of her ballad, — the reply to King Don Fernand.

> "O King Don Fernand, I love thee !
> But — cursed be the day ! —
> I have for master an exacting Moor
> Who holds me in durance,
> A poor, crowned slave,
> Fettered with chains of gold,
> In his tower with the silver keys!"

II.

THE COURIER OF LOVE.

WHILE the spinner was singing this last stanza, the horseman had drawn so near that, by raising her head, she could distinguish his costume and his features.

He was a comely young man of twenty five or six, with a broad-brimmed hat, whose flame-colored plume followed the curve of the crown at first, then parted from it to wave proudly in the air.

Beneath the shadow projected by his hat brim on his face, which was thus in a sort of half-light, could be seen the gleam of two black eyes which it was easy to divine would readily light up with the flame of anger or the fire of love. His straight, perfectly shaped nose surmounted a pair of mustaches slightly curved at the ends, and between them and the beard on the chin could be seen two rows of magnificent teeth, white and sharp as a jackal's.

He was enveloped, in spite of the heat, perhaps because of the heat, in one of those Cordovan cloaks, cut like a South American *poncho*, with a slit in the middle for the head to pass through, which cover the horseman from the shoulders to the toes of his boots. This cloak, of the same flame-color as the plume in the hat, and trimmed with gold embroidery around the outer edge and around the opening at the neck, covered a costume which, if one could judge from the small portion of it that was visible, — that is to say, from the ends of the sleeves and the ribbons on the short-clothes, — was of the greatest elegance.

As for his horse, which he managed like a consummate horseman, he was a beautiful animal, five or six years old, with graceful neck, waving mane, sturdy quarters, tail sweeping the ground, and coat of the priceless shade that the last queen of Castile, Isabella, had brought into fashion; it was a marvellous thing in very truth that, in view of the ardent nature by which both were animated, horse and rider had succeeded in riding over the rough paths we have tried to describe, without being hurled ten times over into the precipices of Alcaacin or Alhama.

A Spanish proverb says that there is a god for drunkards and a goddess for lovers.

Our cavalier had not the appearance of a drunken man; but it must be said that he was as much like a lover as one drop of water is like another.

A fact that rendered that resemblance incontrovertible was that the cavalier passed our young girl without looking at her, and probably without seeing her, his eyes were gazing so intently straight ahead and his heart had so entirely gone from his keeping; and yet certain it is that King Don Carlos himself, virtuous and continent as he was despite his nineteen years, would have ventured to draw rein before her, she was so lovely as she raised her head to look at the handsome traveller and murmured:

"Poor boy! it's a pity!"

Why did the spinner pity the traveller? To what danger, present or prospective, did she allude?

That is something that we shall probably ascertain if we accompany the elegant caballero to the inn of the Moorish King.

To reach that inn, which he seemed in such haste to reach, he had to pass two or three other hollows substantially like that in which the young girl was sitting when he passed without seeing her, or rather without looking at her. In the centre of each of these little valleys, through which the road ran, no more than eight or ten feet wide, cutting through a dense undergrowth of myrtle, mastics, and arbutus, stood two or three crosses, indicating that the proximity of the inn had by no means preserved travellers from the fate which seemed so common that they who passed over the roads on which so many others had perished must have had their hearts protected by that triple steel of which Horace speaks, apropos of the first navigator. As he approached those ill-omened spots, the horseman contented himself by making sure that his sword was still hanging at his side and his pistols at his saddle-bow; and when he had so assured himself with a mechanical rather than anxious movement, he passed the evil place — *el malo sitio*, as they say in Spain — at the same gait and with the same tranquil face.

When he reached the highest point of the road, he stood up in his stirrups to obtain a better view of the inn; then, having seen all he wanted, he drove the spurs into his horse, who, as if the desire to do his rider's bidding had made him incapable of fatigue, plunged down into the little valley as the vessel plunges into the trough of the sea after rising to the crest of a wave.

The scant attention that the traveller paid to the road along which he was riding, and his evident eagerness to reach the inn, probably produced two results.

The first was that he did not notice — lying in ambush as they were in the underbrush on both sides of the road, for a space of a quarter of a league or more, like hunters beating a preserve — a half-score of men flat on the ground and taking great pains to keep alight the matches of their carbines, which also lay on the ground, close beside them. At the sound of the horse's hoofs, these invisible men raised their heads, supported themselves on the left arm and knee, took their smoking carbines in the right hand, and mechanically carried the weapons to their shoulders.

The second result produced was that, when they saw the rapidity with which the horse and rider passed, the men in ambush said to one another in whispers that the horseman, being in all probability expected at the inn, was certain to dismount there, and that it was useless, therefore, to make a great uproar on the highway, which might frighten off some considerable convoy likely to afford more bounteous plunder than they could obtain from a single traveller, however rich and magnificent he might be.

These prostrate men were none other than the purveyors for the roadside graves, upon which, like good Christians, they erected crosses, after having interred the travellers who were imprudent enough to try, at the risk of their lives, to defend their purses, when the excellent brigands saluted them, carbine in hand, with the sacramental phrase which is almost the same in all tongues and among all peoples: "Your money or your life!"

It was to this danger probably, of which she was not unaware, that the young spinner alluded, when, as she watched the handsome traveller pass, she let fall the words, accompanied by a sigh, —

"It's a pity!"

But, as we have seen, the men in ambush, for one reason or another, had given no sign of their presence. But, just as hunters who are beating a wood, to whom we have compared them, rise from their posts when the game has passed, so some of them, first putting out their heads, then their whole bodies, came forth from the

woods behind the traveller and walked toward the inn,
the horse and his rider having meanwhile galloped hastily
into the courtyard.

A *mozuelo* was standing in the yard ready to take the
horse's rein.

"A measure of barley for my horse! a glass of Xeres
for myself! a dinner, the best you can provide, for them
who follow me!"

As the traveller finished this apostrophe, the host appeared at his window and the men from the underbrush
at the gate.

They exchanged a meaning glance which signified, on
the part of the men from the woods, "So we did well
not to stop him?" and, on the part of the host, "You
could n't have done better!"

As the guest, being busily occupied in brushing off the
dust that covered his cloak and boots, had seen nothing
of this double glance, the host said to him:—

"Walk in, my gentleman! Although in the heart of
the mountains, the *posada* of the Moorish King is well
provided, thank God! We have every sort of game in
the larder except the hare, which is an unclean beast:
we have an olla-podrida on the fire, a *gazpacho* that
has been soaking since yesterday; and, if you choose to
wait, one of our friends, a great hunter of that sort of
animals, is on the track of a bear that came down from
the mountain to eat my barley; we shall soon have fresh
bear's meat to offer you."

"We have n't time to wait for the return of your
hunter, though the suggestion is most alluring."

"Then I will do my best, my gentleman."

"Good; and although I am sure that the señora whose
courier I have constituted myself is a veritable goddess,
who lives by inhaling the perfume of flowers and drink-

ing the morning dew, nevertheless prepare the best you
have, and tell me in which room you intend to receive
her."

The host opened a door and showed his guest a large
room with whitewashed walls, white curtains at the
windows, and oaken tables.

"In this room," he said.

"'T is well!" replied the traveller; "pour me a glass
of Xeres, see if my horse has his measure of barley, and
cull me a bouquet of the loveliest flowers in your garden."

"It shall be done," said the host. "How many
covers?"

"Two: one for the father, one for the daughter. The
servants will eat in the kitchen after serving their masters; spare not the Val de Peñas."

"Have no fear, my good sir; when one talks as you
talk, he is sure to be well and promptly served."

And the host, presumably to prove his assertion, left
the room, shouting, —

"Holà, Gil, two covers! Has the horse his barley,
Perez? Amapola, run to the garden and cut all the
flowers you can find!"

"Very good!" murmured the traveller, with a smile of
satisfaction; "now it is my turn."

Thereupon, detaching from the chain about his neck a
little golden ball about as large as a pigeon's egg, of
carved openwork, he opened it, placed it on the table,
went to the kitchen for a hot coal, placed it in the golden
box, and scattered on the coal a pinch of powder, the
fumes of which spread at once through the room, exhal-
ing the sweet, penetrating odor that caresses one's sense
of smell as soon as one enters an Arabian woman's
chamber.

At that moment the host reappeared, holding in one

hand a plate on which was a glass of Xeres, and in the
other a freshly opened bottle; behind him came Gil
with a table-cloth, napkins, and a pile of plates; lastly,
behind Gil, was Amapola, concealed behind an armful of
the brilliant-colored flowers which have no equivalent
in French horticulture, but are so common in Andalusia
that I have been unable even to learn their names.

"Make a bouquet of the best flowers, my girl," said
the cavalier, "and give me the others."

Amapola selected the finest specimens, and asked
when the bouquet was completed, —

"Will that do?"

"Perfectly," said the traveller; "now tie it."

The young girl looked about for a piece of string or
thread.

But the traveller took from his pocket a gold and purple ribbon with which he had apparently provided himself for the purpose, and cut off a piece of it with his
dagger.

Then he gave the ribbon to Amapola, who tied the
bouquet, and, in accordance with the young man's orders, placed it on one of the two plates which Gil had
placed on the principal table.

He then set about scattering the other flowers on the
floor with his own hands, in such way as to make a
flower-strewn path from the courtyard door to the table,
like the path prepared for the Blessed Sacrament on
Corpus Christi Day.

After which he called the host and said, —

"My friend, here is a gold philip for the trouble I
have caused you."

The host bowed.

"Now," continued the young gentleman, "if Don
Inigo Velasco de Haro asks you who ordered his dinner,

you will say that it was a man whose name you do not know. If Doña Flor asks you who strewed these flowers for her, who prepared this bouquet, who burned these essences, you will reply that it was her love courier, Don Ramiro d'Avila."

And, leaping lightly upon his beautiful horse, whose bit the *mozuelo* held, he darted from the courtyard of the inn and continued his journey at a gallop toward Granada.

III.

DON INIGO VELASCO DE HARO.

FROM the position she occupied, at the bottom of one of the hollows we have described, the lovely maiden with the goat was unable to see the young horseman enter the inn or leave it; but she seemed to listen attentively for any sound that might indicate what was taking place there, and several times she raised her beautiful eyes questioningly, as if astonished that the passage of the rich and well-favored youth was followed by no extraordinary occurrence.

The fact was that, not having left her place, and not having heard the dialogue between the traveller and the innkeeper, she naturally knew nothing of the wholly selfish considerations on the part of the frequenters of the inn to which the fair Doña Flor's love courier was indebted for his escape, safe and sound, from their hands.

Meanwhile, and just as Don Ramiro d'Avila, having taken all necessary steps to make sure that the inn of the Moorish King should be worthy to receive Don Inigo Velasco and his daughter, galloped out of the courtyard and rode on toward Granada, the vanguard of the caravan heralded by the gallant quartermaster began to become visible to the gypsy's eyes.

The caravan in question was divided into three distinct parts.

The first — which served as a vanguard and, as we have said, was just coming in sight on the western slope of the little mountain — consisted of a single man, belong-

ing to the domestic household of Don Inigo de Velasco;
but, like the *campieri* in Sicily, who are servants in
times of peace and become soldiers in the hour of peril,
this man was dressed in a half-military, half-livery costume, carried a long shield at his side, and held straight
in the air, like a lance, with the butt resting on his knee,
an arquebus whose lighted match left no question as to
the purpose of the party to defend itself in case it should
be attacked.

The main army, which marched about thirty paces
behind the vanguard, consisted of an old man of sixty to
sixty-five years and a girl of sixteen to eighteen.

Lastly, behind them, at the same distance as the man
who did duty as a scout, came the rearguard, composed
of two servants, with shields at their sides and smoking
arquebuses on their knees.

In all, two masters and three servants.

As the servants are destined to play an unimportant
part in this narrative, whereas, on the other hand, their
master and mistress are to fill the leading rôles, we may
be permitted to pass over Messieurs Nuñez, Camacho,
and Torribio, in order to devote our special attention to
Don Inigo Velasco de Haro and Doña Flor, his daughter.

Don Inigo Velasco was, as we have said, an old man
of some sixty to sixty-five years, although the appellation
" old man " is hardly appropriate perhaps for one who,
although he may be beyond middle age, is still young in
body.

As a matter of fact, his beard, just beginning to turn
gray; his hair, which he wore quite long after the fashion
of Philip the Fair and Ferdinand the Catholic, and which
was hardly touched with the winter's snow, — denoted a
man of from fifty years to fifty-five, at most.

And yet he had the disadvantage, shared by all those

who have had an illustrious youth, of being unable to
conceal his age, because he had, more than once, and at
different periods, left a deep mark on the history of his
country. At thirty years of age, Don Inigo Velasco,
inheritor of one of the most illustrious names and heir of
one of the richest families in Castile, with a thirst for
adventure due to the love aroused in his heart by a young
woman whom he could not marry, — inasmuch as the
father of Doña Mercedes de Mendo (such was the name
of that queen of beauty) was his father's enemy, the two
having sworn eternal hatred to each other, — at thirty
years of age, we say, Don Inigo Velasco, who had had
for his governor Père Marchena, one of the first priests
who, at the risk of assuming an attitude of opposition to
the Holy Scriptures, had been convinced, by the demon-
stration of Christopher Columbus, that the world was
probably round, — Don Inigo Velasco had, from despair
rather than from conviction, adopted the theories and
supported the demands of the Genoese navigator.

We know what that poor man of genius, whom the
least ill-disposed advisers of Ferdinand and Isabella
treated as a visionary and a madman, had to endure at
the court of the Catholic monarchs, when, after he had
unavailingly set forth at Genoa, his native country, the
plan he had conceived of reaching the Empire of Cathay,
mentioned by his predecessor, Marco Polo, by sailing
west; when, after being repulsed by King John II.,
who treacherously and secretly sent a man to attempt
that expedition which he characterized in public as fool-
hardy, he appeared before Ferdinand, King of Arragon,
and Isabella, Queen of Castile, offering to endow Spain,
not with a city, not with a province, not with a kingdom,
but with a world!

Eight years passed in fruitless manœuvring and petitions.

Luckily for the illustrious Genoese — we have already philosophized more than once upon this text so rich in small causes and great results — luckily for the illustrious Genoese, we say, Providence decreed that, at the moment when Christopher Columbus wished to start upon his voyage, at the moment when the Empire of the Caliphs in Spain fell with the fall of its last rampart, the nephew of one of the queen's dearest friends fell madly in love with a girl whom he had no hope of marrying.

We humbly ask love's pardon for ranking it among small causes.

But, small or great, the cause produced a great result.

We have mentioned the cause; now let us tell the result.

The nephew's name we already know; he was Don Inigo Velasco de Haro.

The aunt was Beatrice, Marchioness of Moya.

Now, Queen Isabella had no dearer friend, no closer confidante, than the Marchioness of Moya. We mention that fact by way of memorandum; we shall recur to it anon.

As for Velasco, he had determined to have done with life; and, if he had not been killed ten times over, it was only because death had recoiled before him, as before all resolute hearts. In the wars the Catholic kings had waged against the Moors, he had constantly fought in the front rank: he was at the assault on the fortresses of Illora and Moclin, those two strongholds of the queen city, esteemed of such importance that they were called the eyes of Granada; he was at the siege of Velez when Abdallah attempted to raise the siege and was repulsed with terrible loss; he was at the capture of Gibalfaro, when Ibrahim's city was stormed and given over to pillage; and he was under the walls of Boabdil's capital

when, after they had, as the Spanish said, eaten the pomegranate (*granada*) grain by grain, — that is to say, conquered the kingdom town by town, — the Catholic kings
surrounded the city they were blockading with a new city,
with houses, churches, and ramparts, and called it Santa
Fé, in token of their hopes and of the vow they had
made not to abandon the siege of Granada until Granada
had surrendered.

Granada surrendered November 25, 1491, the year
897 of the Hegira, the 22d day of the moon of Moharrem.

To Columbus, who had been waiting eight years, it
seemed the proper moment to return to the charge; King
Ferdinand and Queen Isabella had finished the work
begun by Pelagius seven centuries before: they had
driven the infidels from Spain.

Columbus urged his expedition, proposing as its principal object the conversion of the infidels of a new world.

To accomplish that object he asked for two caravels, a
hundred men to man them, and three thousand crowns.

Lastly, in addition to the religious purpose, he suggested as a possible material result inexhaustible placers
of gold and mines of priceless diamonds.   What, then,
could prevent the greedy Ferdinand and the pious Isabella from undertaking an enterprise which, both from a
temporal and spiritual standpoint, offered every promise
of a lucky speculation, the existence of this unknown
world being admitted?

We will proceed to tell what it was that prevented
them.

Christopher Columbus, placing the reward upon the
level of the service to be performed, demanded the rank
of admiral of the Spanish fleets, the title of viceroy of all
the countries he might discover, the tenth part of the
profits to be derived from the expedition, and that his

heirs male should inherit the titles and honors to be
accorded him.

These demands seemed the more exorbitant in that
Columbus — although he claimed descent from one of
the most illustrious families of Plaisance, and although
he wrote Queen Isabella that, if she should make him an
admiral, he would not be the first admiral in his family
— Columbus, we say, had failed to produce proofs of his
noble birth, and it was a common rumor at court that he
was simply the son of a poor weaver of Cogoreo or Nervi.

His demands therefore had roused the indignation of
Ferdinand de Talavera, Archbishop of Granada, to whom
Their Catholic Majesties had submitted the project of the
" Genoese pilot," as Christopher Columbus was generally
called at court.

That tenth part of the profits, representing just the
tax that the Church collected under the name of " tithes,"
was the thing that especially wounded the religious sus-
ceptibilities of Don Ferdinand de Talavera.

Poor Columbus was extremely unlucky, for his other
three demands — to be raised to the rank of admiral, to
be made viceroy, and to have that title made hereditary,
as in a royal or princely family — had wounded the pride
of Ferdinand and Isabella, sovereigns at that epoch not
being accustomed to treat a private individual as their
equal, and Columbus, poor and obscure as he was, speaking with as much pride as if he already wore upon his
head the golden crown of Guacanagari or Montezuma.

The result was that after an animated discussion in the
council, where Columbus had but two partisans, Don
Luis de Saint-Angel, collector of the ecclesiastical revenues
of Arragon, and Don Alonzo de Quintanilla, director of
the finances of Castile, the proposition was definitively
rejected, to the great satisfaction of King Ferdinand, the

man of doubt and of material mind, and to the great grief of Isabella, the woman of poesy and faith.

As for Columbus's enemies — and they were numerous at court — they looked upon the decision as irrevocable, and firmly believed that they were rid forever of the absurd dreamer who made all services theretofore rendered seem of little account beside the services he promised to render.

But they had reckoned without Don Inigo Velasco, Count of Haro, and without his aunt Beatrice, Marchioness of Moya.

On the day following that on which the refusal of Their Catholic Majesties was transmitted to Columbus by the Archbishop Don Ferdinand de Talavera, — a refusal of which Don Luis de Saint-Angel and Don Alonzo de Quintanilla had tried to lessen the force, but which had none the less left the poor navigator without hope, — Doña Beatrice entered the queen's oratory, and, in a voice betraying deep emotion, requested an audience for her nephew.

Isabella, amazed at her friend's almost embarrassed manner, gazed at her for a moment; then, in the gentle tone that was habitual with her when she was talking with her chosen friends, she asked, —

" What do you say, my child ? "

" My child " was an affectionate title which the Queen of Castile ordinarily bestowed, but not too lavishly, upon her particular friends.

" I say that my nephew, Don Inigo de Velasco, has the honor of soliciting Your Highness for an audience of leave-taking."

" Don Inigo Velasco ? " repeated Isabella, evidently trying to recall the person in question to her mind; " is not he the young captain who so distinguished himself

during our last war, at the assaults upon Illora and
Moclin, at the siege of Velez, at the capture of Gibalfaro,
and on many other occasions? "

"That is he!" cried Doña Beatrice, overjoyed and
proud that her nephew's name had awakened such memories in the queen's heart; "yes, yes, Your Highness,
that is he!"

"And you say that he is going away?" said Isabella.

"Yes, Your Highness."

"For a long journey?"

"I fear so."

"Will he leave Spain?"

"I think so."

"Oho!"

"He gives as his excuse that there is no longer anything for him to do for Your Majesty's service here."

"And where is he going?"

"I venture to hope," replied Doña Beatrice, "that the
queen will deign to permit him to answer for himself
upon that point."

"'T is well, my child; tell him that he may enter."

And while the Marchioness of Moya, preparing to act
as her nephew's introductress, walked toward the door,
Queen Isabella seated herself, and, rather to keep herself
in countenance than to do any real work, she took up a
banner she was embroidering in honor of the Virgin, to
whose intercession she attributed the fortunate surrender
of Granada, which took place, as is well known, by
capitulation and without bloodshed.

A moment later the door reopened; the young man
entered under the escort of Doña Beatrice, and halted
respectfully, hat in hand, a few steps from Isabella.

IV.

FERDINAND AND ISABELLA.

DON INIGO VELASCO — whom we have just intro-
duced to our readers as a magnificent old man of some
sixty or sixty-five years — was, at the time of the fall
of Granada, a handsome young man of thirty to thirty-
two, with great eyes and long black hair; his pale face
was strongly marked with the tinge of melancholy that
indicates an unhappy love-affair, and consequently is
always a powerful recommendation to a woman, even
though the woman be a queen.

A wound, then scarcely healed, but whose scar had
since vanished from sight in the first wrinkles of old
age, made a red furrow across his brow, and bore witness that he had fought the Moors at close quarters and
face to face, for a scimetar had left that ghastly mark.

The queen, who had often heard him spoken of as a
gallant knight in love and a doughty captain in war,
but who then saw him for the first time, gazed at Don
Inigo with the twofold interest attaching to him, first,
as the nephew of her best friend, and secondly, as a
cavalier who had fought so valiantly for the cause of
his God and his kings.

"You are Don Inigo Velasco?" demanded Isabella,
after a moment of observation, during which profound
silence reigned in the oratory, although a dozen or more
persons were present, seated or standing, near her or at

a distance, according to the degree of familiarity with which they were honored or the rank they held.

"Yes, Your Highness," Don Inigo replied.

"I thought that you were a *rico hombre.*"

"And so I am, Your Highness."

"Why, then, do you not remain covered in our presence?"

"Because my respect for the woman forbids me to exercise the privilege of which the queen deigns to remind me."

Isabella smiled and continued, using the familiar form of address which the kings and queens of Castile are even now accustomed to use with those who in our day are called "grandees of Spain," and who were then called *ricos hombres,* —

"And so, Don Inigo, you propose to travel, my child?"

"Yes, Your Highness," the young man replied.

"Why so?"

Don Inigo was silent.

"It seems to me," continued Isabella, "that there are numerous places at my court well suited to a young man of your years and a conqueror of your merit."

"Your Highness is mistaken in regard to my age," replied Don Inigo, shaking his head sadly; "I am old, madame."

"Old?" exclaimed the queen, in amazement.

"Yes, madame; for one is old, whatever his real age, on the day when he loses his last illusion; and, as to the title of conqueror you are graciously pleased to bestow upon me, as upon another Cid, I should soon lose it, for, thanks to the fall of Granada and the last Moorish king, Abu-Abdallah, you have no more enemies to conquer within your kingdom."

The young man uttered these words in a tone of such profound sadness that the queen looked at him in amazement, and Doña Beatrice, who, doubtless, was aware of her nephew's disappointment in love, wiped away a tear that rolled silently down her cheek.

" Where do you intend to go ? " the queen asked.

" I intend to go to France, Your Highness."

Isabella frowned slightly.

" Pray, has King Charles VIII.," she asked, reverting to the more formal mode of address, " invited you to his nuptials with the heiress of Bretagne, or has he offered you a commission in the army he is raising, so it is said, for the conquest of Italy ? "

" I do not know King Charles VIII., madame," Don Inigo replied; " and I should refuse any offer that he might make me to serve in his armies, for that would certainly involve serving against my beloved queen."

" Why are you going to France, if not in search of a master who will suit you better than we ? "

" I am accompanying thither a friend whom you have driven hence."

" Who is this friend ? "

" Christopher Columbus, madame."

There was a moment's silence, during which there was a barely audible sound, caused by the partial opening of the door of the king's cabinet.

" We have not driven your friend away, Don Inigo, God forbid ! " rejoined Isabella, with a sadness that she could not control; " but our council has declared that the conditions imposed by the Genoese are so exorbitant that it is impossible for us to accept them without failing in what we owe to ourselves and our two crowns. If your friend would have consented to make some concession, Don Inigo, King Ferdinand's good-will, and

the interest which I myself took in it, would have
rendered easy the execution of a project whose ill-success
he owes to himself alone."

Isabella paused, awaiting Don Inigo's reply; but Don
Inigo did not reply.

"Moreover," she continued, "to say nothing of the
fact that the theory of the Genoese accords but ill with
the text of the Holy Scriptures, you know that the
greatest scholars in the kingdom look upon Christopher
Columbus as a visionary."

"It is not like a visionary, Your Highness," replied
Doña Beatrice's nephew, "to renounce his hopes rather
than his dignity.   Columbus is treating for an empire
ten times greater, so he claims, than Spain, and his
demands rise to the level of their subject.   I can
understand that."

"Nephew!" murmured Doña Beatrice.

"Can it be that I have unwittingly failed in respect
to the queen?" asked Don Inigo.   "I should regret it
most profoundly."

"No, my child, no!" said Isabella, hastily.

Then, after a moment's reflection, she continued, —

"So you think that there is something serious, possible, real, behind this pilot's dreams?"

"I am too ignorant to answer Your Highness in the
name of science, madame," said Don Inigo; "but I will
answer in the name of faith: Columbus's deep conviction has convinced me, and just as Your Highness made
a vow not to leave Santa Fé until you had taken Granada,
so I have made a vow not to leave Columbus until he
has set foot on the soil of this unknown world which he
desired to present to Your Highness and which Your
Highness has refused."

"But," said Isabella, affecting to treat the matter

lightly, although the young man's grave words deprived her of the power, if not of the will to do so, — "but since you have such unbounded faith in the learning of the Genoese, and he needs only two caravels, a hundred sailors, and three thousand crowns to carry out his enterprise, why have you not built the two caravels, hired the hundred sailors, and advanced the three thousand crowns from your own fortune, which amounts to three times as much as your friend requires? Under those circumstances, owing nothing to anybody, Columbus might have made himself king and you vice-king of his imaginary kingdom."

"I offered to do it, Your Highness," said Don Inigo, gravely, "not in the hope of so eminent a reward, for I am not ambitious; but Columbus declined my offer."

"Columbus declined the means of realizing a project which he has been following for twenty years, when those means were offered him?" cried Isabella. "Ah, no, no, you cannot make me believe that, my child!"

"It is the truth, none the less, Your Highness," replied Don Inigo, bowing with respect.

"And what reason did he give for declining?"

"He said that he must have the name and patronage of a great king to consecrate such an undertaking, and that, since he was not permitted to attempt it under the flag of Portugal or Spain, he would see if Charles VIII. would not take it under the protection of the three *fleurs-de-lis* of France."

"The Genoese has gone to France? The Genoese has gone to lay his project before Charles VIII.? Are you sure of that, Señor Don Inigo?" demanded Ferdinand of Arragon, suddenly making his appearance and taking part in the conversation, to which he had already been listening for some minutes.

At his unexpected entrance, every one turned with a
slight exclamation, or at least a gesture of surprise.

Don Inigo alone, as if he had heard the noise made
by the door and had guessed who opened it, manifested
nothing but respect, bowing before the king as he had
previously done before the queen.

But, in order, doubtless, to assert his privilege of
remaining covered before the King of Arragon, he
replaced his hat upon his head, removing it again almost immediately as he turned once more to Isabella,
from whom, as his only sovereign, he seemed to await
his dismissal.

But she was trembling with delight to see with what
heat Ferdinand, ordinarily so calm, received the humili-
ating intelligence that Columbus had gone to invoke
the protection of another monarch.

And as Don Inigo made no reply to King Ferdinand's
question, —

"Do you hear what the King of Arragon asks you?"
she said to the young man; "he asks you if it is certainly true that the Genoese has started for France, and
if he has, in good faith, gone to offer his services to
King Charles VIII."

"I left Columbus this morning at the Bara gate,
madame; he was to go along the coast in the hope of
finding at Alicante, Valencia, or Barcelona some means
of transport by sea to Provence."

"And then?" said Ferdinand.

"Then, sire," replied Don Inigo, "I came to ask the
queen's permission to accompany that great man; to set
sail with him and to share his fortunes, good or bad."

"You propose, then, to join him?"

"As soon as I shall have received my gracious sovereign's permission," replied Don Inigo.

"Doubtless he takes his departure crushed by the ill-success of the solicitations he addressed to us?"

"He takes his departure with head erect and tranquil features, Your Highness; for, although regret and disappointment weigh upon his heart, his heart offers a foundation broad enough to support the double burden!"

Ferdinand remained silent for a moment in face of that haughty response; then, passing his hand across his brow, now lined with thought, he murmured with a sigh, —

"I fear that my councillors were too hasty in rejecting this man's propositions. What do you say, madame?"

But, at the first words the king uttered, Isabella had risen.

"Oh, monseñor," she said, walking quickly to his side, with clasped hands, "I bowed to the decision of the council because I thought that that decision emanated from you; but, if I was mistaken, if you still retain some sympathy for the man who inspires such devotion, who arouses such enthusiasm, — why, we must take counsel only of you, your genius, and your grandeur!"

"Do you think, Don Inigo," asked Ferdinand, in a voice that made every word fall upon Isabella's heart like a drop of iced water, — "do you think that Columbus, even assuming that he discovers Cathay and the kingdom of Cipango, will find in that new world spices, aromatic plants, precious stones and gold in sufficient quantity to cover the enormous outlay such an expedition necessitates?"

Isabella felt the perspiration standing upon her forehead; she felt what all poetic hearts feel when a person who is entitled to their love or their respect forgets for

3

a moment to speak in language corresponding with his exalted rank and lofty station.

She had not the courage to reply. Don Inigo replied for her.

"Does Your Highness call the expense of fitting out two caravels with crews amounting to a hundred men, enormous? As for the three thousand crowns, that is a sum which some gentlemen in Your Highness's service have spent more than once in a single night of gaming or dissipation."

"And furthermore," Isabella made haste to add, "if the necessary money for the expedition is the only obstacle, I will furnish that myself."

"You! how so?" demanded Ferdinand.

"Why, from the chest of the treasurer of Castile, I trust," was Isabella's reply; "and, if it does not contain even that trifling sum, I shall be quite prepared to pawn or sell my own jewels rather than see Columbus carry to another king and another nation a project which, if it succeeds, will make the kingdom that has taken Columbus under its protection the richest and most powerful kingdom in the world!"

Ferdinand gave vent to a murmur which expressed neither approbation nor disapprobation; the Marchioness of Moya uttered an admiring exclamation; Don Inigo bent his knee before the queen.

"What are you doing, Don Inigo?" queried Isabella, with a smile.

"I am adoring my sovereign as she deserves to be adored," said the young man, "and I am waiting for her to bid me go and stop Christopher Columbus and bring him back to Santa Fé."

Isabella cast an imploring glance at the King of Arragon.

But the cold, shrewd politician was not the man to allow himself to be carried away, without due reflection, by the outbursts of enthusiasm in which he grudgingly permitted women and young men to indulge, and which, in his view, should always be kept at a respectful distance from the minds of ministers and the hearts of kings.

" Tell this young man to rise, madame," he said, " and do you come with me and discuss this important affair."

Isabella went to the king and took his arm; they did not leave the oratory, but withdrew to the embrasure of a stained-glass window representing the triumph of the Virgin.

The young man extended both hands toward the image of the Madonna.

" O blessed Mother of God," he said, " send down into the king's heart the divine light that crowns thy brow! "

Doubtless Don Inigo's prayer was heard; for he saw Ferdinand's icy mask gradually melt before Isabella's urgent entreaties; he bent his head as if in assent, and said, raising his voice, —

" Very good; let it be as our dear Isabella wishes! "

Every breast, relieved from the pressure of suspense, dilated in a sigh of satisfaction.

" To horse, young man," continued Don Ferdinand, " and go and tell the obstinate Genoese that kings must needs yield, since he will not."

" And so, madame — ? " said Don Inigo, desiring to have the queen's approbation as well as the king's.

" We agree to everything," said Isabella, " and your friend Columbus may return without fear of being con-fronted with fresh difficulties."

"Oh, can it be true, madame; have I heard aright?" cried Don Inigo.

"Here is my hand," said Isabella.

The young man hastily seized that royal hand and respectfully touched it with his lips; then he rushed from the room, crying, —

"My horse! my horse!"

Five minutes later the pavement of the courtyard rang beneath the galloping feet of Don Inigo's horse, but the sound soon died away in the distance.

ISABELLA.

THE BRIGAND, 37.

V.

DOÑA FLOR.

DON INIGO overtook Columbus within ten leagues of Santa Fé, and took him back to the court of Their Catholic Majesties.

The Genoese's mind was overflowing with irritation and suspicion, but the good news Don Inigo had brought him, which he refused to believe, was speedily confirmed by the king and queen with their own mouths.

Thereupon he received all necessary orders, and set out for the seaport of Palos de Moguer, — a village situated at the mouth of the Tinto, near the city of Huelva.

The motive that led Ferdinand to select that port was not, as one might suppose, the fact that it was upon the Atlantic coast, and therefore shortened the voyage, but that the village of Palos, as the result of a judicial decree lately pronounced against it, was required to furnish the king with two fully equipped caravels.

Thus Ferdinand had no other outlay to incur than the three thousand crowns. Let us be just, however, and state that, early in June, Columbus was informed that, at the request of Isabella, his declared patroness, a third vessel had been granted him.

It is true that Ferdinand had learned that Henry VII. of England, yielding to the persistent applications of Bartholomew Columbus, brother to the famous navigator, had offered him all the inducements that had been granted him in Spain.

As for Don Inigo, after accompanying his friend to Palos he returned to Cordova, in pursuance of a letter he had received by special courier, making Columbus promise that he would not leave Spain without him, and that he would send word to him at Cordova of the precise day fixed for his departure.

Columbus owed too much to that faithful friend not to make the required promise. In the course of the month of July, 1492, he sent word to Don Inigo that he should sail on August 3.

On the 2d of August the young man arrived, more depressed, but more determined than ever.

Don Inigo accompanied his friend Columbus through all the perils of that first voyage. He was on deck during the night of October 11 and 12, when the look-out on the "Pinta" cried, "Land ho!" He was the second man to land on the island of San Salvador, in the midst of the astonished natives, who gazed in silence at those strangers arriving from an unknown world: the first was Columbus, who had reserved for himself the honor of planting the standard of Castile on the land he had discovered. He went with him to Cuba and Santo Domingo; returned with him to Spain in March, 1493; set sail with him again in September of the same year, the instances of his aunt as well as those of Queen Isabella and King Ferdinand being powerless to keep him at court; visited in his company the Lesser Antilles, Dominica, Guadeloupe, St. Christopher, and the Windward Islands. He fought with him against the caciques, and against Columbus's rebellious companions, and set sail with him a second time when the accusations of his enemies compelled the illustrious Genoese to leave his viceroyalty in order to return and justify himself before those whom he had made the richest princes in the world. At last, on May 30, 1498, he set out with Columbus on a third voyage; but that time he did not return to Spain with him. On the other side of the ocean he learned of the disgrace of Columbus and his brother Bartholomew, their imprisonment, and finally their death.

In Spain, those persons who still remembered that there existed somewhere in the world a certain Don Inigo Velasco, learned about 1504 or 1505 that he had penetrated into the interior and had been received at the court of a cacique, whose daughter he had married, and that the cacique had given her for her dowry all the gold that the nuptial chamber would hold; then that the father-in-law had died, and that Inigo had declined the crown, which the people of the country had wished him to assume; finally, that his wife too had died, leaving a daughter so lovely that he could think of no other appropriate name for her than that of Doña Flor.

Now, some three years before the epoch at which our narrative opens, a short time after the death of that King Ferdinand who had rewarded Columbus by imprisonment and destitution for the gift he had made him, the report suddenly became current that Don Inigo Velasco had arrived at Malaga with his daughter, upon a vessel ballasted with gold ingots. But Queen Isabella was dead; Doña Beatrice was dead; there was no one left who was interested in Don Inigo, as there was no one in whom he was interested. A single one of his friends, Don Ruiz de Torrillas, came to Malaga to see him. Twenty-five or twenty-six years before, they had served together against the Moors and had taken part together in the capture of that same city of Malaga, where they now met once more. Don Ruiz lived at Granada; he urged Don Inigo to come and make his home in the same city with him; but all his instances were unavailing.

But when, after Ferdinand's death, Cardinal Ximenes, Archbishop of Toledo, was appointed regent, the two-fold reputation, for wealth and probity, that had accompanied Don Inigo in his travels and had returned to Spain with him, led the cardinal, at that time eighty years of age, to request him to join him at Toledo, in order to assist him in affairs of state, and especially in the matter of the relations to be established by the new king, Don Carlos, between Spain and the West Indies.

The welfare of the country was at stake; Don Inigo did not hesitate; he left Malaga with his daughter, went to Toledo, and there, in respect to all matters pertaining to the Spanish dominions over sea, he shared the government with Cardinal Ximenes and Adrian of Utrecht, Don Carlos's former tutor, whom he had sent to Spain in advance of his own coming.

This three-headed regency governed Spain for about a year; then suddenly it became known that Don Carlos had landed at Villa-Viciosa, a small seaport in the Asturias, and was on his way to the convent of Torde-sillas, where, since the death of his father, Philip the Fair,—which took place on Friday, September 25, 1506, — his mother, Joanna, had resided, known in Castilian legend by the name of " Joanna the Mad."

When he heard that news, nothing would induce Don Inigo Velasco to remain at Toledo; and, giving as a pretext for his determination that Don Carlos's arrival in Spain made a council of regency useless, he took leave of his two colleagues, notwithstanding their efforts to detain him, and returned with his daughter to his paradise at Malaga.

He was living there in perfect tranquillity, believing

himself to be safely hidden from all eyes, when, early in June, 1519, a messenger from King Don Carlos made his appearance, announced that the king proposed to visit the cities in the south of Spain, Cordova, Seville, Granada, and invited him to wait upon him at the last-named place.

The same messenger handed him a parchment, sealed with the royal seal, which proved to be nothing less than his appointment to the post of Grand Justiciary.

That appointment, so Don Carlos wrote him with his own hand, was an act of homage rendered by Cardinal Ximenes on his death-bed, and by Adrian of Utrecht, not only to the enlightened mind of Don Inigo Velasco, but to that stern and lofty probity of which no one in Spain denied him the possession.

Regretting his Malaga paradise from the bottom of his heart, Don Inigo Velasco made his preparations for departure; and when the appointed day arrived, he set forth, taking Doña Flor with him, and preceded, although he did not suspect it, by Don Ramiro d'Avila, a passionate worshipper of the beautiful girl, who hoped, thanks to a few stray glances exchanged through the interstices of a blind, that he was not altogether indifferent to her.

He was accompanied also by three servants, posted, as we have said, so that one served as scout and the other two as rearguard.

Indeed, if common report was to be believed, that escort, and even one much more considerable, would not be useless; the road was said to be infested by brigands in whom a new leader, daring to a degree hitherto unheard of even among those daring men, had inspired such insolent audacity within the past year that more than once the leader in question, attended by ten, twelve

or fifteen men, had made incursions, on one side of the
mountains, as far as the gates of Malaga, and on the
other side as far as the gates of Granada.

Whence came this leader? Nobody knew. Who was
he? Nobody could say. His family name and his
Christian name were alike unknown; it had not even
occurred to him to adopt a *nom de guerre*, as that
sort of people often do. He was known simply as *El
Salteador;* that is to say, The Brigand.

All the tales that were told of this mysterious rover
of the high-roads had, as we have seen, influenced in
some degree the precautions taken by Don Inigo; and
when the little party became visible to the young gypsy,
it had all the appearance of travellers in fear of attack
and ready to defend themselves.

Now the reader will perhaps wonder why, in view of
the evil reports that were current concerning the road
across the mountain; why, in view of his love for his
dear Doña Flor, Don Inigo had taken that road rather
than make a détour, and why, having taken it, he had
not provided himself with a more numerous escort.

To these questions we will reply that on two occasions,
not long before that of which we are writing, Don Inigo
and his daughter had crossed the same mountains without meeting with any accident; and, furthermore, it is
an incontestable truth that man becomes accustomed to
danger, and, by dint of being constantly exposed to it,
becomes indifferent to it.

How many perils of every description had Don Inigo
defied in the course of his adventurous life! — perils of
war against the Moors, perils of shipwreck in crossing
the ocean, perils of mutiny on shipboard, perils of assas-
sination amid the savage natives of an unknown continent! Compared with those, what were the perils to

be encountered in the heart of Spain, in that short space of barely twenty leagues that lay between Malaga and Granada?

At those perils, therefore, Don Inigo shrugged his shoulders.

Nevertheless, it was most imprudent in him to venture among such narrow defiles with a treasure of youth and beauty like that which rode at the grand justiciary's right.

The reputation for marvellous loveliness, which had preceded Doña Flor from the new world to the old, had exaggerated nothing. Doña Flor at sixteen — she had just reached that age — would have left far behind the most highflown comparisons that Spanish, or even Arabian poets could have conceived in her regard: in her were combined the brilliancy of the flower and the velvety softness of the fruit, the grace of the mortal and the dignity of the goddess; just as, in the young gypsy, who watched her draw nigh with an expression of artless admiration, one was conscious of the mingling of the Arab and the Spanish races, so, in Doña Flor, one could distinguish the type, not only of two magnificent races, but of all that was purest and noblest in those two races. The child of Mexico and of Spain had the lovely dead-white complexion, the ravishingly beautiful arms, the fascinating hands, the miraculous feet of the Andalusian, with the dark lashes, the velvet eyes, the long flowing hair, the flexible figure of the Indian, daughter of the sun.

Her costume seemed to have been selected expressly to set off the lovely traveller's magnificent outlines and enchanting face. It consisted of a dress of sky-blue silk, dotted with pink and silver, and buttoned from top to bottom with pearls, each of which was worthy a

place in a countess's coronet; the dress marked the
outline of her bust, and the upper part of her arms, like
the Spanish costumes of the beginning of the fourteenth
century; but the sleeves became fuller at the elbow,
and fell away from the arms on each side of the body,
leaving bare, except for waves of Murcia lace, the hands
and forearms, which, having braved the sun of Mexico
with impunity, could safely brave the sun of Spain, but
which had naught to fear from it for the moment, being
concealed in an ample cape of white wool, as fine and
soft as our modern cashmeres, and cut, as to the lower
part, after the style of the Mexican cloak, and as to the
hood, beneath which the girl's face glowed in a warm
half-light, after the style of the Arabian burnous.

Urging on their mules, who tossed their heads constantly under their plumes of scarlet wool, Don Inigo
and Doña Flor came on at a sharp but not precipitate
trot, Doña Flor seeming to be as well used as her father
to journeys across the mountains and to the adventurous
life of the time.

But it was evident that the servant who acted as
scout was less confident than his masters; for, when he
caught sight of the young gypsy, he stopped to question
her, and the others rode up as the prudent domestic was
inquiring if it would be safe for them to halt at the
little inn which they had just lost sight of, having
ridden down into a hollow, but which they had espied
on the horizon as they descended the mountain they had
just left behind them.

When Don Inigo and Doña Flor arrived, the worthy
retainer's hesitation was increased rather than dimin-
ished by the ambiguous and almost mocking replies of
the young gypsy, who had retained her seat and continued to spin while she talked with him, but rose when

she saw his master and mistress approach, laid aside her distaff and spindle, leaped the little brook as a gazelle or a wagtail might have done, and took her stand on the sloping bank beside the road, while her goat, an inquisitive creature, came down from the hill, where she was browsing on the leaves of briars, and ran up and gazed at the equestrians with her great intelligent eyes.

"See what a lovely child, father!" said Doña Flor, stopping the old man and gazing at the girl with the same admiration she herself aroused.

Don Inigo nodded his head approvingly.

"Shall we speak to her, father?" asked Doña Flor.

"Do as you please, my child," said the old man.

"What is your name, my lovely child?" asked Doña Flor.

"The Christians call me Ginesta, and the Moors Aïssé; for I have two names, — one before Mahomet, the other before Jesus Christ."

As she pronounced the blessed name of Our Saviour, the girl crossed herself, thereby proving that she was a Christian.

"We, being good Catholics," said Doña Flor, with a smile, "will call you Ginesta."

"Call me what you please," said the gypsy, "and my name will always seem sweet to me from your lovely mouth, pronounced by your sweet voice."

"Well, well, Flora," said Don Inigo, "the person who had told you that you would find the nymph Flattery in this desert would have been treated by you as a liar, would he not? And yet you see that he would have told the truth!"

"I do not flatter; I admire," said the gypsy.

Doña Flor smiled and blushed at the same time, and, to give a different turn to the conversation, which was becoming embarrassing in its eulogistic artlessness, she asked, —

"What answer did you give to Nuñez, my lovely child?"

"Inquire first what question he asked me."

"Well, what question did he ask you?"

"He questioned me about the road, asking me if the road was safe, asking me if the inn was a good one."

"And you replied?"

"I replied by singing the traveller's song."

"What is the song?"

"Listen."

And the gypsy sang the following stanza from an Andalusian ballad, as the bird sings, — that is to say, without effort, — and to an air which seemed nothing more than a simple modulation of her ordinary voice:

> "If the skies are clear,
>   Take care!
> If the path be sure,
>   Beware!
> May the Virgin with eyes of blue
>   Watch o'er thee!
> Adios, travellers, adios!
> Go, and God's peace be with thee!"

"That is what you said to Nuñez, my dear child," said Doña Flor; "but what have you to say to us?"

"To you, lovely señora," replied the gypsy, "to you I will tell the truth; for you are the first lady from the town who has spoken to me kindly and without contempt."

Thereupon she walked a few steps nearer, and said, placing her right hand on the mule's neck and the fore-finger of her left hand on her lips, —

"Go no farther!"

" What, go no farther ? "

" Turn back ! "

" Girl, are you making sport of us ? " said the old man.

" God is my witness that I give you the advice I would give my own father and sister ! "

" Will you not return to Alhama with two of our servants, my child ? " said Don Inigo.

" And you yourself, father ? "

" I shall continue my journey with the third. The king will be at Granada to-morrow; he has ordered me to be there to-day, and I will not make the king wait for me. "

" And I will go where you go; where you lead, father, I will follow. "

" 'T is well ! Forward, Nuñez. "

And Don Inigo took a purse from his pocket and offered it to the girl.

" There is no purse well filled enough to pay for the advice I give you, señor traveller," she said with a queenly gesture; " so keep your purse: it will be welcome where you are going. "

Thereupon Doña Flor unfastened the clasp at her neck and beckoned to the girl to come nearer.

" Will you accept this ? " she said.

" From whom ? " asked the gypsy, gravely.

" From a friend. "

" Oh, yes. "

And she came nearer, offering Doña Flor her neck and her forehead.

Doña Flor fastened the brooch at the gypsy's neck, and hastily touched the lovely child's brow with her lips, while her father, who was too good a Christian to tolerate such familiarity on his daughter's part with a semi-infidel, was giving a last order to Nuñez.

Nuñez was already thirty yards in advance.

"Let us go!" said Don Inigo.

"I am ready, father," Doña Flor replied.

She resumed her place at the old man's right hand, as he rode forward, waving his hand in farewell to the gypsy, and shouting to his three men, — those in the rear as well as the one in front, —

"Attention, you fellows!"

As for the gypsy, she remained standing where she was, looking after the beautiful girl who had called her her friend, and murmuring in an undertone the refrain of her ballad: —

> "Adios, travellers, adios!
> Go, and God's peace be with thee!"

She followed them thus with her eyes, with evident and increasing disquietude, until they had all disappeared, masters and servants, behind the little eminence that limited her horizon; then, being unable to see them any longer, she leaned forward, listening.

Five minutes passed, during which the gypsy's lips repeated mechanically: —

> "Adios, travellers, adios!
> Go, and God's peace be with thee!"

Suddenly she heard the report of several arquebuses, followed by threatening shouts and cries of pain; then one of the two servants who formed the rearguard appeared on the crest of the hill, bleeding freely from a wound in the shoulder, lying close to his horse's back, and driving his spurs into his sides, and passed the girl like a flash of lightning, crying, —

"Help! help! murder!"

The gypsy stood for a moment as if in uncertainty· then she seemed to resolve upon a decisive step: she ran to her distaff, tied her girdle to one end of it by way of banner, and, rushing toward the mountain, which she ascended so rapidly that the goat could hardly follow her, she bounded from rock to rock to the top of a cliff which overlooked the whole valley, and there, waving her bright-colored scarf, she called three times with all the force of her lungs, —

"Fernand! Fernand! Fernand!"

VI.

THE INTERIOR OF THE MOORISH KING INN.

THOUGH we were to hasten toward the spot where the catastrophe of which we have heard the tumult had taken place, as swiftly as Don Inigo's servant rode away from it; though we were to leap to the summit of the little eminence which overlooks the road, with the agility displayed by the gypsy and her goat in reaching the top of the cliff from which Ginesta was waving her girdle, — we should arrive too late to be present at the catastrophe which had drenched with blood the narrow path leading to the inn.

All that we could see would be the bodies of Nuñez and his horse blocking the path, while Torribio, grievously wounded, crawls toward one of the crosses we have described, and supports himself against it, almost dying.

Don Inigo and his daughter have disappeared within the inn, the door of which has closed upon them and the party of brigands whose prisoners they are.

But we, who, in our quality of novelist, have the power, either, like Mephistopheles, to make walls transparent, or, like Asmodeus, to raise roofs, will not permit anything that takes place within our domain to remain concealed from the eyes of our readers, and, touching with our pen the door of the inn, which will open as before the wand of a magician, we will say to them. " Look! "

The pavement of the courtyard presented, at first glance, traces of the struggle which, having begun in the road outside, had continued within. A trail of blood, which could be followed for more than two hundred yards, passed through the gateway and led to a corner of the wall, where a brigand wounded by the arquebus of one of Don Inigo's men was being cared for by Amapola, the same chambermaid whom we saw bringing flowers to the room prepared for the travellers, and by the *mozuelo* who held the rein of Don Ramiro d'Avila's horse.

Don Inigo's velvet cap and a piece of Doña Flor's white cloak, lying on the steps that led from the yard to the kitchen, indicated that the struggle had been renewed there; that the two travellers had been taken in that direction, and consequently must be sought there.

At the outer door of the inn, which opened on those two steps, began the carpet of flowers strewn by the fair Doña Flor's love courier; but the carpet was trodden under foot, marred by the contact of heavy sandals, by the dust from the cloaks of the combatants, and by some drops of blood, which glistened here and there, on a rose, or a lily, or an anemone, like quivering liquid rubies.

The door between the kitchen and the room in which, by Don Ramiro's forethought, the table had been laid for the two travellers, and in which the odor of the perfumes burned there a moment before could still be detected in the air, — that door was open and the doorway blocked by servants of the inn, who were brigands in disguise, ready to bear aid to the brigands of the road; and through the opening, shrieks, threats, groans, and imprecations poured forth like torrents of wrath.

There it was that the terrible scene was in progress
and would in all probability reach its *dénouement*, — the
scene of which the little gypsy had a horrified premoni-
tion when she advised the two travellers to turn back.

If one could have pushed aside the living barricade
that closed the door, and have broken out a path into
the room, this is the spectacle that would have met his
eyes: —

Don Inigo, lying prostrate on the floor, was still trying to defend himself with the useless stump of a sword,
whose blade, before it was broken, had struck down two
brigands; it was their blood that stained the flowers
strewn on the floor.

Three men could with difficulty hold him, although
one of them had his knee upon his chest and was holding his Catalan knife to his throat.

The other two were searching him, not so much for
the purpose of robbing him, perhaps, as to take away
any concealed weapons that he might have.

Two steps away from him, leaning against the wall
for support, stood Doña Flor, with her hair unbound and
floating, the hood of her cloak in tatters, the priceless
buttons torn from her dress.

It was evident that, while thus laying profane hands
upon the beautiful traveller, they had, for reasons readily
understood, shown more consideration for her than for
the old man.

Doña Flor was, as we have said, gloriously lovely,
and the leader of the band, the hero of this narrative,
the *Salteador*, was reputed to be a man of gallantry,
more terrible, perhaps, under such circumstances than
the most pitiless cruelty would be.

The young girl made a superb picture, her head resting against the white wall, with her magnificent eyes,

which, from beneath their long velvety lids, emitted flashes of wrath and indignation rather than the timid gleam of fear and entreaty.

Her bare white arms were hanging by her side, — in snatching the priceless clasps from her sleeves they had torn the sleeves themselves, — and seemed like bas-reliefs carved by a skilful sculptor on the surface of the wall. Not a word, not a complaint, not a groan, had escaped her from the moment she was seized; the wailing and groaning that filled the air came from the two brigands wounded by Don Inigo's sword.

Doubtless the pure and lovely girl still believed that she was in danger of nothing more than death, and she deemed it unworthy a noble Spanish woman to lament and groan and entreat in face of that danger.

Sure that she could not escape them, and having taken almost everything valuable that she had, the brigands formed a circle about the fair traveller, and eyed her with glances and laughter that would have made her lower her eyes, had not those eyes, open to their fullest extent and lost in space, sought, through the ceiling, the walls, and the firmament, the invisible God to whom alone she, a noble Christian woman, deigned to appeal for help.

Perhaps, too, Doña Flor was thinking of the handsome gallant whom she had noticed, for a year past, prowling about under her chamber window as soon as evening came, and who inundated her balcony with the loveliest flowers in Andalusia during the night.

But, although she was silent, there was, as we have said, a great tumult of shouts and insults and threats about her, and especially about her father.

"Villains!" cried the old man, "kill me, murder me; but I warn you that I met, a league this side of

Alhama, a party of soldiers whose commander I know.
He knows that I am on my way to Granada by command
of King Don Carlos; and when he learns that I have
not arrived there, he will suspect that I have been murdered, and in that case you will not have a man of sixty
and a girl of fifteen to deal with, but a whole company
of soldiers, and we shall see, brigands! we shall see,
bandits! if you are as brave against the king's troops,
man to man, as you are here, twenty to one!"

"Bah!" retorted one of the brigands, "let the king's
troops come. We know them; we saw them pass yesterday; we have a strong underground fortress with subterranean passages leading into the mountains."

"And, after all," interposed another, "who says that
we mean to murder you? If you think that, you are
mistaken. We kill only the poor devils we can get nothing out of; but we take the greatest care of noble lords
like you who can pay a ransom, and we have proved it
by not making the slightest scratch on you, ingrate,
although you fought hard with your sword and wounded
two of us."

At that point a voice as sweet and clear as an angel's
mingled with those coarse and threatening voices. It
was the girl's voice, speaking for the first time.

"Very well!" she said; "if it is only a question of
paying a ransom, it shall be paid. Make it equal to a
prince's ransom, and you shall not fail to receive it."

"By St. James! we reckon on it, my pretty child!
That, you see, is why we would like to have your
worthy father cool down a little. Business is business, deuce take it! — you can settle it by discussion,
but you mix it all up by fighting. And here's your
father still at it, you see!"

In truth, Don Inigo at that moment renewed his

efforts to free himself, and wounded one of the brigands in the face with the stump of his sword, which they had been unable to take from his hand, whose grasp was like that of an iron vice.

"Body of Christ!" shouted the man who held the knife at the old man's throat, "do that once more, and you will have to discuss your ransom with God and not with us, my gentleman!"

"Father!" cried the terrified girl, stepping forward.

"Yes," said one of the brigands, "listen to the pretty young lady; she talks gold, and her mouth is like the Arabian princess's that only opened to let fall a pearl or diamond with every word she said. Don't you be alarmed, my good man; give us your word not to try to escape; give a safe-conduct to our worthy friend the landlord, so that he can go to Malaga without fear of the authorities; there let your steward hand him a thousand, two thousand, three thousand crowns, as your generosity tells you, — we don't tax travellers, — and when the landlord returns with the money you will be free. It is understood, of course, that if he does n't return you will answer for him tooth for tooth, eye for eye, body for body."

"Father, father! pray listen to what these men say," persisted the girl, "and do not endanger your precious existence for a few bags of gold."

"Do you hear, do you hear, Señor Prince? — for you must be a prince, if not a viceroy or a king or an emperor, for this lovely young woman to speak so fluently and nonchalantly of worldly wealth, — do you hear?"

"But while your worthy accomplice the host," said the old man, consenting for the first time to descend to discussion with enemies whom he had hitherto contented hímself with insulting or striking, — "while your worthy accomplice the host goes to find my steward with a letter from me, what will you do with us in this den of thieves?"

"Den of thieves? Oho, Señor Calabazas, do you hear what he calls the Moorish King? A den of thieves! Come here and show this excellent hidalgo his error."

"What will we do with you?" replied another brigand, without giving Don Calabazas time to defend the honor of his inn, — "what will we do with you? That's a very simple question, and we will tell you. In the first place, we will ask you for your word of honor as a gentleman not to try to escape."

"A gentleman doesn't give his word of honor to brigands."

"A gentleman gives his word to God, father," said Doña Flor.

"Just listen once for all to what this pretty child says, for the wisdom of heaven speaks through her mouth."

"Well, when I have given you my word, assuming that I do give it to you, what will you do?"

"Well, in the first place, we won't lose sight of you."

"What!" cried Don Inigo; "on the faith of my word you won't allow me to continue my journey?"

"Oh!" retorted the brigand, "the days have gone by when the Jews of Burgos loaned the Cid a thousand gold marks on a box filled with earth; and instead of doing like the good Israelites, who didn't look into the box until they had paid over the money, we will look into it first."

"Villains!" muttered Don Inigo.

"Father," continued Doña Flor, still trying to calm the old man, — "father, in heaven's name!"

"Well, what will you do in addition to keeping me in sight?"

"We will fasten you to yonder iron ring with a good strong chain."

As he spoke the brigand pointed to a ring set in the wall, evidently placed there for use on such occasions.

"You will chain me like a Moorish slave?"

And at that threat, which aroused all the waves of his pride, he attempted and accomplished a movement, so violent and at the same time so rapid, that he over-turned the brigand who was kneeling on his chest, and rose threateningly on one knee.

But, just as a rock repels a wave to be almost instantly submerged by it anew, five or six brigands threw them-selves upon Don Inigo in a twinkling, and with a wrench that would have broken his arm if it had not yielded, tore from him the hilt of the sword and the remaining six inches of steel, while the man with the knife, ashamed to have been thrown down by the old man's efforts, rushed at him, brandishing his weapon, and swearing by his God that the prisoner's last moment had come.

When she saw the gleam of the knife-blade, Doña Flor uttered a terrible cry and rushed toward her father.

But one brigand held Doña Flor, while another held his companion's hand.

"Vicente! Vicente!" cried he who arrested his com-rade's hand at the risk of having the threatening knife turned against himself, — "what the devil do you mean to do?"

"Why, to kill the madman, of course!"

"You are mistaken; you won't kill him."

"What's that, I won't kill him! Ah! by St. James, we'll see whether I will or not."

"You won't kill him, I tell you! if you do, you'll just make a hole in a bag of gold, and all his ransom will run out through the hole. Vicente, you have a detestable disposition, I have always told you so! Let me talk with this worthy nobleman, and you'll see that I will make him listen to reason."

The brigand whom his comrade had called by the name of Vicente doubtless realized the justice of those words, for he withdrew, grumbling, to be sure, but still he withdrew.

When we say that he withdrew, we mean, not that he left the room, but that he stepped back a few feet, — like the wounded jaguar, ready at any moment to leap again on his prey.

The brigand who had assumed the rôle of negotiator took Vicente's place.

"Come, Señor Caballero, be reasonable," he said; "we won't fasten you to the iron ring, we'll content ourselves by putting you in the cellar, where the choice wines are kept, which has as stout a door as the dungeons of Granada, with a sentinel outside the door."

"How now, villain! you propose to treat a man of my rank in that way?"

"I shall be with you, father! I will not leave you!" cried Doña Flor. "Two or three days are soon passed, you know — "

"Ah! my pretty child," said one of the brigands, "we can't promise you that."

"What? What is it that you can't promise me?"

"That you will remain with your father."

"Great Heaven! what do you intend to do with me, in God's name?" cried the girl.

"What do we intend to do with you?" replied the negotiator. "Oh, we are not great noblemen, to tell you that; young ladies of your age and rank and charm are our chief's booty."

"Oh, my God!" murmured Doña Flor, while the old man uttered a roar of wrath.

"Don't you be alarmed," laughed the brigand; "our chief is young and handsome, — ay, and of a good family, too, so they say. And so, whatever happens, you will have one consolation, my good man! you can say to yourself, even if you 're as nobly born as the king, that there is no mésalliance."

Not till the last words were uttered, did Doña Flor realize to the full the horror of the fate for which she might be reserved; she uttered a cry, and, with a movement swift as thought, drew from her garter a tiny dagger, sharp as a needle, and instantly turned the gleaming blade toward her breast.

The brigands saw the movement and recoiled a step, and Doña Flor once more stood alone against the wall, calm but resolved, like the statue of Determination.

"Father," she said, "what do you bid me do?"

And the virtuous child's eye, as well as her voice, indicated that, at the first word from the old man, the keen blade would disappear to the hilt in her heart.

Don Inigo did not reply; but the critical situation of affairs restored for a moment his youthful strength, and with a powerful and unexpected movement he threw aside the two brigands who were holding him down, and with a single bound stood upon his feet, with open arms, crying, —

"Here, my child! come here!"

Doña Flor darted to her father's side and slipped the little dagger into his hand, saying in an undertone, —

"Father, my father! remember Virginius the Roman, whose story you have told me!"

The words had hardly left her mouth, when a brigand, who had put out his hand toward her, rolled at Don Inigo's feet, struck to the heart by the fragile weapon, which seemed a plaything rather than a means of defence.

On the instant a terrible cry of wrath resounded through the inn. Ten knives opened, ten daggers flashed from their sheaths, ten swords left their scabbards and were brandished menacingly at the two prisoners, who, seeing that the moment had come for them to die, exchanged a last kiss, whispered a last prayer, and, together raising their arms to heaven, cried in the same breath, —

"Strike!"

"Death! death!" roared the brigands, rushing upon the father and daughter with uplifted weapons.

But suddenly they heard the crashing sound of a window broken by a powerful blow with the fist. A young man with no other weapon than a Basque dagger, which he wore in his belt, leaped lightly into the room and said in a voice evidently used to command, —

"Holà! my masters, pray, what is happening here?"

At the sound of that voice, which, however, had not risen above the ordinary diapason of human speech, the cries died away, the knives closed, the daggers disappeared in their sheaths, the swords returned to their scabbards, and the whole band drew back in silence, leaving the father and daughter entwined in each other's arms, in the centre of a great circle, facing the new-comer.

VII.

THE BRIGAND.

THE individual whose sudden arrival — evidently as
unexpected to those who threatened as to those who
were threatened — had produced such an extraordinary
reaction, deserves, by reason of his manner of appearing
on the scene and by reason of the part he is destined to
play in this history, that we should interrupt the recital
of events in which he is to take part, to place his portrait before our readers' eyes.

He was a young man of some twenty-seven or twenty-
eight years. His costume — that of an Andalusian
mountaineer — was of extreme elegance. It consisted
of a broad-brimmed gray felt hat, adorned with two
eagle's feathers, a doublet of embroidered leather such
as the hunters of Cordova still wear on their excursions
in the Sierra Morena, an Algerian belt of watered silk
and gold, short clothes of orange velvet with carved
buttons, boots of leather like that of the doublet, laced
on the sides, but only at the ankle and the knee, being
open all along the calf so that the stocking could be
seen.

A plain dagger like that carried by the bear-hunters of
the Pyrenees — that is to say, with a handle of carved
horn embellished with silver nails, a blade two fingers
wide and eight inches long, sharpened at the point and
on both edges, and contained in a leather sheath with
silver ornaments — was, as we have said, the only weapon

of the young chief; for chief he unquestionably was, since his voice had such a direct and immediate influence upon the men of blood and rapine who had recoiled before him.

The remainder of his costume consisted of a cloak with horizontal stripes, in which he bore himself as majestically as an emperor in his purple robes.

As to the new-comer's physical qualities, the brigand who had asserted, to soothe Don Inigo's sensitive feelings, that the captain was not only young and handsome and refined, but had such a noble bearing that he was generally looked upon as a hidalgo, that brigand had said none too much, and his portrait rather failed to do justice to its subject than flattered him.

When her eyes fell upon the young man, Doña Flor uttered an exclamation of amazement which resembled a cry of joy, as if the new-comer's appearance, instead of being a reinforcement to the brigands, were succor sent from heaven to her father and herself.

As for Don Inigo, he understood that from that moment he had nothing more to do with the rest of the band, and that his daughter's fate and his own depended thenceforth upon this young man.

But, as if he were too proud to speak first, he simply placed the bloody point of the dagger against Doña Flor's breast and waited.

The brigand therefore was the first to speak.

" I do not doubt your courage, señor," he said; " it seems to me, however, great presumption on your part to think that you can defend yourself with that needle against a score of men armed with swords and daggers."

" If I had any desire to live," replied Don Inigo, " it would indeed be madness; but as I have no other purpose than to kill my daughter, and myself after her, that seemed and still seems to me not only possible, but easy of accomplishment."

"And why do you propose to kill the señora and yourself after her?"

"Because we are threatened with outrages to which we prefer death."

"Is the señora your wife?"

"She is my daughter."

"At what price do you estimate your life and her honor?"

"My life at a thousand crowns; but her honor is beyond price."

"I make you a present of your life, señor," replied the brigand; "and as for the señora's honor, that also is as safe here as if she were in her mother's chamber and under her protection."

A murmur of discontent made itself heard among the brigands.

"Leave the room, every man!" said the *Salteador*, putting out his hand, and holding it in that position until the last man was outside the door.

When they had all disappeared, the *Salteador* secured the door and returned to Don Inigo and his daughter, who followed his movements with astonishment mingled with anxiety.

"You must forgive them, señor," he said; "they are vulgar creatures, and not gentlemen like ourselves."

Doña Flor and Don Inigo gazed with less anxiety but with greater astonishment at this brigand who called himself a gentleman, and who, by the nobility of his manners and the dignity of his bearing, even more than by his words, proved that he told no falsehood.

"Señor," said the girl, "my father is, as I can under-stand, without words to thank you; permit me, therefore, to offer our acknowledgments in his name and my own."

"Your father is right, señora; for, coming from such a lovely mouth, they will have a force that not even a king's lips could give them."

Then, turning to the old man, he added, —

"I know that you are in haste to continue your journey, señor. Where are you going?"

"I am going to Granada, whither the king has summoned me."

"Ah, yes," said the brigand, with a half-bitter, half-mocking smile, "the rumor of his arrival has reached even our ears; we saw the soldiers who are beating up the mountains pass yesterday; he proposes, so they say, that a child of twelve shall be able to start from Granada and go to Malaga, with a bag of gold in either hand, and not meet on the road a single person who will say anything more to him than the customary traveller's salutation, ' Go, and God's peace be with you!' "

"Such is, in truth, his purpose," said Don Inigo, "and I know that orders have been given in accordance therewith."

"What period does King Don Carlos assign for this conquest of the mountain?"

"It is said that he has given the grand justiciary only a fortnight."

"What a misfortune that you did not pass this way three weeks hence instead of to-day, señora!" rejoined the brigand, addressing the young girl; "on this road, where you have been so terrified by brigands, you would have met none but honest people, who would have said, ' Go, and God's peace be with you!' and, at need, would have done escort duty!"

"We have been more fortunate than that, señor,"

replied Don Inigo's daughter, "since we have met a gentleman who has restored our liberty."

"You must not thank me for it," returned the brigand, "for I obey a power greater than my will, stronger than my nature."

"What power is that?"

The brigand shrugged his shoulders.

"I cannot say," he answered; "unfortunately I am a man ruled by first impressions. There is between my heart and my head, my head and my hand, my hand and my sword, a mysterious sympathy which leads me sometimes to good, sometimes to evil, — oftener to evil than to good. That sympathy, as soon as I saw you, plucked the wrath from my heart and hurled it far away from me; so far that, on my honor as a gentleman, I have sought it with my eyes and have been unable to find it!"

Don Inigo had kept his eyes on the young man while he was speaking, and, strange to relate! that feeling of sympathy which the brigand described as best he could in the half-jesting, half gentle and tender words he uttered, — that feeling was made clear to the old man by an analogous sensation that crept into his own heart, against his will.

Meanwhile Doña Flor had slowly drawn closer to her father, not through fear, but on the contrary, because while listening to the young man's voice she was conscious of a strange sensation that made a sort of shudder run through her veins, and, like the innocent child she was, she sought in her father's arms shelter from this unfamiliar sentiment that was taking possession of her.

"Young man," said Don Inigo, replying to the brigand's last words, "I have the same feeling toward you that you have felt toward me; it was not my evil

5

star, but my good fortune, therefore, that caused me to
pass over this road to-day rather than three weeks hence;
for perhaps it would then be too late for me to render
you a service equal to that you render me at this
moment."

"Render me a service?" said the brigand, with a
smile.

And his features contracted slightly, as if to say,
"The man must be omnipotent who will render me the
only service that any one can render me!"

As if he understood what was taking place in the
young man's mind, Don Inigo continued: —

"The merciful Lord God assigned to every one his
place in the world: he gave kings to kingdoms, and to
kings he gave the nobles who are their natural escort;
he gave to cities the people who dwell in them, — trades-
men, merchants, common people; he gave to the sea the
daring navigators who cross oceans to find lost worlds or
discover unknown worlds; he gave to the mountains the
men of blood, and in those same mountains placed beasts
of prey and carnage, as if to imply that he likened them
to each other by giving them the same abode, and that
he placed them on the last rung of the social ladder."

The brigand made a gesture.

"Let me continue," said Don Inigo.

The young man bowed in token of assent.

"And so," the old man went on, "in order that we
may meet with men outside of the circle in which God
has enclosed them, like flocks of individuals of the same
species, but of different worth, there must have been
some great social cataclysm or some great family disas-
ter, which has violently hurled them out of the circle
in which they belonged into a circle that was not intended for them. So it happens that we, for example,

who were born to be gentlemen in attendance upon kings, have, each in our own way, followed a different destiny. My destiny made of me a navigator; yours has made of you — ”

The old man stopped.

“ Finish your sentence,” said the young man, with a smile; “ you will tell me nothing that I do not know, and I can listen to anything from you.”

“ Your destiny has made of you a brigand ! ”

“ True; but you know that the same word is used for outlaw and brigand.”

“ Yes, I know it, and be sure that I do not confound the two. You are an outlaw ? ” he added in an interrogative tone.

“ But who are you, señor ? ”

“ I am Don Inigo Velasco de Haro.”

At those words the young man removed his hat and threw it on the floor.

“ Your pardon,” he said; “ I remained covered, and I am not a grandee of Spain.”

“ I am not the king,” replied Don Inigo, with a smile.

“ No, but you are as noble as the king.”

“ You know me, then ? ” asked Don Inigo.

“ I have heard my father speak of you a thousand times.”

“ Then your father knows me ? ”

“ He has told me more than once that he had that honor.”

“ Your father's name, young man ? ”

“ Oh, yes, yes,” murmured Doña Flor, “ his name ! his name ! ”

“ Alas! señor,” replied the brigand, with an air of profound melancholy, “ it would be no joy or satisfaction to my father to hear from the mouth of such a man

as I am the name of a Spaniard of ancient race who
has n't a drop of Moorish blood in his veins; do not ask
me, therefore, to add that sorrow and shame to the sorrow
and shame he already owes to me."

"He is right, father!" cried the young girl, eagerly.

The old man glanced at Doña Flor, who lowered her
eyes and blushed.

"Does not your opinion coincide with the fair
señora's?" the brigand asked him.

"It does," replied Don Inigo. "Keep the secret of
your name, therefore; but if you have no equally strong
motive for concealing from me the cause of the strange
life you have taken up; if your banishment from society
and your taking refuge in these mountains are, as I pre-
sume, the result of some youthful folly; if you have, I
will not say the shadow of remorse, but the appearance
of regret for the life you are leading, — I pledge my
word, before God, to act as your protector, ay, as your
guarantor."

"Thanks, señor! I accept your word, although I
doubt whether it is in the power of any man except
him who has received supreme power from God to
restore me to the place I once occupied in the world,
and yet I have nothing shameful with which to reproach
myself. Hot blood, a heart too quick to take fire,
impelled me to commit certain faults; those faults drove
me to crime. To-day, the faults are committed, the
crimes are consummated; they are so many bottomless
pits lying open behind me; so that I cannot return by
the road by which I came, and it would require some
superhuman power to prepare a different road for me.
Sometimes I dream of the possibility of such a miracle;
I should be happy to see it accomplished, doubly happy
to see it accomplished by you, and to return, like young

Tobias, to my father's house, under the guidance of an angel! Meanwhile, I hope — for hope is the last friend of the unfortunate, although it is often as deceitful, more deceitful, than the others — I hope but I do not believe. I live on, plunging deeper every day in the steep and barren road of revolt against society and the law. I ascend, and because I ascend I believe that I am exalting myself. I command, and because I command I believe that I am king. But sometimes, at night, in my hours of solitude, in my moments of sadness, I reflect, and then I understand that, if one ascends to reach the throne, one ascends also to reach the scaffold."

Doña Flor uttered a stifled shriek.

Don Inigo offered the brigand his hand.

But he, without accepting the honor the old gentleman bestowed upon him, bowed and placed one hand upon his breast, pointing with the other to a chair.

"Then you mean to tell me everything?" said Don Inigo, seating himself.

"Everything, except my father's name."

The old hidalgo, in his turn, invited the young man to be seated, but he declined.

"What you are going to hear is not a story, but a confession," he said. "To a priest I would make that confession on my knees; but to a man, be that man Don Inigo or the king himself, I will make it standing."

The young girl leaned against her father's chair, and the brigand, humble but erect, in a melancholy but tranquil voice, began the following narrative.

VIII.

THE NARRATIVE.

" In the first place, señor," the brigand began, " I think I may make this assertion: that there always is, in the beginnings of a man who has become a criminal, — no matter how great a criminal he may have become, — a force independent of his will that causes him to take the first steps outside of the straight road.

" To make the man turn aside from that road, a powerful hand is needed, and sometimes the iron hand of destiny itself is none too strong.

" But to lead the child astray, whose sight is feeble and whose step is uncertain, sometimes requires only a breath!

" That breath blew upon my cradle.

" That breath was my father's indifference, I might almost say, his hatred of me."

" Señor," murmured the girl, " do not begin by accusing others, if you wish God to forgive you."

" I do not accuse, God forbid! my errors and my crimes are my own, and on the day of the last judgment I shall not seek to charge them upon any other than myself; but I must tell things as they are.

" My mother was once one of the loveliest girls in Cordova, and to-day, at forty-three, she is still one of the loveliest women in Granada.

" I have never known the causes that led to her marriage to my father; what I can say, what I have always noticed, is that they lived rather as strangers to each other than as husband and wife.

"I was born. I have often heard their mutual friends say that they had hoped that my birth would bring them nearer together; but their hopes were disappointed. Cold to the mother, my father was cold to the child; and from the day that I opened my eyes, I felt that one of the two props that God has given to man to support him on his entrance into life was taken from me.

"It is very true that my mother, to conceal from me the error made by destiny, so to speak, in arranging my life, enveloped me with a love so tender and so strong that it might well have taken the place of the love that was withheld from me, and of itself have counted for two.

"But, dearly as my mother loved me, she loved me with a woman's love; in the somewhat less tender but more virile affection of the father, there is something that speaks to the caprices of the child and to the passions of the young man, as God speaks to the Ocean to say, 'Thou shalt rise no higher; thou shalt go no farther!' Those caprices, moulded by a father's hand, those passions, held in check by the hand of a man, take the form that the mould of society impresses upon them; whereas everything overflows in the child brought up under the indulgent eye and guided by the wavering hand of woman. Maternal indulgence — as boundless as maternal love — made of me the high-spirited, ungovernable horse, who needed but one prick of the spur, alas! to spring from the city to the mountain.

"However, if my character was the worse for that unbridled freedom, my strength gained by it. Not having a father's stern hand to close the house door upon me, laughing in anticipation at the feeble reprimand that awaited me on my return, I was always wandering about in the company of the mountaineers of the Sierra Morena. I learned from them how to attack the wild boar with the spear, the bear with the dagger. When I was but fifteen, those animals, which would have terrified another boy of that age, were in my eyes adversaries with whom the combat might be longer or shorter, more or less dangerous, but who were conquered in advance. As soon as I came upon a trail in the mountain, I knew what animal had made it, followed him, unearthed him, attacked him. More than once I crawled like a snake into some cavern, where, when I was once inside, I had no other guide or light than the blazing eyes of the beast I had come to fight. Ah! those were the times — although no one save God alone would witness what was about to take place there in the bowels of the earth between the animal and myself — those were the times when my heart beat fast with pride and joy! Like Homer's heroes, who attacked the enemy with their tongues before attacking him with sword, or javelin, or lance, I mocked and defied the wolf, the boar, or the bear I had come to seek. Then the struggle would begin between man and beast, — a fierce, silent struggle while it lasted, but ending in a roar of agony and a cry of triumph. Then, like Hercules, the vanquisher of monsters, to whom I compared myself, I returned to the light, dragging behind me the body of the victim, which I heaped insults upon in my savage joy, glorifying my triumph in some wild song which I improvised, and in which I called the torrents that came leaping down from the mountains my friends, and the eagles that soared above my head my brothers !

"Then came the age at which those pleasures were

succeeded by passions, and the passions followed their course with the same fury that had characterized the pleasures. To the passion for gaming and the passion of love my mother tried, but fruitlessly as always, to oppose the weak barrier of her will. Then she called my father to her assistance.

"It was too late; being little wonted to obey, I resisted even my father's voice. Moreover, that voice, speaking to me in the midst of the tempest, was unknown to me. I had grown, I had matured, in the wrong direction; the shrub would have bent, perhaps; the tree, become inflexible, resisted, and continued to feel the burning sap of evil flowing beneath its bark, as rough and gnarled as that of an oak.

"Oh, I will not tell you — it would be too long a story, and then, too, in the presence of your pure daughter, respect closes my mouth — I will not tell you of the long series of quarrels, nocturnal orgies, foolish intrigues, by which I came to be the cause of my father's ruin and a source of bitter grief to my mother. No, I pass over the thousand events that compose the tissue of my life, more diversified with brawls, love-making under balconies, and duels at street corners, than is this cloak I wear with its bright colors; I pass over all those incidents to come to the one which definitely decided my future.

"I loved — I thought that I loved a certain woman, the sister of one of my friends. I would have sworn, I would have maintained against the whole world, — forgive me, señora, I had not seen you! — that she was the loveliest of women; when one night, or rather one morning, as I returned home, I found at my door that friend, the brother of her I loved, mounted, and holding a second horse by the bridle.

"I had a presentiment that he had discovered the secret of my love.

" ' What are you doing here ? ' I asked.

" ' You see: I am waiting for you.'

" ' Here I am.'

" ' Have you your sword ? '

" ' It never leaves me.'

" ' Mount this horse and follow me.'

" ' I do not follow: I accompany or I precede.'

" ' Oh, you won't precede me,' he said, ' for I am in a hurry to arrive where I am going.'

"He put his horse to the gallop.

"I did the same with mine, and, side by side, we rode at full speed into the mountains.

"In about five hundred yards we came to a little clearing, where the soft grass grew on a sort of esplanade that seemed to have been levelled by the hand of man.

" 'This is the place,' said Don Alvar.

"That was my friend's name.

" ' So be it! ' I replied.

" ' Dismount, Don Fernand,' he said, ' and draw your sword; for you suspect, I fancy, that I have brought you here to fight ? '

" ' I suspected it at once,' I replied; ' but I have no idea what can have changed our friendship to hatred. Brothers yesterday, enemies to-day ! '

" ' Enemies, for the very reason that we are brothers! ' said Don Alvar, drawing his sword; ' brothers through my sister ! Come, draw, Don Fernand ! '

" ' That, as you well know,' I replied, ' is an invitation that no one ever offers me twice; but, in your case, I shall wait until you have told me your reason for bringing me to this spot. Indeed, Don Alvar, I would be glad to know what excites you so. What subjects of complaint have you against me?'

"'I have so many that I prefer not to mention them; for, when I recall them, I renew the insult, and I am forced to repeat the oath I have taken to wash out that insult in your blood. Come, draw your sword, Don Fernand!'

"I did not know myself, I was so calm in face of his wrath, so unmoved in face of such provocation.

"'I will not fight with you,' I said, 'without knowing why I am fighting.'

"He drew a package of letters from his pocket.

"'Do you recognize these papers?' he demanded.

"I shuddered.

"'Throw them on the ground,' I said, 'and I will pick them up.'

"'Here, pick them up and read them.'

"He threw the letters on the ground.

"I picked them up and read them; they were indeed mine.

"It was impossible for me to deny them; I was at the mercy of an outraged brother!

"'Oh, woe to the man,' I cried, 'who is mad enough to intrust the secrets of his heart and a woman's honor to paper! it is an arrow shot into the air; we know whence it comes, we do not know where it will fall nor whom it may strike!'

"'Do you recognize those letters, Don Fernand?'

"'They are in my handwriting, Don Alvar.'

"'Then draw your sword, so that one of us may lie here dead beside my sister's dead honor.'

"'I am grieved that you have taken the matter in this way, Don Alvar, and by your threats have made impossible the proposition that I might have made you.'

" ' Oh, the coward ! ' said Alvar; ' to propose to marry the woman he has dishonored when he sees her brother with his sword in his hand ! '

" ' You know that I am not a coward, Don Alvar; at all events, if you do not know it, I will teach you, if you insist. So listen to me.'

" ' Draw your sword ! When the steel is to speak, the tongue should keep silent ! '

" ' I love your sister, Don Alvar; your sister loves me; why should I not call you my brother ? '

" ' Because my father told me yesterday that he would never call by the name of son a man abandoned to vice and debauchery, and overburdened with debts ! '

" My coolness began to abandon me in the face of such repeated insults.

" ' Your father said that, Don Alvar ? ' I cried, my teeth clenched in wrath.

" ' Yes, and I repeat it after him, and I add: Draw your sword, Don Fernand ! '

" ' You insist upon it ? ' I replied, putting my hand to the hilt of my sword.

" ' Draw your sword ! draw your sword ! ' cried Don Alvar, ' or I will strike you with the flat of mine and not with the point ! '

" You will agree, Don Inigo, — for I am telling you the solemn truth, — you will agree that I had resisted as long as a gentleman could do.

" I drew my sword.

" Five minutes later Don Alvar was dead.

" Dead without confession, and cursing me with his last breath. That is what brought misfortune on me ! "

The brigand paused a moment, letting his head fall forward pensively on his breast.

At that moment the young gypsy appeared at the win-

dow through which the brigand had entered; and in
the breathless voice of the bearer of important news,
she pronounced the name Fernand three times.

Not till the second time did the brigand seem to
hear, and not till the third did he turn.

But, notwithstanding Ginesta's evident haste to announce the news she brought, the brigand motioned to
her with his hand to wait, and she waited.

"I returned to the city," continued Don Fernand,
"and, meeting two monks on my way, I told them
where they would find Don Alvar's body.

"A meeting between two young men followed by a
death by the sword was a very commonplace matter; but
our meeting did not take place under the ordinary duelling conditions. Don Alvar's father, furious with rage
at the loss of his only son, accused me of murder.

"Alas! I am bound to say that my reputation was a
poor safeguard; the charge, infamous as it was, found
credence with the magistrates; the alcalde issued an
order of arrest against me, and three alguazils appeared
at my home to take me into custody.

"I offered to go to prison alone. They refused. I
gave them my word as a gentleman that I would walk a
hundred paces behind them or in front of them, as they
chose.

"They tried to take me by force.

"I killed two of them and wounded the third; I
leaped on my horse without saddle or bridle, taking but
one single thing with me, — the key to the house.

"I had not seen my mother, and I proposed to return
and embrace her once more.

"Two hours later I was safe in the mountains.

"The mountains were full of outlaws of all sorts, all
of whom, being exiled like myself, on account of some

falling-out with the law, had nothing more to expect from society, and were burning with the desire to repay the wrong that it had done them.

"Those men only needed a chief to organize a terrible power.

"I proposed myself as their chief. They accepted me. You know the rest."

"Have you seen your mother since?" asked Doña Flor.

"Thanks!" said the brigand; "you still look upon me as a man."

The girl lowered her eyes.

"Yes," he said; "I have seen her not once, but ten times, twenty times! My mother is the only bond that attaches me to the world. Once a month, on no fixed day, — for everything depends on the closeness of the watch kept upon us, — once a month, at nightfall, I leave the mountain, dressed in a mountaineer's costume, and wrapped in a great cloak, I cross the *vega* unseen — or, if seen, unrecognized, thus far at least — and enter the house which has never been so dear to me as since I have been exiled from it; I open the door of my mother's bedroom, I walk noiselessly to the bed and awaken her by kissing her on the forehead.

"Then I sit down on the bed and pass the night as in the days of my youth, with my hands in hers, my head upon her breast.

"And after passing the night thus, talking of days long past, of the time when I was innocent and happy, she kisses me on the forehead, and it seems to me that that kiss reconciles me with nature, with men, with God!"

"Oh, father, father! do you hear?" said Doña Flor, wiping away two tears that were rolling down her cheeks.

"Hereafter," said the old man, "you shall see your mother, not at night, not furtively, but in the light of day and in the face of all men; I pledge my honor as a gentleman!"

"Oh, you are kind, a hundred times kind, father!" murmured Doña Flor, embracing the old man.

"Don Fernand!" exclaimed the young gypsy, in a tone of the keenest anxiety, "what I have to say to you is of the utmost importance. Listen to me! in God's name, listen to me!"

But as before, only with a more imperious gesture, the brigand ordered her to wait.

"We leave you, señor," said Don Inigo, "and we carry with us the memory of your courtesy."

"Then you forgive me?" exclaimed the brigand, carried away by his strange feeling of sympathy with Don Inigo.

"Not only do we forgive you, but we consider ourselves your debtors, and with God's help I shall be able, I trust, to give you a special proof of my gratitude."

"And do you, señora," the brigand asked in a hesitating tone, "share Señor Don Inigo's sentiments?"

"Oh, yes," cried Doña Flor, eagerly; "and if I too could give you a proof — "

And she looked about as if to see by what visible means, by what palpable proof, she could emphasize her gratitude to the young man.

The brigand understood her purpose; he saw on the plate the bouquet Amapola had picked for Don Ramiro. He took it and handed it to Doña Flor.

She consulted her father with a glance, and Don Inigo bowed his assent.

She took a flower from the bouquet.

It was an anemone, the flower of sadness.

"My father promised to pay you his ransom," she said; "here is mine."

And she offered the flower to the brigand.

He took it, lifted it respectfully to his lips, then placed it in his bosom, and buttoned his doublet over it.

"Farewell until we meet again," said Don Inigo, "and I venture to promise you, in advance, that it will be soon!"

"Act as your kind heart bids you, señor, and may God in his mercy aid you!"

He added, raising his voice, —

"You are free; go, and whoever does not stand aside ten yards from your path is a dead man!"

Don Inigo and his daughter left the house.

Without leaving his place the brigand watched them, through the window looking on the courtyard, mount their mules and ride away from the inn.

Thereupon the young man took the anemone from his breast and kissed it a second time with an expression that could not be mistaken.

At that moment he felt that a hand was laid softly on his shoulder.

It was Ginesta, who had climbed in at the window, light as a bird, and, Don Inigo and Doña Flor having taken their leave, laid claim once more to the attention the brigand refused to bestow upon her in their presence.

She was pale as death.

"What do you want of me?" the brigand asked.

"To tell you that the king's troops cannot be more than a fourth of a league away while I speak, and that you will be attacked in ten minutes!"

"Are you sure of what you tell me, Ginesta?" queried the brigand, knitting his brows.

The words were hardly out of his mouth when they heard the report of a volley of musketry.

"Do you hear?" said Ginesta.

"To arms!" cried the brigand, rushing from the room: "to arms!"

IX.

THE OAK OF DOÑA MERCEDES.

THIS is what had happened: —

Don Inigo had spoken of a detachment of the king's troops whom he had met near Alhama, and whose commander he knew.

The brigands had, it will be remembered, replied laughingly that the detachment had passed the inn the preceding day.

This detachment, consisting of about four hundred men, had orders to scour the mountain and cleanse it at any price of the band of brigands who infested it.

A reward of one hundred gold philips was offered for every brigand, dead or alive, who should be accounted for to the authorities, and a reward of a thousand gold philips for the leader.

King Don Carlos had sworn that he would destroy brigandage in Spain, and drive it back from Sierra to Sierra until he drove it into the sea.

During the two years and a half since he landed in Spain he had pursued that purpose with the obstinacy that was one of the distinctive characteristics of his genius, and had forced the last brigands to bay in the Sierra Nevada, which is in close proximity to the sea.

Thus the fulfilment of his purpose was near at hand.

The leader of this latest detachment had contented himself with exploring the road; he had found nothing unusual except an inn, at whose door his detachment

had halted and refreshed themselves; but the inn had
no other occupants than the host and the usual frequenters of an Andalusian hostelry. The host's countenance was more open, his manner more courteous and
engaging, than those of most Spanish landlords; there
was nothing about the inn to point to it as a rendezvous
for brigands; the commanding officer had ordered his
detachment to resume their march, and they had
passed on.

They went as far as Alhama without discovering anything worthy of note except the crosses more or less
thickly planted by the roadsides; but crosses are so
common in Spain that the soldiers paid but slight
attention to them.

At Alhama the officer commanding the detachment
had made inquiries and had been warned to concentrate
all his attention on the inn of the Moorish King, which
was described to him as the centre of operations and the
lair of the brigands. The result was that the officer,
without loss of time, had started to retrace his steps,
and had ordered his men to follow him.

It was six leagues from Alhama to the Moorish King,
and the troops had already covered half that distance
when they saw coming toward them, at the mad pace of
despair, Don Inigo's servant, wounded and covered with
blood, and calling loudly for help. He told the officer
what had happened.

As Don Inigo had said, the officer was a gentleman of
his acquaintance. When he learned of the dangerous
plight of the illustrious hidalgo and the lovely Doña
Flor, his daughter, he ordered the detachment to march
forward at the double quick.

From the top of the cliff, where she had remained,
Ginesta had seen in the distance the head of the column;

suspecting the motive of the return of the troops, trembling for the safety of the brigand, she had hurried to the inn, entered by the garden gate, — the same through which Don Fernand had passed, — arrived at the window he had broken and leaped through, and there, held in check by the gesture which bade her wait, she had seen what had taken place between Don Fernand and the prisoners, particularly between him and Doña Flor.

Pale as death, and with death in her heart, Ginesta had, in her turn, climbed through the window, and announced to the brigand the coming of the king's troops.

The brigand rushed from the room, shouting, "To arms!"

He expected to find his companions in the kitchen; the kitchen was empty.

He rushed into the courtyard; there was no one in the courtyard.

In two bounds he was at the gateway of the inn. There he found an arquebus on the ground, and beside the arquebus one of those sixteenth-century baldrics to which cartridges were attached all ready for use.

He picked up the arquebus, passed the baldric about his neck, and, standing erect once more, looked around in search of his companions.

The fusillade they had heard had instantly died away, — a proof that they at whom it was directed had offered but a slight resistance.

Suddenly the brigand saw the advance guard of the royal troops appear on the crest of the little hill.

He turned to see if he was entirely abandoned.

Ginesta alone was behind him, deathly pale and with clasped hands. With the eloquent pantomime of terror she implored him to fly.

"I must do it," muttered the brigand, "as the villains have deserted me."

"Perhaps they will join you in the mountains," suggested Ginesta, timidly, drawing him back.

That suggestion restored Fernand's hopes.

"It is quite possible," he said.

And, returning to the courtyard, he closed the heavy gate behind him, and put the iron bar in place.

Then, still followed by Ginesta, he entered the kitchen, passed from the kitchen into a sort of little pantry, raised a trap-door which he let fall behind him when the gypsy had passed through, secured the trap with a bolt, and with no other light than that of the match of his arquebus, descended the stairway and entered the subterranean passage that began at its foot.

It was the passage to which the brigands had alluded when they were enlightening Don Inigo as to their means of defence and flight.

After about five minutes Don Fernand and the gypsy reached the other end of the passage. Fernand lifted with his strong shoulders a second trap-door, concealed on the outside by a flat rock and covered with moss.

The fugitives were in the mountains.

The brigand drew a long breath of relief.

"Ah!" he said, "here we are free!"

"Yes," replied Ginesta, "but let us waste no time."

"Where do you mean to go?"

"To the oak of Doña Mercedes."

Fernand started.

"Very good," he said; "perhaps the Virgin under whose protection it has been placed will bring me good luck."

Both of them, or rather all three, — for the goat had followed the fugitives, — at once plunged into the under-

brush, taking care to follow no other paths than those
made by wild beasts, which were so numerous, however,
and so well beaten, that they were veritable roads.

But in those roads they had to walk, like the animals
who frequented them, with the head close to the ground;
in some places, indeed, where the branches were joined
together overhead, they had actually to crawl; but the
more difficult the passage, the greater the security
afforded by the natural fortress in which the brigand
and the gypsy had taken refuge.

They walked in this way three-quarters of an hour;
but we must not measure the distance travelled by the
time that had elapsed: the difficulty of the road made
their progress slow, and after three-quarters of an hour
the fugitives had made barely half a league. But it
would have taken any others than themselves — that is
to say, men unfamiliar with the mountain, with the
paths of deer and bears and wild boars — a whole day to
make that half a league.

The farther they advanced, the more impenetrable
the underbrush became, and yet neither Fernand nor
Ginesta showed the slightest sign of hesitation. One
could see that they were both headed toward a known
goal, no more lost among those mastics, strawberry-trees,
and gigantic myrtles than the sailor wandering over the
boundless ocean, where he has the compass and the
constellations to guide him.

At last, after ploughing their way through one last
line of yoke-elms, which seemed impenetrable to the
eye, they found themselves in a small clearing some
twenty feet in diameter, in the centre of which rose an
oak, in whose trunk a little statuette of St. Mercedes,
the patron saint of Fernand's mother, was set in a shrine
of gilded wood.

Fernand had placed this tree, in whose shade he often mused and slept, and which he called his summer house, under the protection of his mother's patron saint, or rather under the protection of his mother herself, whom he adored and respected much more than the saint whose name she bore.

The two fugitives had reached the end of their journey, and it was evident that, unless betrayed, they were perfectly safe for the moment.

We say *unless betrayed*, because the brigands knew of this retreat of their leader, although they never came there unless they were summoned; it was a sort of place of refuge whither Fernand, in his hours of melancholy, came to recall the vanished world of the past, and, as he lay wrapped in his cloak, trying to distinguish through the motionless leaves of the oak a fragment of the sky that stretched away above his head, blue as the wings of Hope, to evoke the pleasant memories of his childhood, which formed such a striking contrast to those ghastly memories of deeds of violence and of blood which, as a young man, he was storing up for his old age.

When he had any orders to issue, any information to receive, he took from the hollow in the tree a silver horn, beautifully wrought by some Moorish workman, and blew one long shrill note upon it if he desired the presence of only one of his comrades; two, if he needed ten men; three, if he wished to summon the whole band.

His first care, on entering the clearing, was to go straight to the shrine of the saint and kiss her feet; then he knelt and said a short prayer, while Ginesta, still half a heathen, stood and watched him; then he rose and made the circuit of a part of the trunk of the tree, took from the hole already mentioned the silver horn, and, putting it to his lips, blew three notes as shrill, as piercing, and as prolonged as those which, from a point five leagues away from the vale of Ronce-vaux, startled Charlemagne in the midst of his army, when, stopping suddenly, he said, "Messeigneurs, 't is my nephew Roland calling for help!"

But the notes rang out, grew fainter, and died to no purpose: no one came.

It is not to be supposed that the brigands did not hear; the echoes of Fernand's horn extended a league into the mountains.

Either the brigands were taken, or they had betrayed their chief, or realizing that resistance was useless, in view of the number of their assailants, they had deemed it more prudent to remain scattered, and had fled in different directions.

For about a quarter of an hour Fernand, leaning against the trunk of the tree, awaited an answer to his call; but, seeing that the prevailing silence remained unbroken, he spread his cloak on the ground and lay down upon it.

Ginesta sat beside him.

Fernand looked up at her with infinite tenderness; the little gypsy alone had remained faithful to him.

Ginesta smiled softly.

There was a promise of undying devotion in that smile.

Fernand put out his arms, took the girl's head in his hands, and put his lips to her forehead.

The moment that the brigand's lips and Ginesta's brow came in contact, the girl uttered a cry in which there was almost as much pain as pleasure.

It was the first caress she had ever received from him.

She sat for some moments with her eyes closed, her head resting against the gnarled trunk of the oak, her mouth open, and her breast without respiration, as if she had fainted.

The young man gazed at her, at first in astonishment, then in anxiety; at last he said softly, —

"Ginesta!"

The gypsy raised her head like a child aroused from sleep by its mother's voice, slowly opened her lovely eyes, and murmured as she met the brigand's gaze, —

"O my God!"

"What happened to you, my child?" queried Fernand.

"I do not know," she replied. "Only I thought I was dying —"

She rose unsteadily to her feet, walked slowly away from Doña Mercedes's oak, and disappeared in the underbrush, holding her head in her hands, and all ready to burst into tears, although she had never known such a sensation of joy and happiness.

The brigand looked after her until she had disappeared; but, as the goat remained with him instead of following her mistress, he concluded that she had not gone very far.

Thereupon he heaved a sigh, wrapped himself in his cloak, and lay down with his eyes closed as if he wished to sleep.

After about an hour of sleep or revery, he heard his name called in a soft but urgent tone.

The gypsy was standing before him in the gathering dusk, with her arm extended toward the west.

"Well," said Fernand, "what is it?"

"Look!" said the gypsy.

"Oho!" said the brigand, springing quickly to his

feet, "the sun is setting very red to-night. That means bloodshed to-morrow."

"You are mistaken," rejoined Ginesta; "those are not the beams of the setting sun."

"What are they, then?" asked Fernand, detecting a smell of smoke and a faint crackling sound.

"They are the reflection of a conflagration," the gypsy replied. "The mountain is on fire!"

At that moment a frightened stag, followed by a hind and a fawn, passed like a flash, flying from west to east.

"Come, Fernand!" said Ginesta; "the instinct of those animals is surer than the wisdom of man, and, while they show us in what direction we must fly, they tell us that there is not a moment to lose."

Doubtless that was also Fernand's opinion; for, throwing his horn around his neck, wrapping himself in his cloak, and taking his arquebus in his hand, he hurried away in the direction taken by the stag, the hind, and the fawn.

Ginesta and her goat walked in front of him.

X.

THE FIRE ON THE MOUNTAIN.

THE brigand, the gypsy, and the goat had gone some five hundred yards in that direction, when the goat suddenly stopped, stood upon her hind legs, sniffed the air, and seemed undecided.

"Well, Maza, what is it?" the girl asked.

The goat shook her head as if she had understood, and bleated as if she would have liked to reply.

The brigand listened and inhaled the night air, which was laden with resinous odors.

The darkness was as dense as it can be in Spain on a beautiful summer evening.

"It seems to me," said the brigand, "that I hear the same crackling and smell the same smell of smoke. Can we have made a mistake and be going to meet the fire instead of running away from it?"

"The fire was there," said Ginesta, pointing to the west, "and we have run in as straight a line as could be drawn."

"You are sure?"

"There is Aldebaran, which was, and still is, at our right; the fire must have caught at two different places on the mountain."

"Caught or been set," muttered Fernand, beginning to suspect the truth.

"Wait," said Ginesta; "I will tell you."

And the child of the mountain, to whom the mountain, with its peaks, its gorges, its underbrush, its valleys, and its caverns, was as familiar as the park

belonging to the château where he was born is to a
child, sprang forward to the base of an almost perpendicular cliff, climbed it by clinging to the excrescences
of the rock, and soon stood upon its summit like a
statue on its pedestal.

She required but five seconds for the ascent; she
required but one for the descent.

"Well?" queried the brigand.

"Yes," she said.

"Fire?"

"Fire! Come this way," she added, pointing to the
south; "we must succeed in passing through the gap
before the ends of the two fires meet."

The farther they went toward the south, the wilder
and denser the vegetation became; there were the high
bramble-bushes, the ordinary haunt of boars, wolves,
and wildcats; the weaker animals, like deer and kids,
rarely ventured upon the territory of their terrible foes,
and yet now those animals flew by them in herds, like
flashes of dun-colored lightning, flying in terror from
the fire in the direction which promised them means of
escape.

"This way! this way!" cried Ginesta; "have no
fear, Fernand; there is our guide."

And she pointed to the tricolored star by which she
directed her course.

"So long as it is at our left, as it was just now at our
right," continued the gypsy, "we shall be on the right
road."

After they had gone on so for some ten minutes, the
star disappeared.

"Oho!" said Fernand, "are we going to have a storm?
It would be a fine sight, — a struggle between fire and
water in the mountain!"

But Ginesta had stopped; grasping Fernand's wrist, she said, —

"It is no cloud that has hidden the star."

"What is it, then?"

"Smoke!"

"Impossible! the wind is from the south."

At that moment a snarling wolf, with fire flashing from his eyes, passed within a few paces of the young people, paying no attention to the goat, and running toward the north.

Nor did the goat pay any attention to the wolf; she seemed engrossed by another danger.

"The fire! the fire!" cried Ginesta. "We are too late; we have a wall of fire before us!"

"Wait," said Fernand; "we will soon see."

And he seized the lower branches of a fir and began to climb into the tree.

But his foot had hardly left the earth when a terrible growl was heard over his head.

Ginesta pulled the young man back in terror, and pointed to a dark mass outlined against the sky, about fifteen feet from the ground, in the branches of the tree.

"Oh, it's of no use for you to growl, old bear of Mulahacen," said Fernand; "you won't drive back the fire, and you would n't drive me back either if I had the time —"

"To the north! to the north!" cried Ginesta; "that is the only passage that is still open."

Indeed, all the dwellers of the mountain — stags, hinds, kids, boars, wildcats — were rushing madly in the only direction in which the flames had not yet appeared. Flocks of Guinea fowl and partridges flew at random before the fire, colliding with the branches and falling

stunned at the feet of the fugitives; while the birds of
night, kings of the darkness, saluted with hoarse cries
of terror the strange daylight that seemed to rise from
the earth instead of descending from heaven.

"Come, Fernand! come, come!" cried Ginesta.

"Where? In which direction?" asked Fernand, beginning to be really terrified, less for himself, perhaps,
than for the girl, who, by clinging to him, shared a
danger which she might have avoided by remaining at
the inn.

"This way! this way! there's the north star in
front of us. Let us follow the goat; her instinct will
guide us."

And they began to run in the direction indicated not
only by the domestic animal who was the companion of
their flight, but by the wild beasts as well, who rushed
by as if driven by the burning breath of the sirocco.

Suddenly the goat stopped.

"It is useless to fly farther," said Fernand; "we are
in a circle of flame."

And he seated himself on a rock as if determined to
make no further effort.

The girl went on a hundred paces to make sure if
Fernand had judged aright; then, as the goat at first
lagged behind, and finally stopped altogether, she retraced
her steps, and returned to Fernand, who was sitting with
his head in his hands, apparently resolved to await the
terrible catastrophe without taking another step.

Indeed, there was no longer any possibility of doubt;
for a league around, the sky gleamed blood-red through
a cloud of smoke.

They could hear an ominous hissing sound, which
rapidly approached, indicating the progress of the
conflagration.

The girl stood for a moment beside the brigand, enveloping him in a gaze overflowing with love.

Whoever could have read her mind would perhaps have found there the fear that such a desperate situation was calculated to inspire, but with it a secret longing to throw her arms around the young man and die with him there, on that spot, without the shadow of an effort to save themselves.

However, she seemed to overcome the temptation.

"Fernand!" she murmured with a sigh.

The brigand raised his head.

"Poor Ginesta," he said, "so young, so lovely, so good, and I shall be the cause of your death! Ah! I am accursed in very truth!"

"Do you want to live, Fernand?" the child asked, in a tone that signified, "For my part, I do not."

"Oh, yes, yes!" cried the young man; "oh, yes, I do want to live, I confess."

"For whose sake?" queried Ginesta.

Not till then, perhaps, did he read what was taking place in Ginesta's heart.

"For my mother's," he replied.

The child uttered a joyful exclamation.

"Thanks, Fernand!" she said; "follow me."

"Follow you! What for?"

"Follow me, I tell you!"

"Why, don't you see that we are lost?" said Fernand, shrugging his shoulders.

"We are saved, Fernand! I will answer for everything," replied the gypsy.

Fernand rose, doubting if he had heard aright.

"Come! come!" said she; "as you regret no one but your mother, I do not choose that your mother shall weep for you."

Seizing the young man's hand, she led him away in
another direction.

The young man followed her mechanically, but with
the instinctive ardor that every created being puts forth
for the preservation of his life.

One would have said that even the goat recovered her
courage when she saw the fugitives start off in their
new direction, and consented to act as their guide once
more, while the other terrified animals, finding that
they were hemmed in by a circle of fire, no longer followed any definite course, but ran hither and thither in
every conceivable direction.

The hissing of the fire came nearer and nearer, and
the atmosphere they breathed began to be burning hot.

Suddenly the hissing of the flames seemed to increase
in force, and to become more intense with every step
the fugitives took in the direction they were following.

Fernand called to the girl to stop.

"Why, the fire is ahead of us! Don't you hear it?"
he cried, pointing in the direction from which the sound
came.

"Can it be, Fernand," said the gypsy, with a laugh,
"that you are still so little used to the noises of the
mountain that you mistake the roar of a waterfall for
the hissing of a fire?"

"Oho!" said Fernand, starting on again, "yes, of
course, you are right; we can escape the fire by following the bed of the stream and pass between two curtains
of flame, as the Israelites, by the protection of the Lord,
passed between two walls of water. But don't you believe that the banks of the stream are guarded?"

"Come, come," the girl insisted; "did I not say that
I would answer for everything?"

And she dragged Fernand toward the plateau, from

which the sturdy waterfall, a transparent scarf tossed
against the side of the mountain, by day like a rain-
bow, by night like a moonbeam, plunged downward,
and after rebounding, twenty-five feet below, upon a jutting rock on which its liquid mass broke with a noise
like thunder, continued its downward course in the form
of spray into an abyss some three or four hundred feet
deep, hollowing out a bed for itself at the bottom, where
it formed a mountain torrent, and rushed on, roaring
fiercely, to empty into the Xenil, three leagues away,
between Armilla and Santa Fé.

In a few moments more the fugitives reached the
plateau from which the cascade plunged into the abyss.

Ginesta would have begun the formidable descent on
the instant; but Fernand stopped her. Although his
mind was hardly at rest concerning his own life and his
companion's, he could not, being a poet before everything, resist the desire to measure the full extent of the
peril he had escaped.

Certain hearts derive a ghastly pleasure from emotion
of that sort.

Moreover, it must be admitted that the spectacle was
a magnificent one. The circle of flame had at the same
time drawn closer at the centre and expanded at the
circumference. An immense ribbon of fire, growing
constantly broader, enveloped the mountain and rapidly
approached the fugitives.

From time to time the flames seized upon a tall pine,
twisted like a serpent around its trunk, ran along its
branches, and illuminated it like one of the yew-trees
provided for royal fêtes. For a moment the flames shot
up with a mighty crackling; then, suddenly, the fiery
giant gave way at its base and fell headlong into the vast
sea of flame, sending an eruption of sparks up to heaven.

7

At another time the flames reached a line of resinous mastics, and ran as swiftly as a train of powder, piercing with a lance of flame the dark green carpet that swathed the sides of the mountain.

Again, a rock all laden with burning cork-trees fell from some elevation where the earth, dried by the intense heat of the flames, no longer had the strength to hold it, and rolled over and over like a cascade of fire to the bottom of some gorge, where it stopped, instantly kindling a new fire about it.

The young man stood for a moment in ecstasy before that sea of lava which was rapidly eating away with its fiery teeth the isle of verdure, from whose highest point he watched the progress of the raging tide which would have devoured him bodily within half an hour.

From the portion that was still untouched came cries of every sort, — the braying of stags, the howling of wolves, the mewing of wildcats, the growling of boars, the yelping of foxes; and, if it had been daylight, they would certainly have seen all those animals, with no indications of hatred for one another, engrossed solely by the danger that caused their assembling in that narrow space, tearing madly through the underbrush, over which a hot, floating vapor was already hovering, the precursor of the flames.

But as if she were more alarmed for Fernand than Fernand for her, Ginesta, after waiting a moment, aroused the young man from his dazed contemplation, and, recalling him to a sense of his position, gave him to understand what still remained to be done by leading the way into the chasm, motioning to him to follow her.

XI.

THE DOVE'S NEST.

THE descent, which seemed familiar to Ginesta, was dangerous for Fernand, and would have been impossible for anybody else.

A white mist rolling along the side of the mountain before a gentle breeze would have been no lighter or more graceful than the young gypsy as she placed her foot on the hardly perceptible jutting points of the almost perpendicular cliff.

Luckily tufts of myrtle, mastic, and arbutus grew here and there in the cletts of the granite, and served at need as points of support for Fernand's feet, while his fingers clung to the creepers that crawled along the face of the wall like gigantic centipedes.

There were moments when even the goat seemed at a loss, and halted, hesitating; at such times Ginesta, no one could guess how, passed her and showed her the road, so to speak.

From time to time she turned, encouraging Fernand with her gestures; for the voice was useless, amid the uproar caused by the roar of the cataract, the hissing of the flames, and the desperate yells of the wild beasts, driven closer and closer together by the narrowing circle of the conflagration.

More than once the girl paused, trembling to see Fernand suspended over the abyss, where you would have said that she was upheld by the wings of a bird;

more than once she held out her hand to him; more
than once she reascended a step or two, as if to offer
him the support of her arm.

But he, ashamed to be outdone by a girl, who seemed
to look upon an enterprise in which they were in peril
of their lives not once only, but twenty times, as mere
play, summoning all his strength, all his courage, all
his self-possession, followed the goat and her mistress
down the wild descent.

About twenty-five feet from the top, at the point
where the falling water broke upon the rock, the gypsy
ceased to descend vertically, taking a diagonal course
and approaching the cascade, which she had avoided
at first as a matter of precaution, for the spray that
escaped from the falling stream made the stones in
its neighborhood more slippery, and therefore more
dangerous.

The fire shed such a brilliant glare, however, that it
lighted up the steep path almost as brightly as the sunlight would have done.

But it might well be that the light, instead of les-
sening the danger, made it even greater by making it
visible.

Fernand was beginning to understand Ginesta's project; ere long he had no doubt whatever concerning it.

The goat, in two or three bounds, had reached the
rock on whose extreme projecting point the cataract
broke; the gypsy arrived there almost at the same
moment, and turned at once to assist Fernand, if necessary, to join her there.

Leaning thus toward the young man, and holding out
her hand to him, framed on one side by the dark surface
of the cliff, on the other by the curve of the cataract,
which, in the glare of the fire, resembled the diamond

arch of a bridge from earth to heaven, she seemed the
very genius of the mountain, the fairy of the torrent.

Not without difficulty did Fernand pass over the space
that separated him from her, short as it was. The
gypsy's bare foot clung to all the protuberances on which
the mountaineer's shoes slipped. Just as he was on
the point of reaching the shelf of granite, the daring
young man's footing failed him; and it would have been
all over with him had not Ginesta, with a strength of
which one would have believed the slender creature
incapable, seized his cloak and held him a moment over
the abyss until he had time to recover his balance.

Having regained his footing, with a single spring he
stood beside the girl and her goat.

But, once he was safe upon the rock, Fernand's
strength gave way; his legs wavered, his forehead was
wet with perspiration, and he would have fallen had he
not found the gypsy's trembling shoulder under his arm,
ready to support him.

He closed his eyes for a moment to give the demon of
vertigo time to fly away.

When he reopened them he started back, dazzled by
the magnificent spectacle before his eyes.

Through the sheet of falling water, clear and transparent as crystal, he saw the roaring flames; it was like
an hallucination produced by magic.

"Oh!" he cried, almost in spite of himself, "oh,
look, Ginesta! how grand it is! how beautiful! how
sublime!"

Like the eagle that hovers about Ætna, the poet's
soul flapped its wings above that mountain transformed
into a volcano.

Feeling that Fernand had no further need of her,
Ginesta gently released herself from the young man's

convulsive embrace; and, leaving him absorbed in his
contemplation, she vanished in the depths of the grotto,
which was soon lighted by the pale gleam of a lamp,
making a pleasant contrast to the blood-red glare cast
by the burning mountain.

Fernand had passed from contemplation to reflection.
There was no longer any doubt in his mind: the burning
of the forest was not an accident; it was a plan devised
by the officers of the detachment that had been sent
against him.

The three notes he had blown on the silver horn to
summon his comrades had informed the troops employed
to hunt the brigands in what part of the mountains
their leader was.   Two hundred or more soldiers had
set out, each with a lighted torch in his hand; they had
formed a huge circle, and each had thrown his torch
into some thicket of resinous shrubs or some clearing
covered with dense grass, and the fire had spread with a
rapidity easily explained by the combustible nature of
the material and the intense heat of the preceding
days.

Only a miracle could have saved Fernand. That
miracle was performed by Ginesta's devotion.

He turned about in an impulse of gratitude; for not
until the last few moments had he taken account of all
that he owed the girl.

Then it was that he saw with profound amazement a
grotto whose existence he, the man of the mountain,
had never even suspected, lighted by the pale light we
have described.

He approached it slowly; and as he approached, his
amazement redoubled.

Through a narrow opening leading from the rock into
the grotto, he saw the young gypsy raising a flat stone

in the floor, and taking from a little hole a ring which she placed on her finger, and a parchment which she concealed in her bosom.

The grotto was hollowed out of the mountain; certain portions of the walls were of granite, like the shelf on which Fernand stood; other portions were of earth, or rather, of the dry, crumbling sand which you find everywhere in Spain as soon as the thin upper layer of loam is removed.

A bed of moss covered with fresh heather was arranged in a corner of the grotto; over the bed, in an oaken frame, was a coarse painting, probably dating back to the thirteenth century, and representing one of the black-faced Madonnas which Catholic traditions delight to attribute to the brush of St. Luke.

Facing the bed were two other paintings of a more advanced, but perhaps less pure style than the first; they were in gilt frames, the gilding of which was, however, somewhat the worse for wear. These paintings represented a man and a woman, each wearing a crown, and above the crown a title, a name and a surname.

The woman, who was dressed in strange fashion, — at least so far as one could judge from the little that could be seen of her figure, — and wore a crown as fanciful as that of an Oriental queen, had the swarthy complexion of the daughters of the South. At the first glance, anybody who knew Ginesta would have thought of the young gypsy, and if the beautiful child had been present, would naturally have turned to look at her; for upon comparing the painter's work with the work of God, a striking resemblance between the two was apparent, although it was plain that Ginesta had not yet reached the age at which the original of the painting had posed for the artist.

Above the crown were these words, —

LA REYNA TOPACIA LA HERMOSA.

Which may be literally translated thus, —

QUEEN TOPAZ THE BEAUTIFUL.

The man, dressed in a magnificent costume, wore the royal crown over a black velvet cap; his long fair hair, cut square at the ends, fell on either side of his face; his pink and white complexion, contrasting strangely with that of the woman, at whom his blue eyes seemed to be gazing amorously, betrayed the man of the North; he was, however, as notable an instance of his type of beauty as the woman was of hers. Both well deserved the flattering epithet attached to their names, which was the same in both cases, varying in gender only, —

EL REY FELIPE EL HERMOSO.

Which signified, —

KING PHILIP THE FAIR.

The young man embraced all these objects at a glance; but his eyes, after wandering from the bed of moss to the Madonna, rested more particularly on the two portraits.

The girl had felt rather than heard his approach; she turned just at the moment when, as we have said, she placed the ring on her finger and concealed the parchment in her breast.

Then, with a smile worthy of a princess proffering hospitality in a palace, she said in her figurative language, —

"Come in, Fernand, and transform the dove's nest into an eagle's eyry!"

"But will not the dove first tell me what nest it is?" asked Fernand.

"That in which I was born," replied Ginesta; " in which I was nursed and reared; that to which I return to laugh or weep when I am happy or when I suffer. Do you not know that every created being has an infinite love for its cradle?"

"Indeed I know it, — I who risk my life every month to pass an hour with my mother in the room in which I was born!"

And the young man entered the grotto.

"As Ginesta consented to reply to my first question," he said, "perhaps she will consent to reply to a second."

"Ask it," said the gypsy, "and I will answer."

"Who are those two portraits?"

"I thought that Fernand was a child of the city; am I mistaken?"

"Why mistaken?"

"Does not Fernand know how to read?"

"Indeed, yes."

"Then let him read!"

She raised the lamp and cast its flickering light upon the pictures.

"Well, I have read," said Fernand.

"What have you read?"

"*Queen Topaz the Beautiful.*"

"Well?"

"I know no queen of that name."

"Not even among the zingari?"

"To be sure," said Fernand. "I forgot, the gypsies have kings."

"And queens," said Ginesta.

"But how does it happen that the portrait resembles you?" queried the brigand.

"Because it is a portrait of my mother," the young girl replied.

Fernand compared the two faces, and was more deeply impressed by the resemblance we have mentioned.

"And the other portrait?" he asked.

"Do as you did with the first, — read."

"Very well, I read, and I see: *King Philip the Fair.*"

"Were you also ignorant that there was once a king of Spain called Philip the Fair?"

"No, child, for I have seen him."

"And so have I."

"When you were very young, then?"

"Yes; but there are memories which sink so deep in the heart that we retain them all our lives, whatever the age at which we may have received them."

"True," said Fernand with a sigh; "I know those memories! But why do the two portraits hang side by side?"

Ginesta smiled.

"Are they not portraits of a king and a queen?" she said.

"To be sure; but — "

He stopped, feeling that he was about to wound the girl's pride.

She continued, still smiling, —

"But one, you were going to say, was king of a real kingdom, while the other was queen of an imaginary kingdom."

"I confess that that was my thought, dear Ginesta."

"In the first place, who says that the kingdom of Egypt is an imaginary kingdom? Who says that she who is descended from the lovely Nicaulis, Queen of Sheba, is not as truly a queen as he is a king who descends from Maximilian, Emperor of Austria?"

"But, after all," queried Fernand, "what has Philip the Fair — "

Ginesta interrupted him.

"Philip the Fair," she said, "was the father of King Don Carlos, who is to be at Granada to-morrow. I have no time to lose, therefore, if I wish to sue to King Don Carlos for what he will perhaps refuse Don Inigo."

"What!" cried Fernand, "you are going to Granada?"

"I start at once. Wait for me here."

"You are mad, Ginesta!"

"In this recess you will find bread and dates. I shall have returned before your supplies are exhausted, and you will be in no want of water, you see."

"Ginesta, I will not allow you, for me — "

"Take care, Fernand! if you do not let me start at once, perhaps the fire may not permit me to reach the bed of the torrent."

"But they who are pursuing me, they who have surrounded this mountain, in which they knew that I had taken refuge, with a circle of flame, will not permit you to pass; they will maltreat you, perhaps kill you!"

"What do you suppose they will say to a poor girl who was surprised by the fire in the mountain, and is making her escape with her goat by following the bed of the mountain stream?"

"True, Ginesta, you are right," cried Fernand; "and if you are taken, it is much better that it should be far away from me than with me."

"Fernand," said the girl, in a deep, grave voice, "if I were not sure of saving you, I would remain here to die with you; but I am sure of saving you, and I go. Come, Maza!"

And without awaiting Fernand's reply, she waved her hand to him in farewell, leaped from the rock to the mountain side, and, lightly as a snowflake, with a foot as sure as that of the climbing beast that accom-

panied her, she descended into the abyss whose genius
she seemed to be.

Fernand, leaning over the precipice, followed her
anxiously with his eyes until she had reached the bed
of the stream, where she leaped from stone to stone like
a wagtail, and soon disappeared between the two walls
of flame that rose from its banks.

XII.

KING DON CARLOS.

LET us leave Fernand resting quietly between the
danger he has escaped and the perhaps greater danger
by which he is threatened, and, taking the same road
with Ginesta, glide with her down the flaming slope of
the mountain to the stream whose bed she followed and
in whose windings she disappeared.

The stream, as we have said, was some three or four
leagues in length, and emptied into the Xenil between
Armilla and Santa Fé, having meanwhile become a
small river.

We will not follow it to that point, however, but
will leave it where Ginesta probably left it, at the point
where, about a league from Armilla, it crosses, under a
stone bridge, a road which is no other than the high-
road from Granada to Malaga.

Having reached that point, we no longer have to fear
that we shall lose our way: the road, which deserved
the name of road from Malaga to Casabermeja, but became a mere path, and a path sometimes hardly visible
when it crossed the Sierra, broadened again at the foot
of the western slope, and became a road once more from
Gravia la Grande.

A casual glance will show you that there is a great
fête at Granada: its thousand towers are surmounted
by the banners of Castile and Arragon, Spain and
Austria; its seventy thousand houses are in holiday

attire, and its three hundred and fifty thousand people
— in the twenty-seven years since it passed from the
hands of the Moorish to those of the Christian kings, it
has lost nearly fifty thousand — and its three hundred
and fifty thousand people are massed in the streets leading from the Jaen gate, through which King Don Carlos
is to make his entrée, to the gateway of the Alhambra
Palace, where quarters have been prepared for him in
the apartments that King Boabdil left so regretfully a
quarter of a century before.

So it happens that upon the shaded bank that leads,
up a gentle slope, to the summit of the *Mountain of
the Sun*, where the fortress stands, and where rises the
Alhambra, that palace built by the wizards of the
Orient, the throng is so great that it is with difficulty
held in check by a line of halberdiers, who are compelled from time to time — persuasion being useless —
to use the handles of their pikes to induce the too
inquisitive spectators to go back to the places they have
left.

At this period, the slope, upon each side of which in
a pebbly bed flows a fresh, rippling stream, which is
fed by the melting of the snow, and but yesterday lay
like a white cloak on the shoulders of Mulahacen, so
that the water is more abundant the hotter the weather,
— at this period, we say, the slope is still free throughout its whole extent; for not until later will Don Luiz,
Marquis of Mendoza, head of the family of Mondejar,
erect in the centre of the road, in honor of the fair-
haired, red-bearded Cæsar, the emblazoned fountain that
sends forth a gigantic sheaf of water, to rise in diamond-
like spray and fall back in icy drops after quivering an
instant on the leaves of the young ash-trees whose inter-
lacing branches form an arbor impenetrable to the light.

It is certainly a caprice on the part of the Granadans
that has led them to select for the young king's abode,
from among the twenty or thirty palaces their city contains, the palace that is approached by this cool avenue:
from the gateway of the Granadas, where the jurisdic-
tion of the Alhambra begins, to that of the Judgment,
which leads into the enclosure of the fortress, not a ray
of sunlight will dazzle his eyes, and except for the shrill
note of the grasshopper and the metallic chirp of the
cricket, he might, within sixty leagues of Africa,
imagine himself beneath the cool and shady groves of
his beloved Flanders.

It is true that he would search in vain throughout all
Flanders for a gateway like that built by King Yusef-
Aboul-Hagiag, about the year of our Lord, 1348, which
owes its name of the Judgment to the custom which the
Moorish kings adopted of dispensing justice in the gate-
way of their palace.

When we say "a gateway" we ought rather to say a
tower, for it is a veritable tower, square and high, with
a great hollow, heart-shaped arch, above which King
Don Carlos will see, as an instance of the instability of
human affairs, the double Moorish hieroglyphic representing a hand and a key: if he has his learned governor,
Adrian of Utrecht, at his side, he will tell him that the
key is intended to recall the verse of the Koran which
begins with the words "He has opened," and that the
hand is stretched forth to conjure the *evil eye*, which
plays such scurvy tricks upon the Arabs and Neapoli-
tans. But if, instead of applying to Cardinal Adrian,
the king should apply to the first child whom he iden-
tifies by his olive complexion, his great velvety eye, and
his guttural enunciation, as one of that Moorish race
which he will soon begin to persecute, and which one

of his successors, Philip III., will finally banish from
Spain, the child will reply, hanging his head and
blushing with shame, that that hand and key were
carved there at the instigation of a prophet of old who
predicted that Granada would not fall into the power
of the Christians until the hand should have taken the
key.

And thereupon the devout King Don Carlos, crossing
himself, will smile with contempt at the thought of
those lying prophets to whom the God of the Christians
has so cruelly given the lie by means of the glorious
triumph of Ferdinand of Arragon and Isabella of Castile,
his paternal and maternal ancestors.

That gateway, which one would say was the gateway
of the firmament — for, as you look at it from below, it
seems to open directly upon the sky — that gateway once
passed, King Don Carlos will find himself on the vast
square of Las Algives, where he may pause for a moment,
and, sitting on his horse, lean over the parapet to see,
lost in an abyss of vegetation, the Moorish city in which
he is to dwell for a few days only, and which is entirely
unknown to him; he will perceive, at the foot of a
precipice, the Darro, which flows through Granada, and
the Xenil, which winds around it, — the Xenil with its
drift of silver, the Darro with its waves of gold; he can
follow, across the broad plain that has preserved its
Arabian name of the *vega*, the course of both rivers,
encumbered with cacti, pistachio-trees, and rose laurels,
under which they vanish at intervals, to reappear farther
on, slender and tortuous, and gleaming like the threads
of silk that the first winds of autumn detach from the
spindle of the mother of our Lord.

On that great square, around a well with a marble
curb, the privileged ones walk back and forth, awaiting

the entrée of the king, which will take place as the clock on the Vela Tower strikes two, — some owing their privilege to the title of *rico hombre*, which this same King Don Carlos will change to that of "grandee of Spain," — as he will change to "Majesty" the less pompous appellation of "highness," with which the kings of Castile and Arragon have hitherto been content; others are "dons" and "señors;" but the ancestors of the dons were friends of the Cid Campeador, the ancestors of the señors companions of Pelagius, and the least among them — in fortune, be it understood, for they all claim to be equal in birth — the least among them deems himself to the full as noble as this petty Austrian prince, who, in their eyes, is Spanish (that is to say, a hidalgo) only through his mother, Joanna the Mad, daughter of Isabella the Catholic.

Nor do all these old Castilians expect any good of this young king, whose Germanic origin betrays itself in his fair hair, in his red beard, in his protruding chin, peculiar characteristics of the princes of the House of Austria. They have not forgotten that his grandfather, Maximilian, caring little for his grandson's succession to the throne of Spain, but much for his succession to the imperial crown, had sent for his mother, in her pregnant condition, to come from Valladolid to Ghent, so that she might give birth in that city to a son who would be not only Infant of Castile, but a Flemish burgher also. It is of no use to tell them that all sorts of happy omens had attended the birth of the child of destiny, who came into the world on Sunday, February 22, 1500, St. Matthew's day; that Rutilio Benincasa, the greatest astrologer of the age, had predicted marvellous things concerning him, apropos of the gifts bestowed upon him by his godfather and godmother, the Prince

8

of Chimay and the Princess Margaret of Austria, on
the day when, preceded by six hundred squires, by two
hundred horse, by fifteen hundred torches, and walking upon carpets from the castle to the cathedral, they
had presented the newly born child for baptism by the
name of Charles, in memory of his maternal grandfather,
Charles of Burgundy, called the Bold; it is of no use
to tell them that, Margaret of Austria having given the
child a silver-gilt ewer filled with precious stones, and
the Prince of Chimay a golden helmet surmounted by a
phœnix, Rutilio Benincasa had predicted that the child
who had received those priceless gifts would some day
be king of the countries where gold and diamonds are
taken from the ground, and that, like the bird he bore
on his helmet, he would be the phœnix of kings and
emperors, — it is of no use to tell them all that: they
shake their heads at the memory of the disasters which
attended his youth, and which, from his first appearance in the world, have seemed to contradict flatly the
sublime destiny which, in their opinion, flattery and
not real knowledge of the future had promised him.

And from the Spanish point of view they have some
right to doubt, for it was in the very year of the young
prince's birth, and during his mother's pregnancy, that
she felt the first symptoms of the disease against which
she has struggled, unable to overcome it, for nineteen
years, and which will leave her in history the piteous
name of "Joanna the Mad," — for, hardly six years
after the child's birth, again on Sunday, the 22d day of
February, the day which was said to be so propitious
for him, his father, Philip the Fair, whose mad love-
affairs had caused poor Joanna the loss of her reason;
Philip the Fair, having gone to take luncheon at a
château near Burgos, which he had given to one of his

favorites, one Juan Manuel, — Philip the Fair, we say, after leaving the table, indulged in a game of tennis, and having become very heated, asked for a glass of water, which was handed him by a young man who belonged neither to his suite nor to Don Manuel's household. The king drank that glass of water, and almost immediately was seized with a sharp pain in the bowels; which did not prevent him from returning, that evening, to Burgos, and going out again the next day to conquer the trouble; but instead of his conquering the trouble, the trouble conquered him; so that on Tuesday he took to his bed, on Wednesday he tried in vain to rise, on Thursday he lost the power of speech, and on Friday, at eleven o'clock in the morning, he gave up the ghost.

We need not ask if desperate attempts were made to find the strange man who had handed the king the glass of water. The man did not reappear, and the whole story, as it was told at that time, seemed to partake much more of the nature of fable than of truth. For instance, one of the rumors that were current said that, among the numerous mistresses that Philip the Fair had had, was a gypsy named Topaz, whom her companions believed to be descended from the Queen of Sheba; that she was betrothed to a prince of the gypsies; but that, having fallen in love with Philip — who, as his surname indicated, was one of the handsomest gentlemen not in Spain alone, but in the whole world — she had disdained the love of the noble zingaro, who had taken his revenge by giving Philip the glass of iced water, after drinking which he died.

However it had come to pass, whether as the result of a crime or from natural causes, his death dealt Queen Joanna a fatal blow: her reason, which had already suffered from several attacks of madness, had gone altogether astray. She refused to believe in her husband's death; in her view — and they did as little as possible to controvert it — he was only sleeping, and, in that belief, she herself dressed the body in the garments that were most becoming to him: a doublet of cloth of gold, scarlet short clothes, and a crimson military cloak lined with ermine; on his feet she placed black velvet shoes; on his head a cap with a crown embroidered thereon; she caused the body to be laid upon a state bed and the doors of the palace to be thrown open for twenty-four hours, so that every one could come and kiss his hand as if he were alive.

They succeeded at last in coaxing her away from the body, which was embalmed and placed in a leaden coffin; and Joanna, still believing that she was accompanying her sleeping husband, attended the coffin to Tordesillas, in the kingdom of Leon, where it was deposited in the convent of Santa Clara.

Thus was fulfilled the prediction of a sorceress, who, when Maximilian's son arrived in Spain, had said with a shake of the head, " King Philip the Fair, I tell you that you will travel farther in Castile dead than alive ! "

But, not abandoning the hope that he would one day rise from his funeral bed, Joanna would not allow the body to be placed in a tomb; she caused it to be placed in the centre of the choir, on a platform, where four halberdiers kept guard night and day, and where four Cordelier monks, sitting at the four corners of the catafalque, repeated prayers incessantly.

There it was that, when he landed in Spain, two years previous to the time at which we have arrived, King Don Carlos, who had sailed from Flushing with thirty-six vessels and disembarked at Villa-Viciosa, —

there it was that King Don Carlos found his insane mother and his dead father.

Thereupon, like a devout son, he had caused the coffin, closed eleven years before, to be reopened, had bent over the body, which was clad in a red robe and perfectly preserved, had gravely and coldly kissed it on the forehead, and, after solemnly promising his mother on his oath that he would never look upon himself as King of Spain while she was alive, had resumed his journey to Valladolid, where he had caused himself to be crowned.

In connection with the coronation there were magnificent festivities and tournaments, in which the king personally took part; but in the mêlée that followed the jousting eight noblemen were wounded, two mortally, and the king took an oath never to give his sanction to a tournament again.

Moreover, about that time he was confronted with an opportunity for a genuine combat instead of a make-believe contest in the lists: Saragossa had declared that she proposed to have a Spanish prince for king, and would not open her gates to a Flemish archduke.

Don Carlos received the news without betraying the slightest sign of emotion. His blue eye disappeared for an instant behind its quivering pupil; then, in his ordinary voice, he gave orders to march upon Saragossa.

The young king battered down the gates with cannon-balls, and entered the city with naked sword, bringing in his train, with matches lighted, the heavy guns which, from the moment of their first appearance, earned the title of the *last argument of kings*.

It was from Saragossa that he issued those terrible decrees against brigandage, which, like the thunder blasts of Olympian Jupiter, furrowed Spain in every direction.

We must understand, of course, that, by the word "brigandage," he who was one day to be Charles V. referred particularly to rebellion.

And so the melancholic youth, the Tiberius of nineteen, would accept no excuse for the non-execution of his orders.

He was at that point in that incessant struggle which lasted two years, half fêtes, half battles, when, on the 9th of February, a courier arrived at Saragossa. It had taken him four weeks to make the journey from Flanders, because of the alternate freezing and thawing, and he brought the news that the Emperor Maximilian died on January 12, 1519.

The Emperor Maximilian, naturally a small man, had been made great by his contemporaries. Francis I. and Alexander VI. compelled him to be of their stature.

Pope Julius II. said of him: "The cardinals and electors made a mistake: the cardinals chose me pope, and the electors chose Maximilian emperor; I should have been chosen emperor and Maximilian pope."

The news of the emperor's death caused the young king the greatest anxiety. If he had been present at his deathbed; if those two politicians — and of the two the child was the master — had taken a few steps together, the younger man supporting the older, on the bridge that leads from earth to heaven, and, having halted halfway on the road to death, had agreed upon the plans to be followed by him who was to return to life, — it is certain that Charles's election would not have been in doubt; but nothing of that sort had happened. No precautions had been taken, the emperor's death was so sudden and unexpected; and Don Carlos, deprived of the support of Cardinal Ximenes, who had recently died, surrounded by his grasping, rapacious Flemings, who had, during the last three years, found a way to squeeze eleven hundred thousand ducats out of Spain, — Don Carlos had produced too unfavorable an impression on that country, which he was to enrich in the future, but which he was ruining in the present, to leave to itself, without great dread, the discontent that was springing up under his feet. If he went to Germany, he was not sure of being chosen emperor; if he left Spain, he was sure that he should cease to be king.

And yet several persons urged him to set sail at once and to leave Spain. That, however, was not the opinion of his trusted adviser, Adrian of Utrecht.

The choice lay wholly between Francis I. and himself.

But, although Don Carlos did not himself start for Germany, his most zealous adherents did, intrusted with full power to act for him.

A courier was sent secretly to Pope Leo X.

What were that secret messenger's instructions? Perhaps we shall learn later.

Meanwhile, and in order that the courier who should bring him information of the result of the election might not require four weeks for the journey, Don Carlos announced that he proposed to travel through the Southern provinces, to visit Seville, Cordova, and Granada.

The courier would thus have only to bestride the Alps, travel across Italy, embark at Genoa and disembark at Valencia or Malaga.

Twelve days after the election Don Carlos would know the result.

He had been told that the Sierra Morena and Sierra Nevada were infested with brigands.

He desired to find out whether they were brigands or rebels.

Hence the orders given to cleanse the Sierras,— orders which had been executed with respect to the *Salteador* by the expeditious method of setting fire to the mountain.

XIII.

DON RUIZ DE TORRILLAS.

WHILE the mountain was burning, the people of Granada were awaiting the arrival of Don Carlos.

His entrée was to take place, as we have said, at two o'clock in the afternoon; in a very few minutes the Vela Tower would give the signal; and, awaiting the moment when the grandson of Ferdinand and Isabella should appear, framed in the Moorish gateway like an equestrian statue, the gentlemen of the first families in Andalusia were walking on the square of Las Algives.

Amid all those gentlemen of noble birth, who walked hither and thither, separately, two by two, talking aloud in groups, or in undertones and secretly, one was especially noticeable by his lofty bearing and at the same time by his profound sadness.

He was sitting on the marble curb around the well in the centre of the courtyard.

His head, which was inclined to one side and rested on the palm of his hand, so that his melancholy gaze could lose itself in the blue depths of the sky, was covered with one of the broad-brimmed hats from which modern hats, while changing their shape, have borrowed the name of sombrero; his hair fell in white curls on his shoulders, his grizzled beard was cut square, and around his neck was the decoration, in the shape of a cross, which Ferdinand and Isabella distributed with their own hands after the fall of Granada to those who had gallantly assisted in the expulsion of the Moors.

Although his preoccupied air held indiscreet curiosity or careless loquacity at a distance, a man of about the same age as he whom we have tried to describe scrutinized him closely for a moment as if to make sure that he was not mistaken in his identity.

A movement made by the old man as he raised his hat and shook his head as if to dislodge the weight of sadness that forces mortal necks to bend, however strong they may be, removed all doubt from the mind of the man who was watching him.

Consequently he approached him and said, hat in hand:

"As I have been your friend from my earliest childhood, it seems to me that it would be ill done of me, witnessing your depression, not to offer you my hand and say, 'Don Ruiz de Torrillas, in what way can I serve you? What commands have you to lay upon me?'"

At his friend's first word Don Ruiz de Torrillas raised his head, and, as he recognized the speaker, held out his hand to him.

"I am obliged to you, Don Lopez d'Avila," he said. "We are, indeed, old friends, and you prove, by the offer you have made me, that you are a faithful friend. Do you still live at Malaga?"

"Still; and you know that, far or near, at Malaga as at Granada, I am always at your service."

Don Ruiz bowed.

"When you left Malaga, was it long since you had seen my old friend — and yours, I think — Don Inigo?"

"I saw him every day. I have heard from my son, Don Ramiro, that Don Inigo and his daughter arrived here yesterday, after being exposed to great peril in the mountains, where they were detained by the *Salteador*."

Don Ruiz turned pale and closed his eyes.

"But they escaped from him," he said, after a mo-

ment's silence, during which, by a mighty effort of his
will, he recovered his strength, which had almost failed
him.

"The truth is that this brigand, who has the audacity
to call himself a gentleman, bore himself like a prince
with them, according to what my son tells me: he released them without ransom, and even without promises;
all of which is the more creditable to him because Don
Inigo is the richest nobleman and Doña Flor the loveliest
girl in all Andalusia."

Don Ruiz breathed again.

"He did that?" said he. "So much the better."

"But I talk to you of my son, Don Ramiro, and neglect
to ask you about your son, Don Fernand; is he still
travelling?"

"Yes," Don Ruiz replied in an almost inaudible voice.

"This is a most excellent opportunity to procure a
place for him at the new king's court, Don Ruiz. You
are one of the noblest gentlemen of Andalusia; and if you
should ask a favor of King Don Carlos, I am sure that,
although he has eyes for none but his Flemings, he would
grant it as a matter of policy."

"I have a favor to ask of King Don Carlos," replied
Don Ruiz; "but I very much doubt if he will grant it."

At that moment the clock on the Vela Tower struck
two.

Those two strokes, whose vibrations ordinarily announced nothing more than that the distribution of the
waters was about to take place, bore a different meaning
on that day. Not only did the waters as usual rush
foaming into the canals, gush from the fountains, and
whirl and eddy in the basins; but as, at the same
moment, all the blaring trumpets announced that King
Don Carlos was riding up the slope to the Alhambra

every one hurried to the Yusef gate in order to be there when he dismounted from his horse.

Don Ruiz de Torrillas was left alone where he sat; he did nothing more than rise to his feet. Don Lopez had followed the other nobles.

The fanfares redoubled, announcing that the king was ascending the slope and coming nearer and nearer.

Suddenly he appeared, mounted on his great war-horse, bristling with steel as if in expectation of battle. He himself was clad in a suit of armor damascened with gold.

His head alone was bare, as if it was his purpose to impress the Spaniards by the sight of that portion of his person which was least Spanish.

In truth, as we have said before, the son of Philip the Fair and Joanna the Mad had no suggestion of the Castilian type in his features, which were formed entirely, if we may so express ourselves, of the quarterings of the House of Austria. Of short stature, thickset, his head somewhat sunken between his shoulders, he was compelled, in order to keep that head erect, with its close-cropped fair hair, its red beard, its twinkling blue eyes, its aquiline nose, its ruddy lips, its protruding chin, to hold it as straight and stiff as if it were kept in that position by a steel gorget; so that he had, especially when he was on foot, a rather stiff carriage, which disappeared when he was astride his horse; for he was an excellent horseman, and the more high-spirited the horse the more brilliant his performance.

It will be readily understood that such a prince, who had none of the physical qualities of the Don Pedros, the Henrys, and the Ferdinands, — although, morally speaking, he was as just as the first, as crafty as the second, and as ambitious as the third, — but who, on the other hand, seemed at first glance to be all Hapsburg,

was not the object of frenzied enthusiasm on the part
of the Spaniards, and especially on the part of the
Andalusians.

And so, upon his arrival, the trumpets redoubled their
brassy clamor, less perhaps to do honor to the grandson
of Ferdinand and Isabella than, by their noisy flourishes,
to cause the silence of the human voice to pass unnoticed.

The king cast a cold, expressionless glance upon the
men and upon their surroundings, and gave no sign of
surprise, although both men and surroundings were in
fact entirely unfamiliar to him; drawing in his horse, he
dismounted, not hurriedly, not in order to come in closer
contact with his people, but because the moment for dismounting had arrived as set down in the prearranged
programme.

He did not even raise his head to look at the beautiful
Moorish gate through which he passed; he did not turn
his eyes to read, on the small chapel beside the gate, the
inscription indicating that, on January 6, 1492, his
grandfather Ferdinand and his grandmother Isabella had
passed through that gate, triumphantly marking out for
him, in the presence of all Spain, intoxicated by the success of her sovereigns, the path which he followed
twenty-seven years later, grave and frowning, amid the
silent respect which always accompanies the progress of
kings whose good qualities are as yet unknown, but
whose faults are known.

The fact was that a single thought was boiling incessantly in that brain, as water boils in a brass kettle,
although he betrayed externally no sign of his agitation;
that thought was his ardent craving for the Empire.

What could that ambitious eye see, fixed as it was,
through all the intervening space, upon the city of Frankfort, where the great conclave of electors was in progress,

in the hall of elections, — a conclave upon which the pope, kings, princes, all the great men of the world, in a word, had, like Don Carlos, their eyes fixed, while every ear was open to catch the slightest sound?

"Are you destined to be emperor; that is to say, as great as the pope, greater than any king?" the voice of ambition constantly whispered in Don Carlos's heart.

What mattered human voices to him, when that voice spoke within him?

It was therefore, as we have said, in compliance with etiquette, and not by reason of the spontaneous impulse of his desire, nor to draw nearer to all the gentlemen who surrounded him, that Don Carlos dismounted.

His whole Flemish suite instantly did the same.

That suite consisted of Cardinal Adrian of Utrecht, his tutor, of the Count of Chièvres, his first minister, the Count of Lachan, the Count of Porcian, the Lord of Furnes, the Lord of Beaurain, and the Dutchman Amersdorff.

But before dismounting, Don Carlos, with his apparently vague and abstracted gaze, had noticed a group of gentlemen who remained covered, while all the others were bareheaded.

That group alone seemed to attract his attention.

"*Ricos hombres!*" he said, motioning with his hand to those whom he addressed to take their places in his suite, but after the Flemish gentlemen.

The Andalusian nobles bowed and took the places assigned them, but like men who acted purely and simply in obedience to a command.

Thereupon the king led the way toward the palace of the Alhambra, which, as seen from the square of Las Algives, seems at the first glance to be nothing more than a great square building with a single door and no windows.

Don Carlos was bareheaded; a page carried his helmet behind him.

The path was clear, every one having taken his place, according to his rank, in the king's suite.

A single man stood in the path, his hat upon his head.

The king, although he seemed not to notice him, did not lose sight of him; perhaps he would have passed him without turning his head in his direction or pausing a second, had not the man in question, with his head still covered, knelt upon one knee as the king approached.

The king stopped.

" Are you a *rico hombre?* " he asked.

" Yes, sire."

" Of Arragon or Castile ? "

" Of Andalusia."

" Free from alliance with the Moors ? "

" Of old and pure Christian blood."

" Your name ? "

" Don Ruiz de Torrillas."

" Rise and speak."

" None but royal ears may hear what I have to say to the king."

" Stand back," said Don Carlos, with a wave of his hand.

All those who were near at hand stood back out of ear-shot, forming a semi-circle, with King Don Carlos and the *rico hombre* Don Ruiz de Torrillas in the centre.

" I am listening," said the king.

XIV.

THE GRAND JUSTICIARY.

"Sire," began Don Ruiz, rising, "if my voice trembles, pardon me, for I feel at once confused and ill at ease to have to ask at your hands a favor like that which brings me before you — "

"Speak slowly, so that I may understand you, señor."

"True," replied Don Ruiz, with more pride than courtier-like tact, "I forgot that Your Highness still speaks Spanish with difficulty."

"I will learn it, señor," retorted Don Carlos, coldly. "I am listening," he repeated, after a moment.

"Sire," Don Ruiz continued, "I have a son twenty-seven years of age. He loved a lady; but, fearing my anger — for I have to accuse myself of having been both too indifferent and too stern with the unhappy youth — fearing my anger, he became betrothed to her without my permission, and, although she accorded him a husband's rights, he delayed from day to day giving her the title of wife, which he had promised her. The señora complained to her father; the father was an old man, and as he felt that his arm was too weak to do battle with an arm of twenty years, he left it to his son, Don Alvar, to avenge the insult. Don Alvar refused to listen to the apologies of my son, — who, I am bound to say, bore himself on that occasion with more prudence than I should have anticipated from one of his character, — Don Alvar refused to listen to his excuses; the two young men fought; Don Alvar was killed!"

"A duel!" Don Carlos interrupted. "I am not fond of duels."

"There are occasions, Your Highness, when a man of honor cannot recoil, especially when he knows that at his father's death he will have the right to render an account of his acts to his king, and crave pardon with head covered."

"Yes, I know that that is a privilege enjoyed by you *ricos hombres*. I will regulate all that. Go on."

"The duel took place without witnesses. Don Alvar's father charged my son with murder, and obtained an order for his arrest. Three alguazils appeared at my house to arrest him, and attempted to carry him to prison by force and in broad daylight. My son killed two, wounded the third, and fled to the mountains."

"Aha!" said Don Carlos, adopting the familiar method of address with Don Ruiz for the first time, but rather as a threat than as a mark of affection, "so that you are [thou art] a *rico hombre*, but your son is a brigand?"

"Sire, the father is dead, and his wrath has died with him; sire, the young woman entered a convent, and I paid her dowry there as if she were a royal princess; sire, I arranged matters with the family of the two dead alguazils and with the wounded alguazil; but, in making those arrangements, I exhausted my whole fortune, so that naught remains of all my patrimony save the house in which I live on Viva Rambla. But that matters little, for the price of blood is paid, and with a word from you the honor of the name will arise unsullied from the ruins of the fortune."

Don Ruiz paused, but, as the king said nothing, he continued, —

"Therefore, Your Highness, I implore you, kneeling at your feet; therefore, sire, I beseech you, ay, a

thousand and a thousand times, as the adverse party no
longer pursues him and there is naught against him save
your royal power, — I implore and beseech you, sire, to
pardon my son!"

The king did not reply.   Don Ruiz continued, —

"That pardon, O my king! I venture to say that he
deserves, not, perhaps, on his own account, — although
I say again to Your Highness that I am in great measure responsible for what has happened, — but because of
his noble ancestors, all of whom say to you by my voice,
'Pardon, sire! pardon!'"

Still Don Carlos said nothing.   One would have said,
indeed, that he had ceased to listen; so that Don Ruiz
continued in a more urgent voice, and bowing almost to
his feet, —

"Sire, sire, cast your eye upon the history of our
family; you will see a multitude of heroes of my race
to whom the kings of Spain owe every sort of honor and
glory!   Have mercy, sire, on my white hair, my prayers,
my tears!   If they are not enough to touch your heart,
have pity on a noble lady, an unhappy mother!   Sire,
sire, being what you are, by your happy accession to the
throne of all the Spains, by your mother, Joanna, by
your grandparents, Ferdinand and Isabella, whom I
served gallantly and loyally, as the cross I wear at my
neck attests, — grant me, sire, the favor that I ask!"

The king raised his head; the cloud that seemed to
veil his glance lightened; but his voice was cold and
utterly devoid of emotion as he said, —

"This does not concern me.   Apply to the grand
justiciary of Andalusia."

And he passed on.

The Flemish and Spanish nobles followed him, and
disappeared behind him in the palace of the Alhambra.

Don Ruiz, utterly cast down, remained alone on the square of Las Algives.

We err when we say that Don Ruiz remained alone on the square: one of the nobles in the train of Don Carlos espied the old man, crushed by the weight of a royal refusal, remained behind the others without affectation, and instead of following them inside the Moorish palace, walked rapidly back toward Don Ruiz de Torrillas; and, halting, hat in hand, in front of the old man, who was so absorbed in his disappointment that he had not noticed his approach, he said, —

"If a gentleman may do himself the honor of recalling his former friendships, I pray you to accept, my dear Don Ruiz, the salutations of one of those men who are most tenderly attached to you."

Don Ruiz slowly raised his clouded face; but his glance had no sooner fallen upon him who saluted him in such affectionate fashion than a gleam of joy shone in his eyes.

"Ah, is it you, Don Inigo?" he said. "I am happy to give you my hand, but on one condition — "

"What is that? Tell me."

"That, as long as you remain in Granada, — I will accept no excuses, I warn you in advance, — you will be my guest."

Don Inigo smiled.

"I did not await your invitation for that, Don Ruiz," he said; "and at this moment my daughter, Doña Flor, is already installed with Doña Mercedes, who, notwithstanding our urgent entreaties that she would not inconvenience herself for us, absolutely insisted on giving up her room to her."

"The wife did, in the husband's absence, what the husband would do in the wife's absence. Then all goes

well at home. I wish I could say the same here !" he
added in an undertone, with a deep sigh.

Low as he spoke, Don Inigo heard him.

Moreover, like all the other nobles, he had seen Don
Ruiz kneeling before King Don Carlos in the attitude
of a man imploring a favor, and it was not difficult to
understand that his request had been refused.

" In truth," he said, " it seemed to me that you were
not fortunate in your application to our young king, my
dear Don Ruiz."

" What can you expect, señor? King Don Carlos
himself admits that he does not yet know Spanish, and
I, for my part, confess that I have never learned
Flemish. But to return to you and to your charming
daughter, Don Inigo, — I hope," he continued in a voice
that he could hardly keep from trembling, " that the
unlucky encounter of yesterday in the mountain has
had no deplorable effect on her health?"

" You already know of that?" asked Don Inigo.

" Yes, señor. Anything that happens to a man of
your eminence is an event that flies on eagle's wings.
Don Lopez told me " — here Don Ruiz' voice trembled
more than ever — " Don Lopez told me that you fell
into the hands of the *Salteador*."

" Did he tell you also that that dreaded chieftain,
a lion and tiger to others, behaved like a gentleman,
not like a brigand, and became a lamb and a dog in his
dealings with us?"

" He told me something of that, but I am glad to
have the news confirmed by you."

" I do confirm it, and I say this in addition, that
I shall not consider myself free from debt to that
young man until I have fulfilled the promise I made
him."

"May I know what that promise was?" asked Don Ruiz, hesitatingly.

"I swore by my patron saint that, having become deeply interested in him, I would not allow King Don Carlos a moment's rest until he had granted me his pardon."

"He will refuse you," said Don Ruiz, shaking his head.

"Why so?"

"You asked me just now what I was doing at the king's feet?"

"I did."

"I was imploring that same pardon."

"You?"

"Yes."

"But what interest have you in that young man? Tell me, Don Ruiz; for I shall act with twofold vigor, knowing that I am acting for a friend of thirty years' standing as well as for a friend of yesterday."

"Give me your hand, Don Inigo."

"There is my hand."

"The man of whom you speak is my son!"

Don Ruiz felt Don Inigo's hand tremble in his.

"Your son," he asked in a stifled voice; "your son and Doña Mercedes'?"

"Of course," Don Ruiz replied with a smile of bitter melancholy, "as Doña Mercedes is my wife!"

"And what did the king reply?"

"Nothing!"

"What do you say, — nothing?"

"Or rather, he replied by a refusal."

"Tell me the terms of his refusal."

"He referred me to the grand justiciary of Andalusia."

"Well?"

"Well, the grand justiciary of Andalusia was Don Rodrigue de Calmenare, and Don Rodrigue de Calmenare is dead."

"Don Rodrigue de Calmenare is dead; but within a week the king has appointed his successor, and that successor arrived at Granada yesterday."

"At Granada?"

"Yes; and I promise you, do you understand, Don Ruiz? — I promise you that you are no more sure of yourself than of the man the king has appointed!"

Don Ruiz was about to question his old companion-in-arms, whose confidence in Providence and in the grand justiciary of Andalusia was beginning to comfort him somewhat, when an usher appeared at the door of the palace, from which they were only about twenty feet distant, and cried in a loud voice, —

"Don Inigo Velasco de Haro, grand justiciary of Andalusia, the king desires your presence."

"You, Señor Don Inigo," cried Don Ruiz, amazed beyond measure, — "you are grand justiciary of Andalusia?"

"Did I not tell you," replied Don Inigo, giving his hand to Don Ruiz once more, "that you could count upon the grand justiciary of Andalusia as upon yourself? Indeed, I might have said more than upon yourself, as I am the successor of Don Rodrigue de Calmenare."

And, rightly judging that one must not delay in answering the summons of a king from whom one has a favor to ask, Don Inigo hastened away to obey the summons of Don Carlos, at as rapid a gait as the dignity of a Spanish *rico hombre* permitted.

XV.

THE COURTYARD OF LIONS.

WE beg leave to follow the grand justiciary into the interior of the palace of the Moorish kings, which Don Carlos had just entered or was about to enter for the first time, and which, perhaps, our readers have never entered.

Following the usher who had summoned him in the king's name, Don Inigo began by crossing a first court-yard, called indifferently the Courtyard of Myrtles, because of the great quantity of myrtles that grew there, the Courtyard of the Reservoir, because of the immense basin that forms its centre, and the Courtyard of the Mezouar, or Women's Bath, because the women of the palace used to bathe in that basin in the days of the Moorish caliphs.

If Don Inigo, familiar as his wandering life had made him with the monuments of the old and new worlds, had not been so deeply preoccupied, both in mind and heart, he would certainly have stopped in that first courtyard, on whose threshold, even in our days, the traveller pauses in wonder and hesitation, for he divines that he is about to enter the mysterious and unknown world of the Orient.

But Don Inigo barely raised his eyes, to see upon its pedestal the gigantic and magnificent vase which Spanish neglect leaves to-day to moulder unnoticed in the corner of a museum that nobody visits, but which then formed

the principal ornament of that courtyard, dominated by
the Tower of Comare, which rose above the cedar beams
and gilded tiles of the roof, its red and orange crenelles
standing out against a clear blue sky.

From the Courtyard of the Reservoir Don Inigo passed
into the antechamber of the *Barca*, and thence into the
Hall of Ambassadors; but neither the peculiar shape to
which the antechamber owes its name of *barca* (boat),
nor the intertwining of the arabesques that cover the
walls, nor the magnificent workmanship of the arches,
painted green and blue and red, and hollowed out of the
stucco with the marvellous delicacy that patient nature
exhibits in the stalactites at which she works a thousand
years, — none of these could for an instant divert Don
Inigo's mind from the thoughts that engrossed it.

He passed thus, silent, walking swiftly, through the
charming pavilion called to-day the Queen's Mirror,
from whose windows can be seen the Generaliffe, resembling an immense clump of rose-laurels, with peacocks,
like birds made of gold and sapphires, perching on the
top; tramping heedlessly upon the white marble flags,
immense perfuming pans pierced with numbers of little
holes, which were used to perfume the sultans when
they left the bath; then, without pausing, he crossed
the garden of Lindacaja, to-day an uncultivated tract
and covered with brambles, then a flower-garden brilliant with flowers; passed on his left the sultanas'
bath, still warm from the breath of the fair Chain-
of-Hearts, and the haughty Zobeide, and was ushered
into the Courtyard of Lions, where the king awaited
him.

The Courtyard of Lions has been described so often
that it is almost useless for us to describe it in our turn;
so we will content ourselves with sketching in a few

words its form and principal ornaments, without introducing anything more than the rough model absolutely essential to our *mise-en-scène*.

The Courtyard of Lions is a rectangle about one hundred and twenty feet long and seventy-three wide, surrounded by a hundred and twenty-eight white marble pillars, with capitals in gold and azure.

Galleries twenty-eight feet from the ground surround the immense *patio*, in the centre of which rises the famous fountain of the Lions.

At the moment when Don Inigo was ushered into the Courtyard of Lions, it had been transformed into a tent, and was covered with broad bands of red, black, and yellow stuffs, forming the colors of Spain and Austria, and serving the double purpose of softening the too glaring light and moderating the too intense heat of the sun.

The fountain of the Lions, with water gushing from every opening, served to cool the air in the great banqueting-hall, where the dinner proffered the young king by the people of Granada and the *ricos hombres* of Andalusia was to be served.

Some of the guests were walking in the courtyard itself, others in the salon of the Two Sisters, which adjoins the courtyard, and others in the gallery overlooking the courtyard.

Don Carlos, leaning against the head of one of the golden lions, was listening to his first minister, the Count of Chièvres, glancing abstractedly at the reddish stains in the granite which are said to be the traces of the blood that spurted from the severed heads of the thirty-six Abencerages who were lured into the snare by the Zegris.

Of what was Don Carlos thinking, and why did his

vague and wandering glance denote such a lack of attention to the words of his first minister? Because he
forgot that he was at Granada in the Courtyard of Lions,
and was transported in thought to Frankfort, to the hall
of elections; and the traditions of the civil wars of the
Moors, romantic as they were, disappeared in face of
the question that was repeated by every pulsation of his
heart, "Who will be Emperor of Germany, Francis
or I?"

At that moment the usher approached the king and
announced that the grand justiciary of Andalusia was
following him.

Don Carlos raised his head; a sort of flash darted
from his eyes in Don Inigo's direction, and, as if to
separate himself from his Flemish favorites, who stood
in a circle about him, and to draw nearer the groups
formed by the Spanish gentlemen at the other end of
the courtyard, he walked forward to meet him whom he
had summoned.

Don Inigo, seeing the king come toward him, divined
his purpose, stopped and waited until he should speak
to him.

"Do you know Don Ruiz de Torrillas?" Don Carlos
asked the grand justiciary.

"Yes, Your Highness; he is one of the most nobly
born gentlemen in Andalusia, and he fought with me
against the Moors under your illustrious ancestors,
Ferdinand and Isabella."

"Do you know what he has asked me?"

"He has asked Your Highness to pardon his son,
Don Fernand."

"Do you know what his son has done?"

"He killed, in a duel, the brother of a lady whose
lover he was."

" And then ? "

" He killed two alguazils who came to arrest him, and wounded the third."

" And then ? "

" He fled to the mountains."

" And then ? "

As he uttered those words the third time, Don Carlos's eyes, which were usually veiled and devoid of animation, gazed into Don Inigo's with the tenacity of obstinate determination and the animation of genius.

Don Inigo recoiled a step; he had no idea that human eyes could emit such a dazzling gleam.

" And then ? " he faltered.

" Yes, I ask you what he did after he fled to the mountains."

" Sire, I am bound to confess to Your Highness that, carried away by the impetuosity of his years — "

" He became a brigand! he robbed and stripped travellers! so that he who wishes to journey from my city of Granada to my city of Malaga, or from my city of Malaga to my city of Granada, should make his will before setting out."

" Sire ! "

" Very good. Now, my grand justiciary, what course, in your opinion, should we take with reference to this brigand ? "

Don Inigo trembled, for there was in the voice of this youth of nineteen an accent of inflexibility which alarmed him for the future of his protégé.

" I think, sire, that we must make many allowances for youth."

" How old is Don Fernand de Torrillas ? " inquired the king.

Don Inigo seemed to be searching his memory for a

date that awoke painful recollections, for he sighed as
he answered, —

"He must be twenty-seven, sire."

"Eight years older than I," said Don Carlos.

And his tone implied, "Why do you speak of youth
in connection with a man of twenty-seven? I am nineteen, and I am old!"

"Sire," said Don Inigo, "genius has aged Your
Highness prematurely, and King Don Carlos should not
measure other men by his stature, should not weigh
other men in his scales."

"Your opinion is, then, as grand justiciary — ?"

"My opinion is, sire, that the circumstances are
peculiar; that Don Fernand is guilty, but has some
grounds of excuse; that he belongs to one of the first
families in Andalusia; that his father, a worthy and
honorable gentleman, has fulfilled all the conditions
ordinarily demanded of the murderer by the victim's
family, and that it would be well for Don Carlos to
signalize his journey through Andalusia by an act of
clemency, and not by an act of severity."

"Is that your opinion, Don Inigo?"

"Yes, sire," said the nobleman, timidly, lowering his
eyes before the young king's eagle glance.

"Then I regret having referred Don Ruiz to you.
I will keep this matter in my own hands, and will
decide it with my conscience."

He turned to the nearest group.

"To table, señors!" he said, "and let us fall to at
once! My grand justiciary here, Don Inigo Velasco,
considers me too stern a judge, and I am determined to
prove to him as speedily as possible that I am not *a
judge*, but justice itself."

With that he turned again to Don Inigo, who was in

a measure dazed by this exhibition of so powerful a will in a young man who was hardly more than a boy.

"Sit at my right, Don Inigo," he said. "When we leave the table we will visit the prisons of Granada together, and there we shall surely find an opportunity to grant a pardon to some one more deserving than he for whom you ask it."

He then walked to the chair intended for his use, and placed his hand upon the crown that surmounted its back.

"King! king!" he muttered; "is it worth while to be a king? Ah! there are but two crowns in the world that are worthy to be craved, — the pope's and the emperor's!"

And, King Don Carlos having taken his place at table with Don Inigo at his right and Cardinal Adrian at his left, all the other guests seated themselves according to their respective ranks and dignities.

A quarter of an hour later — a fact which amply demonstrated the king's preoccupation, for he was an enormous eater, and usually spent two hours over his dinner — a quarter of an hour later Don Carlos left the table, and, declining even the escort of his favorites, the Flemish noblemen, went out, attended by the grand justiciary alone, to visit the prisons of Granada.

But when he reached the entrance to the garden of Lindacaja, he met a young girl who, having been unable to obtain leave from the ushers to go farther into the palace, had asked permission to remain there.

The girl, who, although strangely dressed, was remarkably beautiful, knelt upon one knee when she saw the king, and presented him with one hand a gold ring, with the other a parchment.

Don Carlos started in surprise at sight of those two objects.

The gold ring was the ring of the Dukes of Burgundy, and upon the parchment, below a few lines written in German characters, was this signature, well known to all, but especially to King Don Carlos, as it was his father's signature, —

" *Der König Philipp.*"

Don Carlos stared in sheer amazement, first at the ring, then at the parchment, and finally at the lovely girl in the strange costume.

" Read, sire! " she said in the purest Saxon.

It was in itself an adroit bit of flattery to address Don Carlos in the language of that Germany where he had been reared, and which was so dear to him.

And so the king began to read the familiar characters, turning his eyes at every line, almost at every word, from the parchment to the girl, and from the girl to the parchment.

" Don Inigo," he said, when he had finished reading, " an event has happened which compels me to postpone our visit to the prisons to a later hour. If you have aught to do, dispose of your time as you choose; if not, wait for me here."

" I will await Your Highness," replied Don Inigo, who had recognized in the maiden of the gold ring and the parchment the little gypsy of the Moorish King Inn, and who suspected that there was some connection between her appearance and the pardon which he and Don Ruiz had so vainly solicited at the hands of King Don Carlos in favor of the *Salteador*.

The king contented himself by saying to the girl in the same language in which she had addressed him, —

"Follow me!" at the same time pointing in the direction of the Queen's Mirror, which owed its name to the preference of Isabella the Catholic for that little pavilion as manifested during her sojourn at the Alhambra.

XVI.

QUEEN TOPAZ.

WE have already seen how little influence the sight of external objects seemed to have upon Don Carlos when he was preoccupied by the pressure of some insistent thought.   And so he ascended the few steps leading to what was once the dressing-room of the sultanas, but had become, since the conquest of Granada, the oratory of the queens of Castile, heedless of the fantastic carved work on the walls and ceiling, supported by small Moorish columns of curious and delicate workmanship which were quite worthy to attract the notice of a king.

But, as we have said, the young king, following some phantom of his thought, his imagination, or his desire, seemed to close his eyes purposely to all the marvellous things that arose on every hand, evocations of the Orient.

Having arrived at the Queen's Mirror, Don Carlos halted, and turned to Ginesta without a glance at the beautiful panorama spread before him by nature and art.

"I recognize the ring; I recognize the parchment," he said.   "How does it happen that they are both in your hands?"

"My mother is dead; she left them to me," said the girl.   "They were my only inheritance; but, as Your Highness sees, they were a royal inheritance."

"How did your mother know King Philip the Fair?
How is it that my father's letter is written in German?
How do you yourself know German?"

"My mother knew King Philip the Fair in Bohemia,
when he was only Archduke of Austria. Among his
numerous passions, his love for my mother was the only
one that never weakened. When he set out for Spain in
1506, in order to be proclaimed king, he bade my mother
accompany him; but my mother would not consent unless
the king would acknowledge that the child she had
borne two years before was really his. Then it was
that he gave her the parchment you have in your hand,
sire."

"And the child?" demanded Don Carlos, with a
sidelong glance at the girl.

"That child," she replied, without lowering her
proud eyes, "was myself, Your Highness!"

"Very good!" said Don Carlos, "so much for the
parchment; but about the ring?"

"My mother had often asked the king, her lover, for
a ring, which should at least be a symbol of their union
in God's sight, if not before men; and the king had
always promised her, not a ring simply, but this ring,
which he used as a seal, so that, as he said, she might
be able some day to secure the recognition of the daughter of his love by the son of his lawful wife. My
mother relied upon his promise, and did not urge her
royal lover. Why urge him? Why think of appealing
to the son for what the father could do himself? She
was twenty years old, and her lover twenty-eight —
Alas! one day a man galloped along the road from
Burgos to Santivarez; my mother stood in her doorway;
I was playing with the bees and butterflies among the
flowers in the garden.

10

" ' Queen Topaz,' he cried, ' if you want to see your
lover before he dies, you must make haste !'

" My mother stood for a moment dumb and motionless
with alarm; she had recognized a zingaro prince who
had loved her for five years, and for five years had
wanted to marry her, but whom she had always rejected
with disdain. Then, saying no more than the three
words, ' Come, my child !' she took me in her arms
and ran with me toward Burgos. When we reached
the palace, the king had just gone in, and in the distance we saw the gates close behind the last man of
his suite. My mother tried to gain admission; but a
sentinel had been placed at the gate with orders to admit
no one. She sat down with me on the edge of the moat,
the palace and the fortress being in the same enclosure.
A few moments later a man rode swiftly by.

" ' Where are you going?' called my mother.

" It was one of the king's servants; he recognized
her.

" ' I am going to bring the physician,' he replied.

" ' I must speak to the physician, do you understand?' my mother said to him. ' It's a matter of life
or death to the king!'

" And we remained standing, waiting for the physician
to come.

" A quarter of an hour had not passed when the servant and the physician appeared.

" ' There's the woman who would speak with you,'
said the servant.

" ' Who is the woman?' asked the physician. As
his eyes fell upon my mother, he added aloud, ' Queen
Topaz !' then said, in an undertone, but not so low that
his words did not reach us, ' One of the king's mistresses, but the one he loves best! — What have you

to say to me, woman?' he asked my mother. 'Speak quickly; the king awaits me.'

"'I have to say to you,' my mother replied, 'that the king may be either poisoned or assassinated, but that he is not dying a natural death.'

"'So the king is dying?' said the physician.

"'The king is dying!' my mother repeated, in a tone that I shall never forget.

"'Who told you so?'

"'His murderer.'

"'What has become of him?'

"'Ask the whirlwind what becomes of the leaf it whirls away! His horse was carrying him toward the Asturias, and he is ten leagues away ere now.'

"'I hasten to the king.'

"'Go. Let him know that I am here,' she added, turning to the servant.

"'He shall know it,' the servant replied.

"And they both entered the fortress. My mother returned to her seat on the edge of the moat. We passed the evening there, and the night and the next morning. Meanwhile the news of the king's illness had spread abroad, and the crowd, which had collected around us the evening before and had not left us until well into the night, reappeared at daybreak, more numerous, more anxious, more earnest than ever. All sorts of rumors were in circulation; but that which most impressed my mother, as it was the most probable, was that the king, being heated by his exertions at tennis, had asked for a glass of water, and had received it from the hands of a man who disappeared at once. The description of that man accorded so well with that of the zingaro who had ridden by my mother's door, and, as he passed, had uttered the terrible words that brought us thither, that my mother no longer had any doubt, — the king was poisoned!

" There was no definite news, however. The doctor was with the king, and the persons who came out of the castle were not so well informed as to the sick man's condition that one could depend upon what they said. Everybody waited, therefore, in great anxiety, my mother in an agony of apprehension.

" At eleven o'clock the gate was thrown open; and it was announced that the king, being much improved, was coming forth to reassure the people. A few seconds after the announcement, the king appeared on horseback; he was attended only by his physician and two or three officers of his household.

" It was not the first time that I had seen my father, but it was the first time I had seen him when I was old enough to remember having seen him. Oh, I remember him well: he was wonderfully handsome, notwithstanding his pallor; and yet his eyes were bordered by the red circle of insomnia, his nostrils were contracted, and his bloodless lips seemed as if they were glued to his teeth. His horse was walking; but the rider was so weak that he clung to his saddle-bow, and without that support would certainly have fallen. He was looking to right and left as if in search of some one.

" My mother understood that it was she for whom he was looking; she rose and lifted me in her arms.

" The physician, who had recognized us, touched the king's shoulder, and looked in our direction. The king's sight was so dimmed that perhaps he would not have recognized us. He stopped his horse and motioned to my mother to approach. At sight of that woman with a child of three in her arms, the four persons who formed the royal cortége drew apart. The crowd, divining what was about to take place, for my mother was not unknown to many of those who composed it, did the same. Thus we three — the king, my mother, and myself — were left in the centre of a great circle; the physician alone was sufficiently near to hear what the king and my mother said.

"My mother, without a single word, her breast heaving with the sobs she held back, her cheeks bathed in the tears that escaped in spite of her efforts to restrain them, held me up to the king, who took me in his arms, kissed me, and seated me on the pommel of his saddle. Then, resting his nerveless hand on my mother's head, which he turned back slightly, he said in German, —

"'Ah, my poor Topaz, it is really you!'

"My mother could not reply. She rested her head against the horseman's knee and burst out sobbing as she kissed it.

"'I came out for your sake,' said the king; 'solely for your sake!'

"'Oh, my king! my dear, noble king!' cried my mother.

"'My father, my sweet father!' I said in German.

"It was the first time that the king had heard my voice, and it spoke in the language that he loved.

"'Ah!' said he, 'now I can die; I have been called by the sweetest name that can be pronounced by human lips, and in my mother tongue!'

"'Die!' said my mother, 'die! Oh, my dear lord, what word is that?'

"'The word which God, who permits me to die the death of a Christian, has been whispering in my ear since yesterday; for the moment that I drank that glass of iced water, I felt a shudder run through all my veins to my heart.'

" ' Oh, my dear lord ! my dear lord !' murmured my mother.

" ' I thought of you all night, my poor Topaz !' he said. 'Alas ! I could not do much for you while I lived; dead I can do nothing, except protect you with my shadow, if God permits any part of us to survive ourselves.'

" ' My sweet father ! my sweet father !' I repeated, weeping bitterly.

" ' Yes, my child, yes,' said the king; ' I thought of you too. Take this,' he added, hanging around my neck a little leather purse at the end of a silk and gold cord, — ' take this; no one knows what may happen when I am dead. I leave behind me a jealous widow; your mother may be forced to fly. I passed the night taking these diamonds from their settings; they are worth about two hundred thousand crowns. They are your dowry, my dearest daughter ! and if your brother, when he has become King of Arragon and Castile, should some day refuse to recognize you despite the paper I have given your mother and the ring I now give her, why, you will at least be able to lead the life of a wealthy high-born dame, if not that of a royal princess ! '

" My mother wished to take the ring only, and to refuse the purse; but the king gently put aside her hand. So she had the ring and I had the purse. Moreover, fatigue and emotion had exhausted the poor dying man's strength. He turned even paler, which one would have thought impossible, and swayed toward my mother, helpless and almost fainting. My mother held him in her arms, put her lips to his icy forehead, and called for help; she tottered under the weight of that inert body, which was no longer able to support itself. The physician and the retainers hurried to the spot.

"' Go!' said the physician, ' go!'

" My mother did not stir.

"' Do you want him to die here, before your eyes?' he said.

"' Do you think that my presence is fatal to him?'

"' Your presence is killing him.'

"' Come, my child!' she said.

"' My father! my sweet father!' I repeated again and again. And, as I felt that my mother was taking me away in her arms, I exclaimed, ' No, no! I don't want to go!'

"At that moment we heard a loud cry of anguish from the direction of the city. Queen Joanna, all dishevelled, with distorted features, paler than her dying husband, was running toward us, wringing her hands and crying, —

"' He is dead! he is dead! they told me he was dead!'

" I was afraid; I threw myself on my mother's breast, and just as the circle opened at one point to allow my mother and myself to make our escape, it opened at another point to admit Queen Joanna. My mother hurried along for about a hundred yards; then, her strength failing her, she sat down at the foot of a tree, strained me to her breast, and bent her head over me, her long hair enveloping me like a veil. When she raised her head, when her hair fell from my face, when I looked for King Don Philip, the gate of the fortress had closed upon him and Queen Joanna."

Throughout this narrative the king had not uttered a single word, had not shown the slightest sign of emotion; but as the girl, choked by her tears, was unable to continue, he put out his hand and pointed to a chair.

"Be seated," he said; "you are entitled to be seated in my presence: I am not emperor as yet."

But she replied, shaking her head, —

"No, no; let me go on to the end. I have come here in quest of the king, not of my brother; I have come, not to claim my rank, but to solicit a favor. If my strength fails me, I will fall at your knees, sire; but I will not be seated in the presence of the son of Philip and Joanna. Oh, my God!"

She stopped, overcome by the emotion aroused by her memories.

Then, respectfully kissing the hand the king held out to her, she stepped back and continued her story.

XVII.

THE BED OF STATE.

"My mother remained where she had sat down, or rather, where she had fallen.

"The day passed without other news from the king than this, that he had retired upon returning to the palace.

"On the following day we learned that the king had tried, but in vain, to speak. On the next day the king lost all power of speech about two o'clock in the afternoon. On the next day, at eleven o'clock in the morning, there was a great cry from the castle, which seemed to shatter doors and windows in its haste to spread over the city and to fly thence to every corner of Spain, —

"'The king is dead!'

"Alas! sire, at that time I hardly knew what death or life was. And yet at that cry, 'The king is dead!' feeling my mother's chest heave and the tears roll from her face upon mine, I realized that there was in this world a thing that is called unhappiness.

"During the four days that we remained at the castle gate, my mother took care of me and supplied all my needs; but I do not remember to have seen her eat or drink.

"We remained there one more day and night.

"On the following day we saw the gates of the castle thrown open; a mounted herald appeared, preceded by a trumpeter; the trumpeter blew a mournful flourish and then the herald spoke. I did not understand what he said; but he had no sooner pronounced the words he had to say and gone on to make the same announcement on all the squares and public places in the city, than the crowd rushed to the gate, and flowed in great waves into the fortress.

"My mother rose, took me in her arms, and whispered in my ear as she kissed me, —

" 'Come, my daughter, we are going to see your sweet father for the last time!'

"I did not understand why she should tell me that we were going to see my father and weep as she told me.

"We followed the crowd that rushed toward the gate of the castle, and entered with it. The courtyard was already full; two sentinels were on guard at the door, through which the people were admitted, two by two. We waited a long while; my mother held me in her arms all the time, otherwise I should have been crushed. At last our turn came; we entered like the others; but as soon as we were inside, my mother put me down and led me by the hand.

"They who walked before us were weeping; they who walked behind us were weeping.

"We walked slowly through richly furnished apartments; at every door there were two guards who saw that the people passed through two by two.

"We approached a room that seemed to be the goal of our melancholy pilgrimage.

"At last we entered that room.

"Oh, monseñor, I was very young, but I could describe all the furniture, the hangings, the tapestries, the curtains of that room to the smallest details, every object was imprinted so deeply in my memory.

"But the principal object in the room, the one

which, by its mournful solemnity, soon engrossed all my attention, was a bed covered with black velvet. Upon that bed, dressed in a brocade robe, a crimson cloak lined with ermine, a doublet of cloth of gold, and scarlet short clothes, lay a man in the stiffness and immobility of death.

" It was my father.

" Death had restored to his features the serenity which pain had taken from them when I saw him four days before. In death he seemed even more beautiful than when living, if that were possible.

" Beside the bed, robed in the ermine-lined cloak of royal purple, with the royal crown upon her head, wearing a long white dress, her hair falling in disorder upon her shoulders, stood a woman, with staring eyes, unnaturally wide open, motionless features, colorless lips, and paler, if it were possible, than the dead; she held one finger upon her lips, and said again and again, in a voice so low as to be almost inaudible, —

" ' Be careful and not wake him; he is asleep! '

" It was Queen Joanna, your mother, sire.

" When she saw her, my mother stopped; but she soon realized that the queen neither saw nor heard anything, and she murmured, —

" ' She is very fortunate: she is mad! '

" We kept on toward the bed: the dead man's hand was hanging over the side; it was the hand which everybody was allowed to kiss, and which my mother and I, by virtue of that permission, had come to kiss.

" When my mother reached the bedside, I felt her stagger. She has often told me since that she did not want to kiss that hand, but to strain the body to her heart in a last embrace, to open the closed eyes, to warm the cold lips with her own. She had the courage to restrain herself. I did not even hear her weep at that moment. She knelt without a shudder, without a shriek, without a sob, took the dead man's hand, and gave it to me to kiss first, saying, —

" ' Oh, my child, never forget him you see at this moment, for you will never see him again ! '

" ' It is my sweet father sleeping there, is n't it, mamma ? ' I whispered.

" ' It is the father of a whole people, my child ! ' my mother answered, motioning to me to keep silent.

"And she kissed the dead man's hand long and fondly.

"We went out through the door opposite that by which we had entered; and in the room adjoining the one where the bed of state was my mother staggered, uttered a feeble cry, and fell to the floor in a swoon. Two men, who had also passed through the chamber of death, approached us.

" ' Get up; do get up, mamma ! ' I cried, ' or else I shall think you 're asleep, like my sweet father.'

" ' Look,' said one of the men; ' it 's she ! '

" ' Who is she ? ' the other asked.

" ' The gypsy who was the king's mistress; the one they call Queen Topaz.'

" ' Let us take her and her child away from here,' said the second man.

"And one of them lifted my mother in his arms, while the other led me by the hand. We passed through the royal apartments and crossed the courtyard. The man who carried my mother laid her down at the foot of the tree where we had sat three days and nights; the man who held my hand left me beside my mother, and both of them went away. I threw my arms around my mother and covered her face with kisses.

"'Oh, mamma, mamma! don't go to sleep like my sweet father!' I cried.

"Whether because the air revived her, or because the tears and caresses of a child renewed the sources of life in my mother's heart, or because the natural end of her swoon had arrived, she reopened her eyes. For a moment she could not remember what had taken place; then, assisted by my recollections, which my childish lips reproduced in all their cruel ingenuousness, she finally remembered everything, as one remembers a terrible dream.

"'Come, my child,' she then said; 'there is nothing more for us to do here!'

"And we went back to the house.

"That same evening my mother took down from the wall an image of the Madonna for which she had an especially devout veneration, her own portrait, and the portrait of King Philip, and when it was dark we set forth.

"We walked many days — now that I know something of time, I should say for a month, perhaps — stopping only long enough for needed rest; and at last we reached the Sierra Nevada. There my mother fell in with a tribe of gypsies, and made herself known to them. They gave her the house which has since become the Moorish King Inn. The tribe camped in the neighborhood and obeyed her as their queen.

"This state of affairs lasted for several years; but I noticed that a gradual change was taking place in my mother. She was still beautiful, but her beauty changed its character, and I might almost say its form; she had become so pale that it was the beauty of a phantom, not of a living creature. I believe that she would have left the earth long before, like the mists that rise from the mountains in the morning and float heavenward, had not I, in a certain sense, held her back with my hand.

" One day I noticed that neither the Madonna nor the king's portrait nor her own was in her room; I asked her what had become of them.

" ' Follow me, my child! ' she said.

" She led me into the mountains, and, by a path known only to herself, to a grotto hidden from all eyes, out of sight, undiscoverable. In the grotto, above a bed of heather, was the Madonna; at either side, a portrait.

" ' My child,' said she, ' it may be that some day you will have to seek a place of refuge in the mountains; this is inaccessible; do not reveal its existence to anybody on earth! Who can say to what persecution you may be exposed? This grotto is life; ay, more than life, liberty! '

" We passed the night there; the next day we returned to the house; but, as we were returning, I noticed that my mother's gait was slower and less assured; two or three times on the way she sat down to rest, and each time she drew me to her side and pressed me to her heart. At every kiss, at every embrace, my tears overflowed; for, in spite of myself, my thoughts went back to the day when my father rode out from Burgos, pale and swaying in his saddle, when he pressed me to his heart, and for the first time called me his child in words that I could understand.

" My presentiment did not deceive me.

" On the day following that on which we returned from the grotto, my mother took to her bed. From that moment I realized that she was on the road that leads to eternity, and I never left her.

" And she, knowing that the moment was approaching for the long journey that takes us away from all that is dear to us, talked to me of nothing but my father. She reminded me, in such a way that they were engraved so deeply in my mind that I can never forget them, of all the incidents of my youth as I have told them to you, sire. She gave me the ring; she gave me the paper; she told me that I had — pardon me, Your Highness — that I had a brother who would reign some day; that it was for me to judge whether I ought to make myself known to my brother, or to live, unknown but rich, in whatever part of the world it might please me to inhabit, by grace of the diamonds my father had given me.

"I listened on my knees, weeping, at her bedside; for she no longer left her bed, and every day her face became paler, her voice weaker, her eye brighter; and when I questioned the physician of our tribe, who had studied the science of curing disease under Oriental doctors, and asked him, —

"'What is the matter with my mother?'

"'Nothing,' he replied. 'She is going to God!'

"The day on which God opened the doors of eternity to her arrived.

"I was on my knees beside her bed as usual: she was talking to me, not of herself, but of me. One would have said that her eye, on the point of closing forever, was struggling, in an impulse of maternal affection, to pierce the future. Her mind strove with all the strength of her death agony to grasp an indefinite form. A sort of smile played about her lips. She raised her hand, pointing to something like a ghost that had passed before her eyes. She murmured two words, which I took for the beginning of delirium, for they had no connection with any of our common memories. I thought that I must have misunderstood her; I raised my head to hear better; but twice more, in a feeble voice, she repeated, —

"'Don Fernand! Don Fernand!'

"Then she placed her hands on my head. My head bent beneath that last benediction. I waited for her to raise her hands; I waited in vain: she died, blessing me!

"One would have said that she wished to shield me forever with the buckler of her affection!

"If Your Highness ever travels from Granada to Malaga, you will see my mother's grave in a little valley about a mile beyond the Moorish King. You may recognize it by the stream that flows beside the stone surmounted by a cross, — for my mother, by the grace of the Lord Jesus, was a Christian, — and by this inscription, roughly carved with a knife on the stone:

"La Reyna Topacia La Hermosa.

"And Your Highness will reflect that she who rests beneath that stone is not altogether a stranger to you, as she loved King Philip, our father, so dearly that she could not survive him. Oh, mother! mother!" the girl continued, choking back her sobs, and putting her hands over her eyes to conceal her tears.

"Her body shall be removed to some holy monastery," said the young king, in his quiet voice, "and I will found an *obit*, so that the monks shall say a mass every day for the repose of her soul. Go on."

XVIII.

THE BROTHER AND SISTER.

" Some time after my mother's death," said Ginesta,
" the gypsies determined to change their domicile.
From the day that she closed her eyes they looked on
me as their queen. So they came to tell me of the plan
decided upon by the ancients of the tribe, and to request
my assent. I gave it, saying to them that the tribe
might go where it chose; that it was as free as the birds
of the air; but that, for my own part, I would not leave
the stone under which my mother was laid.

" The council assembled, and I was warned that they
had formed a scheme to seize me during the night preceding their departure, and to carry me with them by
force.

" I procured a supply of dates, which I carried to
the grotto; and, two days before the date fixed for the
departure, I disappeared. On the evening when the
plan of seizing me was to be put in execution they
sought me in vain.

" Thus my mother's precautions bore their fruit: I
had a safe, inaccessible retreat, hidden from every eye.

" The gypsies were determined not to go away without me, and I was determined to remain hidden so long
as they remained.

" They delayed their departure a month. During
that month I left my retreat only at night, to pluck a
little wild fruit, and to ascertain, from the top of the

11

cliffs, by the light of their fires, whether the camp was still there.

"One night the fires were no longer burning. It might be a ruse to lure me into some unsheltered spot and take me by surprise; so I remained hidden in a clump of myrtles, from which, by putting out my head, I could overlook the whole road. There I waited for daylight.

"When daylight came it showed me that the house was abandoned and the road deserted. I dared not go down, however, but postponed my explorations till night.

"The night was dark and without a moon; the stars alone twinkled in a sky of such a deep blue that it was almost black. But to us gypsies, daughters of the darkness, there are no shadows so dense that our eyes cannot penetrate them.

"I went down to the road; on the other side was my mother's grave, and I went and knelt there. In the middle of my prayer I heard the step of a horse. The rider could not be one of my comrades, so I waited without fear; indeed, at night, in the mountains, I would have defied the gypsies themselves.

"It was a traveller.

"As he rode by, I rose to my feet, having finished my prayer; doubtless he took me for a spectre rising from its grave. He cried aloud, crossed himself, urged his horse to a gallop, and disappeared.

"The sound of the horse's hoofs grew gradually fainter, then died away altogether. The darkness became silent once more, and the silence was disturbed only by the usual noises of the mountain, the creaking of the trees, the falling of a stone, the howl of a wild beast, the hoot of a bird of night.

"I was very certain that there was no human being in the neighborhood.

"Therefore the gypsies had gone.

"The first hours of daylight confirmed what the darkness had told me.

"I felt as if I were relieved of an immense weight.

"I was free; the mountain was mine, the whole Sierra became my kingdom.

"I lived thus several years, without desires, without needs, living, like the birds, on our wild fruits, the water from our springs, the night air, the morning dew, and the noonday sunlight.

"I was about my mother's size. Her clothes fitted me, her trinkets sufficed me; but I lacked something: it was a companion.

"One day I went as far as Alhama. I purchased a goat and returned.

"While I was absent, an innkeeper had taken possession of our house. He questioned me. I told him who I was, but without telling him where I lived. He asked me for some information, which I gave him, concerning the frequency with which travellers passed.

"Gradually, as a result of the opening of the inn, the mountain became peopled anew. Its guests were men with stern faces and savage manners; they frightened me. I went back into the woods, and never saw the inn or the road except from a distance, and from some inaccessible spot.

"Unusual noises woke the echoes of the mountain; sometimes there were reports of firearms, sometimes yells of rage, sometimes calls for help.

"The gypsies were succeeded by the brigands.

"To me there was no great difference; ignorant of the laws of society, having no notion of what was good or what was evil, seeing the abuse of weakness by force throughout all nature, I believed that the world of cities was made on the same plan as the world of the mountain.

"And yet those men frightened me; I moved farther and farther away from them.

"One day I was walking, as my custom was, in the wildest part of the Sierra; my goat was leaping from rock to rock, and I behind her, but some distance away, stopping every moment to pluck fruit or flowers, or wild berries. Suddenly I heard my dear, faithful companion utter a bleat of pain, then another, but farther away, then a third, still farther away; you would have said a gust of wind was carrying her off, and that, being unable to resist that superior force, she was calling to me for help.

"I rushed in the direction from which the cries came. I heard a shot, perhaps half a mile away. I saw the smoke curling up above the bushes; I ran toward the smoke and the noise, without a thought that I might be running into danger. As I approached the spot where the shot was fired, above which the smoke was still floating in the pure atmosphere of the Sierra, I saw my goat coming toward me: she was dragging herself along, bleeding from wounds in the shoulder and neck; but when she saw me, instead of coming to me, she turned back, as if to urge me to follow her. The poor creature's instinct could intend no harm to me, so I followed her.

"In a clearing near by stood a handsome young man of twenty five or six years, leaning on his arquebus and watching an enormous she-wolf struggle in the agony of death. At that sight everything became clear to me: the wolf had seized upon my goat, and was carrying her away to her cubs, to devour her with them; the young hunter had fallen in with the fierce beast and broken both her hind legs with his ball. The wounded wolf had released the goat; the goat had returned to me, and then, in her gratitude, had led me back to the man who had saved her life by killing her enemy.

"As I drew near the young man a strangely disturbed feeling took possession of me: he seemed to me of a nature superior to everybody I had ever seen. I thought him almost as handsome as my father. He, on his side, gazed at me in amazement; it was evident that he was in doubt whether I was a mortal creature, and that he took me for one of the spirits of the streams, the flowers, or the snow, which, according to tradition, and especially the traditions of our race, wander among the mountains.

"He was waiting, therefore, for me to speak first, in order that he might form an idea, from my words, the tones of my voice, or my motions, what I was, when suddenly a strange thing took place in my mind: although there was nothing to connect the present with the past, although there was no analogy between what I had before my eyes at that moment and what I had had before them five years before, there came to my memory the whole scene at my mother's death-bed, when she, enlightened by the approach of death, raised herself in her bed with her arm extended, pointing to some object that I could not see; and her hoarse voice, as living and distinct as I had heard it on the day of her death, murmured in my ear the same words it had murmured on that day, ' Don Fernand! '

"'Don Fernand!' I repeated aloud, yielding to an inward impulse and without even thinking of what I was saying.

"'How do you know me?' asked the astonished

young man. 'How do you know my name when I don't
know yours?'

"And he glared at me almost angrily, convinced that
I was a supernatural being.

"'Is your name really Don Fernand?' I asked.

"'You must know that it is, as you call me by it.'

"'I called you by that name,' I said, 'because that
name came to my lips just as I caught sight of you;
but, aside from that name, I know nothing of you.'

"And I told him how my dying mother had uttered
that name, and how, ever since that day, it had lain
asleep in my memory, where it had suddenly waked at
that moment.

"Whether it was a case of instantaneous sympathy,
or whether there really exists between us one of the
secret bonds that join the threads of two persons' destinies long before they meet, from that moment I loved
that young man, not as one loves a stranger whom one
meets by chance, and who tyrannically takes possession
of one's thoughts, but as a being whose life, though it
may have been lived entirely apart from yours, is destined sooner or later, after a détour, to unite and be
inextricably mingled with yours, like the brooks that
flow from separate springs, which, after watering two
different valleys, after losing sight of each other and
forgetting each other's voices, suddenly meet at the foot
of the mountain of which each has bathed one slope, and
plunge into each other's arms in mutual recognition.

"I do not know if it was the same with him; but I
do know that from that day to this I have lived in his
life, and it seems to me that, without any effort, I may
almost say without any pain, whatever cut short his
life would cut short mine.

"This state of affairs had lasted two years when I

learned of your arrival in Andalusia by the increased severity of the measures taken against Fernand.

"Day before yesterday Don Inigo and his daughter crossed the Sierra. Does Your Highness know what happened to them?"

Don Carlos, his eyes still veiled, made an affirmative motion of the head.

"Behind Don Inigo and his daughter came the troops who dispersed Fernand's band, and, instead of wasting their time tracking him from Sierra to Sierra, set fire to the mountain and surrounded us with a circle of flames."

"You say us, girl?"

"I say us, yes, Your Highness, for I was with him. Did I not tell you that my life was bound to his?"

"Well, what happened?" inquired the king. "The leader of the brigands surrendered, was captured?"

"Don Fernand is safe in the grotto my mother revealed to me."

"But he cannot remain in hiding forever; hunger will force him to come out of his retreat, and he will fall into the hands of my troops."

"That is what I thought, too, Your Highness," said Ginesta; "that is why I took this ring and this parchment and came to you."

"And when you arrived you learned that I had refused to pardon the Salteador at the solicitation of his father, Don Ruiz de Torrillas, and subsequently at the solicitation of the grand justiciary, Don Inigo?"

"Yes, I learned that, and it confirmed me in my desire to gain access to the king; for I said to myself: 'Don Carlos may refuse a stranger what he asks in the name of humanity or of favor; but Don Carlos will not refuse a sister what she asks in the name of their father's tomb ! ' — King Don Carlos, your sister prays for the pardon of Don Fernand de Torrillas, in the name of Philip, our father."

As she uttered the last words with the utmost dignity, Ginesta knelt on one knee before the king.

The young monarch gazed at her for a moment in that humble posture, without speaking, and without the slightest external indication of what was taking place in his mind.

"And suppose I should tell you," he rejoined after a brief silence, "that the pardon you solicit, which I had sworn to grant to no one, can be granted only on two conditions?"

"Then you grant me his pardon?" cried the maiden, trying to seize the king's hand to kiss it.

"Wait until you know the conditions, girl, before you thank me."

"I listen, O my king! I wait, O my brother!" said Ginesta, raising her head, and looking at Don Carlos with a smile of ineffable joy and devotion.

"What if the first of these conditions were that you must give me the ring, destroy the parchment, and bind yourself by the most terrible of oaths never to mention your royal birth, of which the ring and the parchment are the only proofs?"

"Sire," said the girl, "the ring is on your finger, — keep it; the paper is in your hands, — destroy it; dictate the oath to me and I will repeat it. What is the other condition?"

There was a momentary gleam in the king's eyes, but it vanished at once.

"It is customary among us chiefs of the religion." he continued, " when we pardon some great sinner from the temporal penalty he has incurred, to do so on condition that some pure soul, who can obtain his spiritual pardon, shall pray for him at the altar of the God of mercy. Do you know any chaste and innocent human creature, who is disposed to enter a religious institution, to renounce the world, — to pray night and day, in short, — for the salvation of his soul whose body I will save?"

"Yes," said Ginesta; "tell me at what convent I must take the vows, and I will enter it."

"There will be a dowry to pay," muttered Don Carlos, as if he felt some shame at imposing this last condition upon Ginesta.

Ginesta smiled sadly, and, taking from her bosom the little leather bag stamped with the arms of Philip the Fair, she opened it and poured at the king's feet the diamonds it contained.

"There is my dowry," she said; "it will be sufficient, I trust; for my mother assured me more than once that these diamonds were worth a million."

"So you abandon everything," queried Don Carlos, — "social rank, happiness to come, worldly fortune, — to secure the brigand's pardon?"

"Everything!" replied Ginesta; "and I have but one favor to ask; that is, that I may carry him the pardon myself."

"Very well," said Don Carlos; "you shall have what you wish."

And, going to a table, he wrote a few lines, which he signed with his hand and sealed with his seal.

Then, returning to Ginesta at the same slow and solemn gait, —

"Here," said he, "is the pardon of Don Fernand de Torrillas; hand it to him yourself; he will see, upon reading it, that at your request his life and honor are safe. On your return, we will agree upon the convent you are to enter."

"Oh, sire!" cried the girl, seizing the king's hand; "oh, how good you are, and how earnestly I thank you!"

She ran down the stairs as lightly as if she were upheld by the wings of a bird, crossed the garden, hurried through the apartments, left the Courtyard of the Reservoir behind her, and found herself once more on the square of Las Algives, having neither walked nor run, but soared, as one does in a dream.

When she had gone, Don Carlos carefully picked up the diamonds, put them in the leather purse, bestowed purse, ring, and parchment in a sort of secretary, of which he took the key, then walked slowly and pensively downstairs.

At the foot of the stairs he found Don Inigo, and looked at him in amazement, as if he had no idea of finding him there.

"Sire," said the grand justiciary, "I am here by command of Your Highness, who ordered me to await him here. Has Your Highness no orders to give me?"

Don Carlos seemed to make an effort to remember; forcing back his constant thought of the Empire, which covered up all his other thoughts, as the obstinate, everflowing tide covers the beach, he said, —

"Ah, yes, you are right. Inform Don Ruiz de Torrillas that I have signed his son's pardon."

And while Don Inigo betook himself to the square of Las Algives to announce the good news to his friend, Don Carlos walked on toward the Courtyard of Lions.

XIX.

THE ASSAULT.

GINESTA was already on the road to the mountain.

Let us go before her and see what had happened in the grotto after she left it.

Fernand followed her with his eyes so long as he was able to see her, and not until she had passed completely from his sight did he consider himself alone.

Then he turned his eyes once more upon the conflagration. The whole mountain was enveloped in the blazing sheet; the shrieks of the wild beasts were stifled by the fire and smoke, and naught could be heard save the mighty roaring of the vast furnace, mingled in Don Fernand's ears with the rushing of the cataract.

It was a magnificent spectacle; but, magnificent as it was, it became fatiguing at last. Nero, who had so long desired to burn Rome, finally turned his dazzled eyes away from the burning city and returned to his little retreat on the Palatine, dreaming of his golden house.

Don Fernand returned to his grotto and lay down upon his bed of heather, likewise dreaming.

Dreaming of what?

He would have found it hard to say. Was it of the beauteous Doña Flor, whom he had seen pass before his eyes like a luminous meteor, and whom in his strength he had saved?

Was it of the gentle Ginesta, whom he had followed through the winding paths of the forest, as the lost sailor follows a star, and who had saved him in his weakness?

However that may have been, he ended by falling asleep as tranquilly as if he were not surrounded by five or six leagues of mountains, all burning on his account.

A little before daybreak he was aroused by a strange noise which seemed to come from the bowels of the mountain. He opened his eyes and listened.

A vigorous, continuous scratching was in progress within a few feet of his head; it was as if a miner were working desperately on some underground lead.

Don Fernand did not hesitate a moment as to the cause of the noise: his enemies had discovered his retreat, and, recognizing the absolute impossibility of attacking him in front, were at work in the mountain with a view of attacking him by a subterranean mine.

He rose and examined his arquebus; the match was in good condition, and he had twenty or twenty-five cartridges beside the one with which it was loaded; and when his ammunition was exhausted he had his Pyrenees knife, upon which he relied almost as much, yes, more than upon all the firearms in the world.

He seized his arquebus, therefore, and put his ear close to the wall of the grotto.

The miner seemed to be making constant, if not rapid progress; it was evident that after a few hours more of such assiduous toil he would succeed in putting himself in communication with the grotto.

At daybreak the noise ceased. Doubtless the miner was taking a little rest. But, in that case, why did not one of his companions go on with his work?

That is what Don Fernand could not explain.

Like all logical minds, he did not persist in seeking the solution of a problem he could not understand, saying to himself that the time would come when the mystery would be explained, and that he must wait patiently for that time.

The young man had every reason in the world to wait patiently.

In the first place, he had no fear of famine for five or six days at least: Ginesta, it will be remembered, had placed a supply of provisions at his disposal; he attacked them gallantly an hour or two after sunrise, and it was easy to see, by the ardor with which he applied himself to that duty, that the precarious situation in which he found himself had no influence whatever upon his appetite.

In the second place, he had two grounds of hope for relief from that situation instead of one, — Don Inigo's offer and Ginesta's promise.

Let us admit frankly that the young man relied less on the little gypsy's influence, notwithstanding the hint she had given him of her own story and her mother's, than upon that of Doña Flor's father.

And then, too, the heart of man is ungrateful; perhaps Don Fernand, in his then frame of mind, would have preferred to receive a benefit from Don Inigo's hand than from Ginesta's.

He had understood, by the feeling Don Inigo aroused in him, the force of the feeling that he himself inspired in the noble old man.

There was some strange sympathy, something like the voice of blood between the two men.

Don Fernand was roused from his reflections by the same noise he had heard before.

He put his ear to the wall of the grotto, and with the lucidity that daylight imparts to the human mind, always a little obscured, like nature itself, by the darkness, he became more thoroughly convinced that a skilful miner was working persistently to effect a communication with the grotto.

If the miner accomplished his task, — that is to say, if he established communication between a tunnel, as it is called strategically, and the grotto, — Don Fernand would have to maintain an unequal contest in which he would have no chance of success.

Would it not be better, when night had fallen, to try a sortie, and endeavor, with the assistance of the darkness and his knowledge of the locality, to reach some other part of the mountain?

But had not the fire, which had licked with tongues of flame the vast, almost perpendicular wall, by consuming the mastics, myrtles, and creepers that crawled along the surface or grew in the crevices, removed every semblance of support for the fugitive's feet and hands?

Don Fernand leaned out of the grotto to see whether the path Ginesta had followed before the fire was still practicable.

As he was intent upon that investigation a report rang out and a bullet flattened against the granite within six inches of the spot where his hand was resting.

Don Fernand looked up. Three soldiers, standing on top of a rock, were pointing him out to one another, and a tiny cloud of white smoke floating in the air over their heads indicated that the shot had come from them.

The *Salteador* was discovered.

But he was not the man to receive such a challenge without replying to it.

He took his arquebus, aimed at that one of the three who was just reloading his weapon, and was therefore, presumably, the one who had fired.

He pulled the trigger; the man threw up his arms, dropped the arquebus which had just rendered him such an ill service, and pitched head foremost down the mountain.

A great shout arose. There was no further doubt : the man they were looking for was found.

Fernand drew back into the grotto to reload his arquebus, and, that done, approached the opening once more.

But the two companions of the man he had killed had disappeared, and in the whole vast semi-circle overlooked by the grotto, as far as his eye could reach, he could see nothing. A stone or two, rolling down from the top of the mountain and bounding against its sides, were the only indication that the troops were assembling above Don Fernand's head.

The work on the mine still continued.

It was evident that, the *Salteador's* hiding-place having been discovered, he was to be attacked by every possible means.

He prepared, therefore, for his part, all his means of defence, made sure that his Basque dagger worked easily in its sheath, that his arquebus was well primed, and seated himself on the bed of heather, where he could listen to what was going on behind him and see what was taking place in front.

After about half an hour of suspense, during which his mind had naturally passed from vigilance to revery, he imagined that he saw a shadow pass between himself and the light, that an opaque body was swaying at the end of a rope at the entrance to the grotto.

Being unable to ascend to the grotto from below, the soldiers had undertaken to descend to it from above ; a man, covered with a full suit of armor, almost entirely hidden behind a bullet-proof buckler, had attempted the feat, made fast to a rope, being tempted by the thousand gold philips promised to the man who should capture the *Salteador*, dead or alive.

But just as the soldier, after swinging across the cataract, was about to step upon the rock, a shot from an arquebus filled the grotto with noise and smoke.

The bullet, powerless to pierce the buckler or find a hole in the armor, had contented itself with severing the rope just above the head of the man hanging at the end of it.

The soldier fell headlong into the abyss.

Three more attempts of the same nature were made; all three had the same result.

Each time a terrible shriek arose from the precipice, and was answered by another shriek, like an echo, from the top of the mountain.

Doubtless after these three attempts, fatal to those who made them, the besiegers concluded that they must have recourse to some other method of attack, for the last shrieks were succeeded by absolute silence, and no other soldier appeared.

To be sure, the miner continued his toil underground, and the mine made rapid progress.

With his ear glued to the wall Don Fernand watched the approach of night. The night threatened him with an attack from two directions. Under cover of the darkness the soldiers might succeed in scaling the cliff. At all events, the mine was now so near that within an hour communication would be opened between it and the grotto.

The *Salteador's* experienced ear told him that a single man was at work at the subterranean task, and that man was separated from him by a layer of earth so thin that he could tell when he changed from one hand to the other.

The most astonishing thing was that the noise that reached his ears was neither the blow of a mattock nor the bite of a pickaxe; it was rather like a constant scratching.

One would have said that the miner had no other tool than his hands for his digging.

The noise came nearer and nearer.

For the third time Don Fernand placed his ear to the wall. The miner was so near that he could hear his hoarse, jerky breathing.

Fernand listened more attentively than ever; his eyes shot forth flames that lighted up his face; a smile of joy played about his lips.

He left the back of the grotto, walked out to the slippery edge of the rock, leaned over and looked into the abyss to make sure that he was threatened by no danger from without.

Everything was calm and peaceful; the pall of night, sombre and silent, enveloped the mountain. It was evident that the soldiers had abandoned all idea of attack in the hope of subduing the brigand by starvation.

"Oh, give me but half an hour more," muttered Fernand, "and I will not thank King Don Carlos for the pardon that is being solicited for me at this moment."

Thereupon he rushed back into the grotto, his Basque dagger in his hand, and began to dig on his side, going to meet the person who was coming toward him.

The two workmen rapidly approached each other. After about twenty minutes, the feeble wall that still separated them crumbled away, and Fernand, as in all probability he anticipated, saw in the aperture the monstrous head of a bear, resting on two enormous paws.

The animal breathed heavily. His respiration resembled a roar. It was that noise, well-known to Fernand,

12

which had betrayed the formidable quarry to the fearless hunter.

Upon that respiration, which he had recognized, Fernand had constructed a scheme of flight.

He had said to himself that the bear's den was doubtless contiguous to the grotto, and that it would present a means of exit not likely to be watched.

And so, when he saw that his anticipations were realized by the event, he looked at the monster with a smile.

"Ah!" he muttered. "I know you, old bear of Mulahacen! it was you whose trail I was following when Ginesta called me; it was you who roared when I attempted to climb the tree to look at the fire; and now, willing or unwilling, you are going to let me pass. Come, make room!"

As he spoke he struck the bear's muzzle with the point of his dagger.

The blood spurted out; the animal howled with pain and retreated backward into his den, leaving the opening clear.

Fernand glided through the opening with the rapidity of a snake and found himself within four paces of the bear in his own den; but the animal had so placed himself as to block his path.

"Yes," muttered Fernand; "yes, I know that only one of us two will go from here alive; but it remains to find out which one it will be!"

As if he had understood what the hunter said to him, the bear replied with a threatening roar.

Then there was a moment's silence, during which the two adversaries measured each other with their eyes. Those of the beast seemed like red-hot coals.

Neither the one nor the other budged; you would

have said that each was waiting for the other to make a false step of which he might take advantage.

The man became tired first.

Fernand looked among the ruins of the wall for a stone; chance favored him; he found by his foot a fragment about the size of a paving-stone.

The two blazing eyes served as a target, and the stone, thrown with all the force of a machine of war, struck the animal's head with a dull thud.

A bull's frontal bone would have been crushed by the blow.

The bear fell upon his knees and Fernand saw the gleaming eyes disappear for an instant behind their drooping lids.

Then the animal seemed at last to decide to attack, and with a terrible roar he stood erect on his hind legs.

"Aha!" said Fernand, stepping toward him, "so you have made up your mind at last!"

Resting the hilt of his dagger against his breast while he turned the point toward his adversary, he continued:

"Come on, comrade, let us embrace!"

It was a terrible embrace! the kiss was deadly! Fernand felt the bear's claws sink into his shoulder; but the bear felt the sharp point of Fernand's dagger penetrate to his heart.

The man and the animal rolled together on the floor of the cavern, which the wounded bear inundated with his blood.

XX.

HOSPITALITY.

At nightfall Ginesta entered the mountains.

But before we follow her it will be well for us to pay a visit to the house of Don Ruiz de Torrillas, on the heels of the grand justiciary of Andalusia.

The reader will remember perhaps the few words the king had said to Don Inigo as he descended the stairs from the Queen's Mirror, behind Ginesta.

Don Inigo, without pausing to wonder by what strange influence the gypsy had succeeded in obtaining from the king a favor that the king had refused Don Ruiz and himself, had betaken himself at once to Don Ruiz' house on the square of Viva-Rambla near the Granada gate.

It will be remembered also that the grand justiciary, upon coming to Granada to remain as long as Don Carlos should tarry in the capital of the Moorish kings, would have considered it an insult to his friend Don Ruiz not to go at once and ask at his hands the hospitality which his old companion-in-arms had once offered him at Malaga.

Consequently, as he had told Don Ruiz on the square of Las Algives, he had presented himself with his daughter at his friend's house on the day following his arrival, and had demanded the proffered hospitality.

Doña Mercedes was alone; for Don Ruiz, as we know, had been on the square of Las Algives, awaiting the king, since the morning.

Beautiful still, although past forty, Doña Mercedes had the reputation of a matron of antiquity; her life had been lived in the sight of all men, pure and stainless, and no one in Granada had ever dreamed of suggesting the slightest shadow of a suspicion concerning the wife of Don Ruiz.

When she saw Don Inigo, Mercedes uttered a stifled exclamation and rose; her face, ordinarily pale, was suffused with a sudden flame that disappeared with the rapidity of lightning, leaving the lovely face even paler than before; and, strangely enough! as if the same feeling that had taken possession of Doña Mercedes had acted upon Don Inigo, it was only after a moment's silence, during which Doña Flor gazed in amazement at her father and Mercedes, that he recovered the power of speech.

"Señora," he said, "I have come to pass a few days at Granada, for the first time since my return from America. I should consider that I behaved very ill to an old friend if, after that friend had come to Malaga to offer me the use of his house, I should take up my quarters at an inn or with any other gentleman of my acquaintance."

"Señor," Mercedes replied, with her eyes fixed on the floor, and in a voice whose emotion she tried in vain to master, but whose vibrating tones thrilled Doña Flor, — "señor, you are right; and if you had done otherwise, Don Ruiz would certainly say that either he or his wife had forfeited your esteem, and as he would be very sure that it was not he, he would ask me, as a judge questions a prisoner, if it were not I."

"That, señora," replied Don Inigo, lowering his eyes in his turn, "that, over and above the very natural desire to see a friend of thirty years' standing, is the real motive" — he emphasized the last two words — "the real motive that has brought me to your house."

"It is well, señor," said Mercedes; "remain here with
Doña Flor, upon whom I should be only too happy to
bestow a mother's love, if she would deign for a moment
to let me believe that she is my daughter. I go to see
that the hospitality accorded you ,in my husband's house
is as worthy of you as is possible in the state of decadence
into which this poor household has fallen by reason of
my husband's generosity."

And Mercedes, bowing to Don Inigo and his daughter,
left the room.

In speaking of her husband's generosity, Doña Mercedes alluded to what Don Ruiz had told the king touching the impoverished condition to which he was reduced
through having purchased from their families the blood
of the two alguazils killed by his son, and through having
paid the dowry of Don Alvar's sister at her convent.

This generosity was the more remarkable, and the
more praiseworthy, too, because, as we have said, Don
Ruiz had never had any great fatherly affection for his
son.

A footman, an old retainer of the family, had entered
the room behind Doña Mercedes, bringing pastry, fruit,
and wine upon a plate of gilded copper, embellished with
Arabic paintings.

The grand justiciary waved the plate away with his
hand; but Doña Flor, with the artless greediness of
birds and children, always ready to taste what one offers
them, opened a juicy, red pomegranate, and dipped
her lips, ruddier and fresher if that were possible than
the blood of the fruit, in what was called the wine of
Xeres.

A quarter of an hour later Doña Mercedes, returning
to the room, or rather opening the door, invited her
guests to follow her.

Her bedroom had become Doña Flor's; her husband's had become Don Inigo's.

It did not occur, either to Don Inigo or to Doña Flor, to apologize for the disturbance they caused in Don Ruiz' household; hospitality had its laws, which were respected by him who received as by him who offered it. Don Inigo and Doña Flor would have done as much if they had entertained Don Ruiz and Doña Mercedes, instead of being entertained by them.

Don Inigo installed himself in Don Ruiz' chamber while Doña Flor was doing the same in Mercedes', and, laying aside his travelling costume, dressed to go and meet the king.

We have seen him cross the square of Las Algives in Don Carlos's suite, and return to make known his arrival to Don Ruiz.

We know also that an usher, by summoning the grand justiciary of Andalusia to attend the king, had disclosed to Don Ruiz the title, as yet unannounced, of his old friend.

Don Ruiz returned home so depressed in mind that his wife, who saw him enter the house, did not dare meet him; she withdrew to her new apartment, which was above her former one, leaving the old servant Vicente to wait upon his master, tell him of the change that had taken place in the house, and show him to his new apartment.

The king's manner, when he referred Don Ruiz to the grand justiciary of Andalusia, was so stern that Don Ruiz relied but little even upon Don Inigo's influence to obtain his son's pardon. It was necessary to glance but once at the young king's cold, unmoved face to realize what an unbending will was concealed behind that marble brow; so that Don Inigo's delay did not surprise his host; on the contrary, his surprise knew no bounds when he saw Doña Flor, with beaming countenance, suddenly throw open the door between the two rooms, crying, first to Doña Mercedes, then to Don Ruiz, —

"Oh, come, come! my father is here with a message from King Don Carlos that Señor Don Fernand's pardon is granted."

Thereupon they went down into the common reception-room.

"Good news! good news!" cried Don Inigo, when he saw the husband and wife; "leave the door open for happiness to come in, for happiness is at my heels!"

"It will be the more welcome guest in this house," replied Don Ruiz, "for having been so long a stranger."

"The Lord's mercy is great," said Mercedes, devoutly; "and though I were on my death-bed without having seen the guest whom you announce, señor, I should still hope that it would arrive in time to receive my last breath."

Thereupon Don Inigo narrated the strange event in all its details: how the king had sternly denied his request, and how he had granted the pardon to the little gypsy who, on her knees, had handed him the ring and the parchment.

Doña Mercedes, to whom, as a mother, no one of the details concerning her son was without interest, and who was ignorant of what her husband had learned from Don Inigo, that he and his daughter had fallen into the *Salteador's* hands the day before — Doña Mercedes asked who the gypsy was.

Thereupon Doña Flor took her hand, and said, giving to the noble matron the title she had seemed to crave, —

"Come, mother!"

And she led Doña Mercedes to her room.

There, in order to soften as much as possible the pain-

ful features of what she had to tell. Doña Flor knelt at
the feet of Fernand's mother, and, with her elbows on
Mercedes' knees, her eyes gazing into hers, and her hands
clasped, she narrated, with all the delicacy of which her
heart was capable, what had happened to her father and
herself at the Moorish King Inn.

And Mercedes listened, with bated breath, her mouth
half open, shuddering at every word, passing from joy to
terror, from terror to joy, thanking God with infinite
gratitude, when she learned that the redoubtable *Saltea
dor*, who had so often been described to her, by those who
did not know that they were speaking to his mother,
as a ferocious, implacable assassin, had been gentle and
kind to Don Inigo and his daughter.

From that moment a warm attachment for Doña Flor
had sprung up in Mercedes' heart; for a mother's love is
such a marvellously inexhaustible treasure that, even
while she gives all that love to her son, she still finds a
way to love those who love him.

And Doña Flor, with a joyous heart and overflowing
with fondness for Fernand's mother, passed the evening
with her head resting against Doña Mercedes' shoulder,
as if she were her own mother; while the two old men
walked back and forth under the double row of trees in
front of the house, talking gravely of the probable future
of Spain in the hands of the fair-haired and red-bearded
young king, who bore so little resemblance to the Castilian and Arragonese kings, his predecessors.

XXI.

THE FIELD OF BATTLE.

MEANWHILE, — that is to say, while the two old men were talking together, and Doña Mercedes and Doña Flor smiling in each other's faces, in a silence more expressive than the most eloquent words, — Ginesta, as we said at the beginning of the last chapter, entered the mountain.

Within a fourth of a league of the inn she fell in with a cordon of troops.

This time, however, she was looking for them, not trying to avoid them.

"Oho!" they cried, "here's the pretty girl with the goat!"

The girl went directly to the officer in command.

"Señor captain," said she, "read this paper."

It was the order not to molest the *Salteador*, signed and sealed by Don Carlos.

"The devil!" muttered the officer; "it was hardly worth while to burn up seven or eight leagues of forest and lose four men."

After reading the document a second time, as if the thing seemed so strange to him that he was not convinced by a first reading, he said to the girl, whom he took for an ordinary gypsy, —

"Of course you will undertake to carry this paper to him where he now is?"

"I will," replied Ginesta.

" Off with you, then ! "

Ginesta hurried away.

" Just let me give you one bit of advice," the officer called after her: " be sure that he knows who you are and what your errand is, or he may receive you as he received my soldiers."

" Oh, I have nothing to fear," said Ginesta; " he knows me."

" By St. James!   I don't know whether you ought to boast of the acquaintance, my pretty child! "

And he motioned to her that she was at liberty to continue her journey.

Ginesta was already far away.

Her path was all marked out for her: the torrent offered its foaming, pebble-strewn bed to enter the smoking furnace by the same road by which she had left it when it was a mass of flames.

She followed it to the foot of the waterfall.

There her goat, who was leading the way, took fright and ran back to her.

Ginesta approached.

Her eyes, which were accustomed to the darkness, and could see almost as well as in broad daylight, distinguished the form of a dead body.

It was that of the first soldier who had fallen over the precipice.

She stepped aside to the right, and her foot stumbled against a second corpse.

She darted forward, and was obliged to step over a third.

She could not interrogate death; but the very silence of death told her that there had been a struggle, ay, and a terrible struggle.

What had become of Fernand in that struggle ?

For one moment a cry trembled on her lips, ready to ascend to Fernand; but Ginesta reflected that the roar of the cataract would cover her voice, and that, even if her call did reach him, it might also be heard by those who were besieging him.

And so, silent and light of foot, she darted to the wall, which she must scale before reaching the grotto.

Only a fairy or an angel could undertake such a climb. The time that a bird would have taken to cover the distance, with the help of his wings, was the time taken by Ginesta.

When her feet touched the projecting rock, she put her hand to her heart, for it was beating as if it would break the walls of her chest.

Then she called Fernand.

Ginesta felt the sweat of agony gather at the roots of her hair. A breeze like that which comes through a half-open door froze the drops upon her brow.

She called again.

The very echo remained dumb.

In the darkness it seemed to her that she could detect a new opening at the back of the grotto.

She lighted the lamp.

It was a gaping aperture, and there issued from it that mysterious noise which terrifies one because it is neither the clamor of life nor the silence of death, but the rumbling of the unknown.

She put her lamp to the opening.

The draught extinguished it.

She relighted it, and, sheltering the flame with her hand, proceeded from the first grotto into the second.

The goat would not follow her, but remained on the other side of the opening, trembling and bleating uneasily.

A great heap of earth, all of which had fallen in the second grotto, proved to her that the work of establishing communications had been finished, if not begun, by Fernand.

Then she began to scrutinize the walls of the cavern. During the scrutiny her foot slipped on a damp spot.

She put her lamp to the ground; the ground was all soaked with blood.

The lamp nearly fell from her hand.

But she summoned all her strength, and held the lamp toward the ceiling in order to light up the whole of the den as well as possible.

A black, hairy mass lay in one corner.

At the same time the acrid odor exhaled by wild beasts reached her nostrils.

It was that odor which frightened the goat.

Ginesta drew near the black mass; it did not move. As she approached, she recognized the great black bear of the mountains.

She leaned over him and turned the light of her lamp upon him. He was dead.

The blood was flowing from a deep wound below the breast, just where his heart lay.

The gypsy made bold to touch the creature's body; it was still warm. It was not more than an hour, therefore, since the battle took place.

Thereupon she began to understand. The animal had kept in his contracted claws some fragments of cloth torn from Fernand's cloak. Therefore it was with Fernand that he had fought. Indeed, who but Fernand could have triumphed over such an adversary?

With that everything was made clear to her.

Fernand had been attacked, and had killed the men whose bodies she had found.

Then, fearing to be driven to bay in his retreat, he had dug that opening.

The opening had led him into the bear's den. The bear had barred his passage, and he had killed the bear.

Then he had made his escape through the other entrance, which, being hidden from sight in the burning bushes, had not been discovered.

Her assumption was the more certain because the bloody imprint of Fernand's feet could be traced in the direction of the second opening.

The underground passage leading to the outside world was from a hundred to a hundred and twenty feet in length.

Ginesta, having entered by the opening beside the waterfall, went out by the other opening.

A party of soldiers was stationed on the summit of the mountain, — a proof that Fernand was believed to be still in the grotto.

Here and there some parts of the forest were still in flames. They were the places where the fire had encountered groups of resinous trees.

On all sides columns of white smoke, like tall ghosts enveloped in their winding-sheets and with their feet rooted in the ground, swayed to and fro in the evening breeze.

Ginesta, herself a thread of vapor, vanished among the other vapors.

The next morning, at daybreak, a young girl, wrapped in a mantle that entirely concealed her face, appeared on the square of Viva Rambla, knocked at the door of Don Ruiz' house, and asked to be allowed to speak with Doña Flor.

Doña Flor, still happy and smiling over the good news Don Inigo had brought the day before, welcomed the gypsy as one welcomes even a stranger when the heart is keeping holiday.

Now, when the heart is keeping holiday, the face resembles the windows of an illuminated house; however carefully the curtains may be drawn, however carefully closed the shutters, some rays of the light within always flash through.

And they who pass stop when they see those telltale rays and say, " Happy people live in that house ! "

At sight of that joyous expression, which made Doña Flor more beautiful than ever, the gypsy sighed softly.

Soft as that sigh was, Doña Flor heard it.

She thought that the girl had come to solicit some favor at her hands.

" You asked to see me ? " she said.

" Yes," murmured Ginesta.

" Come nearer, and tell me what manner of service I can render you."

Ginesta shook her head.

" I have come, señora," said she, " to render you a service, not to ask a favor at your hands."

" To render me a service ? " exclaimed Doña Flor, in amazement.

" Yes," said Ginesta; " you wonder, do you not, what service any one can render the daughter of the wealthy and powerful Don Inigo, when she is young and fair and beloved by Don Fernand ? "

Doña Flor blushed, but did not say no.

" Ah, well," continued Ginesta, " one may bestow upon her a gift of inestimable value: one may give her the pardon of the man who loves her."

" But I thought," said Doña Flor, " that the pardon had been carried to Don Fernand, who was in hiding in the mountains."

"Don Fernand," rejoined Ginesta, sadly, "is no longer where I left him; I do not know where Don Fernand is."

"Great Heaven!" cried Doña Flor, trembling from head to foot.

"I know simply that he is out of danger," continued Ginesta.

"Ah!" murmured Doña Flor, joyously, while the smile reappeared on her lips and the carmine on her cheeks.

"And I have brought the pardon to you, so that you may hand it to him."

"The pardon?" stammered Doña Flor. "But I have no idea where Don Fernand is. Whom shall I ask? Where shall I go to find him?"

"You love him, and he loves you!" said Ginesta.

"I cannot say, — I think so; I hope so," murmured Doña Flor.

"Then you will certainly find him, as he will seek you!"

And Ginesta handed Doña Flor the parchment containing Don Fernand's pardon.

But, although she had taken the utmost pains to conceal her identity up to that moment, her hood fell away when she made that movement, and allowed Doña Flor to obtain a glimpse of her face.

"Oh!" she cried, "the little gypsy of the Moorish King Inn!"

"No," replied Ginesta, in a voice in which God alone could read all the suffering; "no, Sister Felippa of the Annonciade."

The Annonciade was the convent selected by Don Carlos for the gypsy to pass her novitiate and take the vows.

XXII.

THE KEY.

ABOUT midnight Doña Flor left the balcony of the apartment she occupied in Don Ruiz' house.

It was, the reader will remember, Doña Mercedes' bedroom; hospitality had offered the guest the best that the house afforded.

Why did Doña Flor leave the balcony so late? Why did she close the blind so late and with such heedless fingers?

What had detained her till midnight, with wide-open eyes and ears on the alert?

Were her eyes awaiting the beautiful star Hesperus, that rises in the west?

Was her ear listening to the nightingale singing his hymn to the night, hidden among the rose-laurels that bloomed on the banks of the Darro?

Or did her eyes see naught, her ears hear naught, and was her mind lost in that dream of sixteen years which people call love?

Ginesta doubtless was weeping and praying in her cell at the Annonciade Convent.

Doña Flor breathed the cool air and smiled. Perhaps she was not in love as yet; but, just as a celestial emanation announced the appearance of the angel Gabriel to the Virgin Mary, so did a strange perfume reveal to Doña Flor the approach of the god Love.

The strangest thing about the young girl was the division of affection in her heart between the two young men who loved her.

The man she feared, the man she would have avoided if he had made his appearance, the man with whom she would have had an instinctive feeling that her maidenly modesty was in danger, was that handsome cavalier, that gallant love courier, as he had styled himself, who had ridden before her on the road from Malaga, — Don Ramiro.

He whom her feet would of themselves have gone out to meet, he upon whose shoulder she would have gone to sleep without fear, he whom she would have gazed at for an hour without a thought of blushing or of casting down her eyes, was the highway robber, the brigand of the Moorish King Inn, — Don Fernand.

Doña Flor was in that frame of mind when the soul is exalted and the body full of languor, as she approached her mirror, the last courtier at night and first in the morning, and nodded to her maid to undress her.

The maid understood so well that any question she might ask her mistress when her mind was so preoccupied would remain unanswered, that she began to prepare the lovely girl's night toilet without uttering a word.

As for Doña Flor, never, perhaps, had her eyes, with the long velvety lashes, her dilated nostrils, her half-opened lips disclosing the enamel line of her teeth, said so plainly to the night, " I am sixteen years old, and I long to love and to be loved."

The maid was not mistaken. Women have a marvellous instinct for divining the presence or even the approach of Love.

She perfumed her mistress, not like a young virgin

about to be put to bed, but like a young bride who awaits the coming of her husband.

Then, with tottering, languid steps, with a thrill at her heart, Doña Flor walked to her bed; and, like the Borghese hermaphrodite, lay down with her neck thrown back a little, and her lovely dark head resting on her beautiful white arm.

She had been slow to reach that point, and yet she was in haste to be alone. She had made a sort of solitude by maintaining perfect silence; but that solitude was not sufficient, — she wished to be actually alone.

She raised her head to follow the last steps of her maid, who walked back and forth in the room, looking about without any idea what she was looking for, remaining in order not to go, and deciding at last to leave the room, not suspecting that, by so doing, she was gratifying her mistress's ardent wish, but, on the other hand, quite prepared to return and apologize for leaving her alone when she seemed so cast down.

The maid took away the lamp, leaving the room bathed in the pale, fantastic light cast by a night-lamp through its alabaster shade.

And yet, soft as it was, that light was evidently too strong for the girl's eyes, for she raised her head a second time, and with a sigh of fatigue drew the curtain of the bed as a barrier between herself and the lamp; so that, while the lower two-thirds of the bed were bathed in a flood of bluish light like moonlight, the upper third was in darkness.

Every woman has at some time been fifteen years old, every man eighteen, and every man and every woman has kept in that corner of the memory that corresponds with the heart the recollection of what he saw through that door of youth opening upon paradise. We will not

try, therefore, to materialize Doña Flor's dreams: the
rose is composed of red and white leaves; a maiden's
dream is composed of hope and love.

Little by little the sweet and lovely child passed from
waking dreams to the dreams of sleep. Her drooping
lids closed, her closed lips opened, something like a
cloud floated between the outer world and her thought;
she heaved two or three sighs, long-drawn and languish-
ing, like sighs of love; then the fluttering agitation of
her breast was succeeded by soft and regular respiration. The angel who was keeping watch over her put
his head between the bed-curtains, leaned over her and
listened.

She was asleep.

Ten minutes passed, and no sound disturbed the
religious silence; then, suddenly, there was the sound
of a key turning in a lock; the door was cautiously
opened and closed; a cavalier, wrapped in a long brown
cloak, appeared in the half-light, turned the key in
order not to be taken by surprise, stole forward on tip-
toe, and deposited a kiss on the sleeper's brow, murmuring, "Mother!"

The sleeper started, opened her eyes, and uttered an
exclamation; the young man, greatly surprised, sprang
to his feet, letting his cloak fall, and stood forth in the
light of the night-lamp in a handsome gentleman's
costume.

"Don Fernand!" cried the girl, drawing the counter-
pane up to her lips.

"Doña Flor!" murmured the stupefied young man.

"Why are you here at this hour, señor? Whom do
you seek? What do you want?"

Before replying, the *Salteador* drew the thick bed-
curtains together until they touched, enclosing Doña

Flor in a tent of brocade; then he stepped back and knelt upon one knee.

"I came, señora," he said, "as truly as you are fair and as truly as I love you, to bid my mother farewell for the last time, and to leave Spain forever!"

"And why do you leave Spain forever, Don Fernand?" the girl asked from her prison of silk and gold.

"Because I am proscribed, hunted, a fugitive; because my life has been saved by a miracle; because I do not wish to inflict upon my parents, my mother especially — whose room I had no idea that you were occupying — the shame of seeing their son upon the scaffold."

There was a moment's silence, during which naught could be heard save the hurried beating of the maiden's heart; then the curtains of the bed moved slightly, and a white hand holding a paper was passed through the opening between them.

"Read!" said a trembling voice.

Don Fernand took the paper without daring to touch the hand that gave it, and unfolded it, while the hand returned behind the curtains, leaving unclosed the opening it had made.

The young man, without leaving his place or changing his attitude, held the paper toward the light and read: —

"We, Charles, by the grace of God King of Spain, Naples, and Jerusalem, do hereby declare to all men that we do grant full and entire amnesty for all crimes and misdemeanors he may have committed to Don Fernand de Torrillas — "

"Oh!" cried Don Fernand, seizing Doña Flor's hand between the curtains and kissing it; "oh, thanks, thanks! Don Inigo has fulfilled his promise, and you,

like the dove of the ark, are commissioned to bring the
olive-branch to the poor outlaw."

Doña Flor gently withdrew her hand, and said with
a sigh, —

"Alas! read on."

Don Fernand, surprised by her words, turned his
eyes once more on the parchment and read on: —

"We do further declare, in order that the person named
in this pardon may know to whom he is indebted therefor,
that it is granted at the solicitation of the gypsy Ginesta,
who has bound herself to enter the convent of the Annonciade to-morrow, and to take the veil there as soon as her
novitiate shall be at an end.

"Given at our palace of the Alhambra, this 9th day of
June in the year of grace, 1519."

"Oh, dear Ginesta!" murmured the brigand; "she
too promised me!"

"Do you pity her?" demanded Doña Flor.

"Not only do I pity her, but I will not accept her
sacrifice."

"But if the sacrifice were made by me, would you
accept it, Don Fernand?"

"Oh, much less; for, if the sacrifice is to be measured
by the loss it entails, you, who are rich, noble, and
honored, would lose much more than a poor little gypsy,
without rank or kindred or future prospects."

"Then that must be why she seemed to be content to
enter the convent!" Doña Flor ventured to say.

"Content!" repeated Don Fernand, shaking his head;
"do you think it?"

"She said so; and for a poor, wandering girl, of
humble birth, who asks alms on the high-roads, a
convent is a palace."

"You are mistaken, Doña Flor," said the young man, distressed by the slighting tone in which Don Inigo's daughter, pure as she was herself, spoke of the devotion of one whom she might look upon as a rival, — "you are mistaken: Ginesta not only is not a beggar, but she is, perhaps, after yourself, one of the wealthiest heiresses in Spain. Ginesta is not of humble birth, for she is the daughter, and the acknowledged daughter, of Philip the Fair. In very truth, for that child of the fresh air and the sunlight, that fairy of the mountain, that angel of the high-road, even a palace would be a prison. Judge, therefore, what a convent is likely to be to her. Ah, Doña Flor! Doña Flor! you will be none the less beautiful and less dearly loved for allowing her love and her devotion to retain all their perfume."

Doña Flor sighed.

"So you refuse your pardon at the price of her sacrifice?" she said.

"Man is a sad coward when he is influenced by an ardent desire," was his reply; "and I am afraid of doing a dastardly thing in order to remain with you, Doña Flor."

The young man heard the long-drawn, shuddering sigh of joy.

"Then I may tell Doña Mercedes of your return, Don Fernand?"

"I came to announce my departure, Doña Flor; tell her that she will see me to-morrow, or rather to-day. You are the angel of good news!"

"Until later in the day, then," said Doña Flor, putting forth her white hand between the curtains for the second time.

"Until later," said Fernand, rising and touching his

lips to the hand held out to him, with as much respect
as if it had been the hand of a queen.

Picking up his cloak, he wrapped himself in its long
folds, and, bowing toward the bed with its drawn curtain as he would have bowed before a throne, he took
the key from his pocket, opened the door, stopped to
cast one last glance toward Doña Flor, who followed
him with her eyes through the opening between the
curtains, and vanished as noiselessly as a ghost in the
dark depths of the corridor.

XXIII.

THE PRODIGAL SON.

THE next day a festal atmosphere, a perfume of happiness was diffused through the house of Don Ruiz de Torrillas.

Doña Mercedes had informed the old retainers of the family — a small remnant as firmly attached to Don Ruiz in his adversity as they had been in his more prosperous days — Doña Mercedes had informed them that she had heard from Don Fernand, and that their young master said that he should arrive that very day from the long journey that had kept him away from Spain for nearly three years.

It goes without saying that Doña Flor was the messenger who brought the good news; so it was that Doña Mercedes treated Don Inigo's daughter as her own child, and gave her, in anticipation, all the kisses she would have liked to give Don Fernand.

About nine o'clock in the morning, Don Ruiz, his wife, and Beatrice — Mercedes' old maid and Fernand's nurse — were sitting in the hall on the lower floor of the house, which they had reserved for their own use.

Doña Flor had come down early in the morning to inform them of Don Fernand's return, without telling how she knew it, and had remained with them as one of the family.

Doña Flor and Doña Mercedes were sitting side by side. Doña Flor had her hand in Doña Mercedes'

hand, her head upon her shoulder. The two women
were talking together in undertones.

There was evident constraint in Mercedes' manner,
however, every time that the young girl uttered Don
Fernand's name in a tone that indicated a feeling a
little warmer, perhaps, than friendship or friendly
interest.

Don Ruiz was walking back and forth, his head bent
forward upon his breast; his long white beard stood out
against his gold-embroidered black velvet doublet; from
time to time, when he heard the sharp ring of a horse's
shoes upon the pavement of the street, he raised his
head and listened with contracted brow and dejected
eye. His face presented a striking contrast to that of
Doña Mercedes, whereon maternal love was displayed
in all its expansiveness, and even to that of old Beatrice,
who had established herself in a corner of the room,
adjusting her desire to see Don Fernand at the earliest
possible moment to the respect which bade her keep at
a distance from her masters and their children. There
was nothing in Don Ruiz' face indicative of the joy of
a father awaiting a son whom he loved so dearly that he
had sacrificed his fortune for him.

What was the explanation of the stern expression
upon Don Ruiz' face? Was it assumed in preparation
for the reproaches he would be justified in heaping upon
the young man, — reproaches which could hardly be rec-
onciled, however, with the earnestness he had displayed
in soliciting his son's pardon? or was it attributable to
some other reason, buried in the depths of his heart,
the secret of which he confided to no one?

Every time that Don Ruiz raised his head at the
sound of a horse's hoofs on the pavement, the two
women broke off their conversation and listened, with

hearts beating rapidly and eyes fixed on the door, while Beatrice ran to the window, hoping to be the first to cry to her mistress, "There he is!"

The horseman passed on; the horse's step, instead of stopping, died away in the distance. Don Ruiz let his head fall on his breast once more, and resumed his march. Beatrice returned, sighing, from the balcony, shaking her head with an expression that said as clearly as possible, "It isn't he!" and the two women continued their confidences under their breath.

Five or six horsemen had passed in this way; five or six times the same sounds had been repeated, to die away in the distance after giving birth to a vain hope in the hearts of those who listened, when they heard once more the hoof-beats of a horse coming from the direction of the Zacatin.

The stage business, so to speak, that had accompanied each previous repetition of the sound, was gone through with once more; but this time Beatrice uttered a loud cry of joy.

"Ah!" she exclaimed, clapping her hands, "it is he! it is my boy! I recognize him!"

Mercedes sprang to her feet, carried away by an outburst of motherly love.

Don Ruiz looked at her with a strange expression as she remained where she stood, without taking a step toward the door.

Doña Flor blushed, then turned pale; she had risen with Doña Mercedes, but, being less strong than she, fell back upon her chair.

A moment later they saw a horseman ride by the windows; and that time the sound of the horse's hoofs did not pass the door, whose bronze knocker rang through the house.

But not one of the persons who, with such different emotions, awaited the arrival of the man who had just raised the door-knocker, changed the attitude he or she had assumed; their faces alone betrayed the thoughts of the three women and the man who, with true Spanish gravity and in accordance with the strict etiquette in vogue in the sixteenth century, not only at court, but in all noble families, held them in subjection with his glance.

They heard the street door open and steps approaching; Don Fernand appeared, but, as if he shared the general feeling of constraint, paused upon the threshold.

He was dressed in a handsome travelling costume, and had all the appearance of a man just returned from a long journey.

He cast a rapid glance about the room, and upon the persons who were awaiting him there. Don Ruiz was the first upon whom his eye fell; then, at Don Ruiz' left and in the foreground, the two women, his mother and Doña Flor, supporting each other; and lastly, in the background, old Beatrice, as motionless in his presence as she had been excited in anticipation of his coming.

In that glance, rapid as it was, every one had his part. For Don Ruiz it was cold but respectful; for Doña Mercedes, loving and eloquent; for Doña Flor, impassioned and full of tender memories; for Beatrice, affectionate.

Then, bowing before his father, Don Fernand began, as if he were returning from an ordinary journey,—

" Señor, blessed be the day when you permit my filial love to kneel at your feet, for that day is the happiest of my life! "

And as he spoke, the young man, with evident repug-

nance, but as if he were performing an obligatory ceremony, put one knee to the floor.

Don Ruiz gazed at him for a moment in that humble
posture, and in a voice that accorded ill with his words,
for the words were affectionate and the voice retained
some harshness of accent, he said,—

" Rise, Don Fernand; welcome to this house, where a
father and mother have long been anxiously awaiting
you."

" Señor," the young man replied, " something tells me
that I should remain on my knees before my father, so
long as he does not give me his hand to kiss."

The old man stepped forward toward his son.

" Here is my hand," he said; " and may God make
you as virtuous as I urgently entreat Him to do from the
bottom of my heart!"

Don Fernand took his father's hand and touched it
with his lips.

" Now," said the old man, " enter the house and kiss
your mother's hand."

The young man rose, saluted Don Ruiz, and approached
his mother.

" Señora, with fear and trembling, and with a heart
overflowing with shame, I appear before your eyes, which
I — may God and you forgive me, señora! — have caused
to shed so many tears!"

Thereupon he knelt on both knees, holding out both
arms to Doña Mercedes, and waited.

She walked toward him, and with the sweet maternal
inflection, which, even when it utters a reproach, still
seems a caress, —

" Fernand," she said, putting both her hands to her
son's lips, " in addition to the tears of which you speak,
I owe to you those I shed at this moment, and, believe

me, my beloved child, if the first were very bitter, the
others are very sweet!" Gazing into his face with the
most loving smile of a woman and a mother, she added,
' Welcome, child of my heart!"

Doña Flor stood behind Mercedes.

"Señora," said Don Fernand, "I know what your
illustrious father, Don Inigo, intended to do for me; in
my eyes the intention is equivalent to the deed; accept,
therefore, in his name, all the gratitude I offer to you
both."

Instead of asking leave to kiss the maiden's hand, as
he had done in the case of Don Ruiz and Doña Mercedes,
the young man took a faded flower from his breast and
passionately pressed it to his lips.

Doña Flor blushed and stepped back: she recognized
the anemone that she had given the brigand at the
inn.

Thereupon the old nurse, impatient for her turn, came
forward.

"Señora," she said to Doña Mercedes, "am not I in a
way the dear child's mother?"

"Señor," said Fernand, turning to Don Ruiz, and at
the same time holding out his arms to his nurse, with
the smile of his childhood days, "will you not permit
me, notwithstanding your respected presence, to embrace
this good woman?"

Don Ruiz nodded.

Beatrice threw herself into his arms whom she called
her son, and pressed him again and again to her breast,
accompanying each embrace with one of those heartfelt,
resounding smacks to which the common people have
given the tender name of nurse's kisses.

"Ah me!" murmured Doña Mercedes, seeing in the
nurse's arms the child who, in Don Ruiz' presence,

had dared to do no more than kiss her hand, "she is certainly the happiest of us all!"

And two envious tears rolled down her maternal cheeks. Don Ruiz had not for an instant removed his melancholy glance from the picture we have tried to sketch.

At sight of the tears on Doña Mercedes' cheeks, his features contracted, and he closed his eyes for an instant as if some memory, like a venomous serpent, had bitten him to the heart.

He made a violent effort over himself; his mouth opened and closed; his lips trembled, but no sound issued from them.

You would have said that his stomach was making fruitless efforts to throw off the poison he had swallowed.

But Doña Mercedes' eyes had taken in every detail of the scene, even as Don Ruiz' had done.

"Don Fernand," she said, "I think that your father wishes to speak to you."

Don Fernand turned to the old man, and, with downcast eyes, signified by a movement of his head and shoulders that he was listening.

But a visible impatience was concealed beneath his apparent humility, and any one who could have translated the thoughts that the impulses of his heart communicated to his mind, might have seen that the sermon the prodigal son was expecting to receive, inevitable as it seemed to him, was none the less disagreeable, especially in Doña Flor's presence.

With the delicacy of perception peculiar to her sex, she detected that feeling.

"Excuse me," she said; "I think I heard the door. Probably it was my father coming in; I will go and tell him the good news of Don Fernand's return."

Thereupon she pressed Mercedes' hand, saluted the
old man, and left the room without looking at Don
Fernand, who, with bowed head, awaited the paternal
discourse with more resignation than respect.

But when Doña Flor had gone, his breast dilated,
and he breathed more freely.

The old man himself seemed more at his ease the
moment that the auditors and spectators were reduced
to the members of his family.

"Don Fernand," he said, "you must have noticed,
upon entering the house, the changes that have taken
place during your absence; our fortune is exhausted;
our property — and that is what I least regret — is
either sold or pledged; Don Alvar's sister having consented to enter a convent, I provided a dowry for her;
the families of the dead alguazils having accepted a
pecuniary penalty, I paid them a considerable sum in
cash and agreed to pay a certain yearly sum in addition;
but, in order to do it, your mother and I were compelled
to reduce ourselves almost to poverty."

Don Fernand made a movement that expressed regret,
at least, if not penitence; but Don Ruiz continued with
a noble gesture, accompanied by a melancholy smile, —

"We will say no more of that; it is all forgotten
since you are pardoned, my son! and I thank King Don
Carlos most humbly for that pardon.   From this moment
I bid adieu to past sorrows, and they are to me as if they
had never existed; but what I wished to ask you, with
tears in my eyes, Don Fernand, what I wished to ask
you with affectionate entreaty, what I would ask you,
kneeling at your feet, if it were not repugnant to nature
to see the father kneeling to the son, the old man abased
before the young man, white hair imploring dark hair, —
what I wished to ask you, my son, is this: that you

would work, and I will assist you with all my strength, to reconquer public esteem; so that even your enemies may see that the bitter lessons of misfortune are never wasted with a noble heart and an intelligent mind. Thus far, Don Fernand, we have been simply father and son; that is not enough; from this time forth, let us be friends! It may be that there are some unpleasant memories between us; do you banish them, and so will I; let us live at peace, doing all that we can for each other. I will try to bestow upon you the three sentiments that a father owes his son: love, regard, devotion; I ask of you only a single one in exchange; at your age, the age of headstrong passions, a man has not the same power over himself as a man advanced in years; I ask nothing of you save obedience, binding myself never to ask of you anything that is not fair and honorable. Excuse me if I have been longer than I intended, Don Fernand; old age is loquacious."

"Señor," replied Don Fernand, bowing, "I pledge you my word that from this day you shall have no cause to reproach me, and that I will turn my misfortunes to such good account that you will rejoice that they befell me."

"It is well, Fernand," said Don Ruiz; "now you have my permission to embrace your mother."

Mercedes uttered a joyful cry and held out her arms to her son.

14

XXIV.

DON RAMIRO.

THE spectacle of a mother embracing her son, with tears of love, however touching it may be to other men, evidently made a painful impression upon the dejected glance of Don Ruiz, for he left the room silently, and old Beatrice alone saw him go.

Left alone with his mother and his nurse, the young man told his mother all that had taken place the night before, and — without saying aught of the strange feeling he had for Doña Flor — how he had come to see her during the night, as usual, and had found her room occupied by her fair guest.

Thereupon Doña Mercedes led her son to her new apartment. His mother's room in that house was to Don Fernand what the sanctuary in a church is to a devout heart. There it was that as a child, as a boy, as a young man, he had passed his pleasantest hours; there only had his capricious heart beaten at ease, his vagabond thoughts dared to take their flight, like the birds, born in one hemisphere, which at a certain season of the year, take flight to unknown regions in the other.

There, lying at her feet as in the days of youth and innocence, kissing the maternal knees in that fulness of happiness which he had not felt for so long a time, Fernand, with more pride than shame, told his mother of his adventurous life, from the moment of his flight to that of his return to the house.

Hitherto he had constantly avoided the subject in his interviews with his mother; a man does not tell of a painful dream while the dream lasts, but when he is once awake, the more terrible the dream has been, the more delight he has in relating it and laughing at the nocturnal mirage that terrified him so.

Mercedes listened to her son, hanging on his lips; but, when he came to his meeting with Don Inigo and Doña Flor, the interest taken by Mercedes in his narrative seemed to become even greater than before, the color came and went in her cheeks. Don Fernand could feel her breast rising and falling under his head; and when he spoke of the strange sympathetic feeling that had taken possession of him at the sight of Don Inigo, the almost irresistible impulse to throw himself, a suppliant, at Doña Flor's feet, she put her hand over his mouth as if to beg for a truce.

It was evident that she was at the end of her strength and could bear no more.

Then, when she had removed her hand, came the story of the danger he had incurred, the flight to the mountain, the fire, the taking refuge in the gypsy's grotto, the attack by the troops, and, lastly, the battle with the bear.

When the last words had died away on Fernand's lips, Mercedes rose, pale and trembling, and tottered to a corner of the room, which she had transformed into an oratory, and there she knelt and prayed.

Don Fernand stood watching her, with deep respect, when he felt that a hand was laid softly on his shoulder. He turned. It was his old nurse's hand. She came to inform him that one of his best friends, Don Ramiro, having heard of his return, was in the salon and desired to speak with him.

The young man left Mercedes to her prayers; he was well aware that she was praying for him.

Don Ramiro, arrayed in a bewitching morning costume, was lolling carelessly in a large easy-chair, awaiting his friend's coming.

The two young men, who had formerly been very close friends and had not seen each other for three years, exchanged a warm embrace.

Then ensued the inevitable questions.

Don Ramiro knew of Fernand's amour with Doña Estefania, his duel with Don Alvar, and his flight after his adversary's death; but at that point all certain information stopped.

The general report, however, was that Don Fernand had visited France and Italy after the duel; he had been seen, it was said, at the court of Francis I. and of Lorenzo II., whose great fame is due to his having been the father of Catherine de' Medici, and to his having left behind him a bust of himself carved by Michael Angelo.

That is what Don Ramiro believed.

No one had been sufficiently near to Don Ruiz and the king to hear their conversation; consequently, even those who had seen the old man kneeling at Don Carlos's feet supposed that he had asked for nothing more than his son's pardon for the murder of Don Alvar.

Fernand left Don Ramiro in his error.

Then, partly from curiosity and partly to change the conversation, he took his turn at questioning Don Ramiro.

"You are welcome," he said; "I should have sent word to you of my return."

But Don Ramiro shook his head with a melancholy expression.

"I can hardly be welcome," he said, "as I bear in my

heart a sentiment that has caused me more trouble than joy up to the present time."

Fernand saw that Don Ramiro, unlike himself, had a full heart and asked nothing better than to confide to him the feelings with which it was filled.

He smiled and held out his hand.

"My dear friend," he said, "we are of those whose hearts and passions need fresh air. It is stifling in this room; would you not prefer to tell me of your adventures in the fine tree-lined avenue in front of the house?"

"Yes," said Don Ramiro, "especially as I may perhaps see *her* while I am talking with you."

"Oho!" rejoined Don Fernand, with a laugh, "so *she* lives on this square?"

"Come," said Ramiro. "In a moment you shall know not only all that has happened to me, but the service I expect of you."

The young men went out arm in arm, and began their promenade, which, as if they had agreed beforehand, did not extend beyond the façade of the house in either direction.

From time to time, moreover, each of them looked up at the windows on the first floor. But as neither inquired of the other the cause of that movement, it led to no explanation during the silence that they both maintained at first.

At last Don Ramiro could contain himself no longer.

"Fernand, my friend," he said, "I believe we came out here, you to listen to what I had to say, and I to say it."

"Therefore, dear Ramiro, I am all attention," said Fernand.

"Ah, my friend," rejoined Ramiro, "what a cruel tyrant Love is, and how like slaves he treats the hearts over which he reigns!"

Don Fernand smiled as if he were of the same opinion.

"And yet," he said, "when one is loved — "

"Ay," said Ramiro; "but, although I have every reason to hope that I am, I doubt it still."

"You doubt it, Don Ramiro? Why, if I remember aright, at the time of our separation modesty in matters of love was not placed by the ladies in the list of faults with which they charged you."

"That was because I had never loved until I saw *her*, Don Fernand! "

"Well, well," said Don Fernand, "tell me how you fell in with this marvel of beauty whose influence has transformed the haughty Don Ramiro into the most modest man in Andalusia."

"Why, my dear fellow, I first saw her as one sees a flower lost among the leaves, a star veiled by a cloud: I was walking through the streets of Toledo one evening, when, through a half-opened blind, I saw the most won-derfully beautiful face that ever made glad the heart of man. I was on horseback; spell-bound, I stopped my horse. She evidently mistook for impertinence what was simply admiration, for she closed her blind, although, lost in wonder and with clasped hands, I begged her not to do it."

"Oh, the cruel creature! " laughed Don Fernand.

"I remained more than an hour in front of that win-dow, always hoping that she would open it again; but my waiting was fruitless. Then I looked for the en-trance door of the house; but I saw that the façade I was facing had no other openings than windows."

"Was it an enchanted house, pray? "

"No, and I understood at once, as it was a deserted side street through which I was riding, that the house must be entered from another street. It was because she was protected by that isolation, doubtless, that my fair unknown had ventured to open her window. I concluded from that circumstance, however, that she was not under the guardianship of a very stern father or a very jealous governor, as she was allowed to open the blind of a window only twelve or fifteen feet from the ground. As for her being married, I did not so much as think of it; she seemed to be hardly fourteen years old."

"But I know you, Don Ramiro!" said Fernand: "you are not, or rather, for love seems to have wrought a great change in you, you were not, the man to argue long with yourself over the solution of such a problem. Every maiden — it is a favor that we owe to nature or to society — every maiden has a duenna; every duenna has her failing; that failing has a lock, and that lock is opened with a golden key."

"I thought so too, dear Don Fernand; but that time I was mistaken."

"Poor Don Ramiro, that was playing in hard luck! so that you were not able even to find out who she was, eh?"

"Oh, yes, I was, and I had no need to bribe valet or duenna for that; I made the circuit of the quarter, and I found myself in a wide, handsome street on the other side of the house. It was a veritable palace. I inquired among the neighbors and I learned that it belonged — "

"The girl or the house?"

"Both, i' faith! — that they belonged to an enormously rich stranger, returned from the Indies within a year or two, whom, in view of his reputation for wisdom and justice, Cardinal Ximenes had summoned from Malaga, where he lived, to join the council of regency. Can you guess who he was, Don Fernand?"

"Faith! I have not the least idea."

"Impossible!"

"You forget, my dear Don Ramiro, that I have been absent from Spain two years, and that I know almost nothing of what has happened in those two years."

"True; and your ignorance will assist me very materially, I confess, in the latter part of my story. There were two ways of reaching my fair unknown: to take advantage of my birth and position to obtain an introduction to the father and through him to the daughter; or else to watch for the opening of that blind through which shone the rays of her beauty, as the prisoner, at his barred window, watches for a ray of sunlight. I employed the first method. My father in his youth had known the illustrious personage with whom I had to do. I wrote to him. He sent me a letter. I was cordially received; but it was the daughter, not the father, whom I wished to see; and, whether by her father's command or from love of retirement, the daughter obstinately remained shut up in her own apartments. I resorted to the second method, the mysterious method, which was to surprise a glance from her at night, when, believing herself alone, she inhaled at her window the fresh, perfumed air that blows from the Tagus. Indeed, is not that method always the best, and does not every maiden gaze with greater interest and attention on the gallant who draws rein under her balcony on a lovely starlit night or a night of tempest, than on him who is presented to her in a boudoir or salon?"

"You have always been a very keen observer where women are concerned, Don Ramiro. Go on, I pray; for I doubt not that you succeeded."

Don Ramiro shook his head.

"I neither succeeded nor failed altogether," he said. "Two or three times, hidden by a corner of the wall, I

succeeded in drawing back out of sight swiftly enough to
be able to see her; but no sooner did I show myself than
the open blind was closed, without undue haste, without
anger."

"And could you not see whether she continued to look
at you through the blind?"

"That, I confess, was the one hope that sustained me
for a long while; but one day, after an absence of a week
which I could not avoid, I returned and found the house
tightly closed, doors and windows. Neither old man nor
maiden nor duenna appeared by day; no light shone
within the house at night; you would have said it was a
tomb. I made inquiries. The council of regency having been dissolved by the arrival of King Don Carlos in
Spain, and by his approach to Toledo, the father of my
infanta had returned to Malaga. I followed him to
Malaga; I would have followed him to the end of the
world. There the same expedients were renewed, but, I
hope, with better success. In the first place, she withdrew less quickly and I was able to say a few words to
her; then I threw bouquets on her balcony; at first she
pushed them away with her foot, then seemed to take no
notice of them, and at last picked them up. Once or
twice she even answered my questions; but as if confused
by her complaisance, as if terrified by the sound of her
voice, she withdrew almost instantly, and her words were
rather like the lightning flash that makes the night less
dark than like the dawn that ushers in the day."

"And matters went on so —?" queried Don Fernand.

"Down to the moment when her father received the
king's command to come to Granada."

"O poor Don Ramiro!" laughed Fernand; "so that,
one fine morning, you found the house at Malaga closed
like that at Toledo?"

"Nay! That time she did me the favor to inform me of the hour fixed for their departure and the route they were to take; so that, instead of following her, I determined to go before her. That gave me a great advantage, you see; every halt that she made would recall me to her memory; every room in which she stopped would speak to her of me. I became a courier — but a love courier."

"Aha!" said Fernand; but Ramiro was so intent upon his story that he did not notice the change that had taken place in his friend's voice since he last spoke.

"Yes, you know, there is almost nothing ready in our wretched inns; so I ordered their meals. I knew her favorite perfume, — I carry it around my neck in a gold box; I burned it in the halls she would have to pass through, in the rooms in which she would rest. I knew her favorite flowers, and from Malaga to Granada she walked on nothing but flowers!"

"And how does it happen that so gallant a knight as Don Ramiro can need the help of a friend, having so many resources in himself?" asked Don Fernand, in a voice over which he had less and less control.

"Ah, my dear Don Fernand, chance, no, I am wrong, Providence has combined two coincidences which should, unless some unforeseen catastrophe interferes, lead me straight to happiness."

"What are these coincidences?" queried Fernand, passing his hand across his forehead to wipe away the perspiration that covered it.

"The father of her I love is your father's friend; and you, my dear Fernand, like an angel of salvation, arrived this morning."

"Well, what then?"

"Why, as your father has offered his hospitality — "

"So," said Don Fernand, grinding his teeth with jealousy, "she whom you love — ?"

"Why, do you not guess, my dear friend?"

Don Fernand frowned upon the young man who chose so ill his time to call him by that name.

"I guess nothing," he retorted with a threatening expression, "and you must tell me everything. What is the name of your beloved, Don Ramiro?"

"Is it necessary to tell you the name of the sun, when you feel his warmth and are dazzled by his rays? Look up, Don Fernand, and endure, if you can, the sight of the star that burns my heart!"

Don Fernand raised his eyes and saw Doña Flor leaning over her balcony and looking at him with a sweet smile; but, as if she were waiting only until she should be discovered, she had no sooner exchanged a swift glance with Don Fernand than she drew back and they heard the sound of her window closing.

But the window did not close so quickly that a flower did not fall from it.

That flower was an anemone.

XXV.

THE ANEMONE.

THE two young men darted forward, moved by a common impulse to pick up the flower that had fallen, by chance or by design, from the girl's hand.

Don Fernand, being nearer to the window, obtained possession of the anemone.

"Thanks, dear Fernand," said Ramiro, putting out his hand; "give me that flower."

"Why should I give it to you, pray?" demanded Fernand.

"Why, because I am inclined to think that it was dropped for me."

"Who told you that?"

"No one; but who tells me that it was not?"

"Some one who is not afraid, perhaps, to tell you so to your face."

"Who?"

"I!"

Don Ramiro stared at Don Fernand in bewilderment, and noticed then, for the first time, his pallor and the convulsive trembling of his lips.

"You!" he said, recoiling a step; "why you?"

"Because — this woman that you love — I also love her!"

"You love Doña Flor?" cried Don Ramiro.

"I love her!" Don Fernand repeated.

"Where did you see her? How long ago did you first see her?" demanded Ramiro, turning as pale as the other.

" What does it matter to you?"

" Why, I have loved her two years!"

" Perhaps I have known her only two days; but suppose that in those two days I have done more than you in two years?"

" Prove that to me, Don Fernand, or I will proclaim aloud that you have insolently attacked a young girl's reputation."

" You told me that you rode before her from Malaga to Granada, did you not?"

" I told you so."

" You passed the Moorish King Inn?"

" I stopped there."

" You ordered dinner for Don Inigo and his daughter; you burned perfumes and left a bouquet there?"

" Yes."

" There was an anemone in the bouquet."

" What then?"

" She gave me that anemone."

" With her own hand?"

" Even so! — and it is here on my heart, where it has withered as this one will wither there."

" You stole the anemone, took it from the bouquet without her knowledge, picked it up on the road where she accidentally dropped it; confess that, and I will pardon you."

" In the first place, only from God or the king would I accept a pardon," replied the young man, proudly; " and as for the flower, she gave it to me."

" You lie, Don Fernand," said Ramiro; " and you have stolen this second flower, just as you stole the first!"

Don Fernand uttered a wrathful exclamation, and, drawing his sword with his right hand, threw the fresh flower and the faded one at Don Ramiro's feet.

"Very well, so be it!" he said; "given or stolen, there they both lie on the ground. The one who is living five minutes hence may pick them up."

"Agreed!" said Don Ramiro, stepping back and drawing his sword. "That is the sort of bargain I like!"

With that he addressed the gentlemen who were walking on the square, and who, attracted by the gleam of naked swords, had turned toward them.

"Holà! caballeros," he said; "come this way, so that we need not fight without witnesses, and, if Don Fernand kills me, it may not be said that he murdered me, as it has been said that he murdered Don Alvar."

"So be it, let them come," said Don Fernand; "for I swear to God, Don Ramiro, that what they will see will be well worth seeing!"

And the two young men, standing five paces apart, lowered the points of their swords and waited until a circle was formed about them.

When the circle was formed, a voice exclaimed,—

"Begin, señors."

Water does not rush forward more madly when it breaks its dike than the young men rushed upon each other. At that moment a shriek rang out from behind the blind; but while it made both combatants raise their heads, it not only did not stop the combat, but seemed to have no other result than to augment its violence.

Don Fernand and Don Ramiro were two of the most fearless and most skilful young gentlemen on earth. Neither of them certainly had any rival in respect of those two qualities in Andalusia, and, to encounter any serious resistance, they must needs fight each other.

And so, as Don Fernand had predicted, what the gentlemen saw was worth seeing.

The two swords met and crossed with such rapidity and ferocity that one might well have thought for a moment that the steel, from which sparks flew in showers, was animated by the same passions as the men who held it. All the resources of art, address, and strength were displayed during the few minutes that the first passage lasted, during which neither of the combatants, motionless as the trees in whose shade they were fighting, made a single backward step; indeed, it almost seemed as if there were no further danger, and as if the spectators might watch the battle, desperate as it was, with the same feeling that they would watch a bout with buttoned foils at a fencing school. It is true, also, that such encounters were a part of the manners of the time, and that few days passed without such a spectacle as that presented by Don Fernand and Don Ramiro. The interval was short. Time to breathe was all that either asked, and, despite the shouts of, "Take your time! take your time!" from the spectators, they hurled themselves upon each other with renewed fury. But the swords had hardly met the second time when a breathless voice was heard exclaiming, —

"Stay, Don Fernand! stay, Don Ramiro!"

All heads were turned in the direction from which the voice came.

"Don Ruiz de Torrillas!" cried the spectators, standing aside.

And, in a moment, Don Ruiz stood in the centre of the circle on his son's side. Warned, doubtless, by Doña Flor, he had hurried out to separate the combatants.

"Stay your hands!" he repeated imperatively.

"Father!" muttered Don Fernand, impatiently.

"Señor!" said Don Ramiro, with respect.

"I have no commands to lay upon Don Ramiro," said the old man; "but you, Don Fernand, are my son, and to you I say, 'Stay your hand!'"

"Stay, señors!" echoed all the bystanders.

"How now, unhappy boy!" cried Don Ruiz, clasping his hands before him; "can you not conquer your fatal passions? Pardoned only yesterday for duelling, can you think of committing a like crime to-day?"

"Father! father!" murmured Don Fernand, "let me alone, I beg you!"

"Here, in the street, in the broad light of day!" cried Don Ruiz, wringing his hands.

"Why not? It was here, in the street, in the broad light of day, that the insult was offered. They were witnesses of the insult; let them be witnesses of the vengeance!"

"Sheathe your sword, Don Fernand!"

"On guard, on guard, Don Ramiro!"

"Do you disobey me?"

"Do you think that I will allow you to deprive me of the honor you have transmitted to me, as your father received it from his ancestors?"

"Oh!" cried Don Ruiz, "would to God you had retained a spark of the honor I transmitted to you!"

The old man turned to Don Ramiro.

"Señor Don Ramiro," he said, "as my son has no respect for the white hairs and trembling hands that appeal to him, although they are those of a father, do you listen to me, and let those about us see that a stranger shows greater respect to me than my own son."

"Yes! yes!" said the spectators; "listen to him, Don Ramiro!"

Don Ramiro stepped back, lowered his sword, and bowed.

"You have done well to appeal to me, Don Ruiz de Torrillas," he said; "you have done well to rely upon me, señores. The world is wide; the mountains are deserted; I shall meet my adversary in some other place."

"Ah!" cried Don Fernand, "that is a clever way of disguising one's fear, upon my word!"

Don Ramiro, who had already sheathed his sword and had already stepped back, was on guard again in an instant, sword in hand.

"I afraid?" he said.

The spectators murmured, evidently blaming Don Fernand, and two of the oldest or wisest among them made a movement as if to intervene between the young men.

But Don Ruiz de Torrillas, with a gesture, begged them to stand aside.

The two gentlemen obeyed in silence.

Again the clash of the swords was heard.

Don Ruiz took one step toward his son.

Don Fernand, with clenched teeth and flashing eye, pale with rage, attacked his adversary with a violence that would have been fatal to a man less sure of his hand than he.

"Madman," said his father; "what! when you see that a stranger respects and obeys me, do you disobey me and defy me?"

With that he raised the cane he held in his hand.

"By the living God!" he cried, in an outburst of excitement that made his eyes flash with the fire of youth, "I do not know why I refrain from teaching you your duty in public."

15

Don Fernand turned half around without removing his blade from his opponent's.

He saw the cane raised in his father's hand; his face, which was deadly pale, became purple, his blood poured so swiftly into his heart and rushed violently thence to his extremities.

There was something very like hate on the old man's face; Fernand's imitated it, and assumed a similar expression.

It seemed as if any one who had been imprudent enough to pass between the flashes that shot from their eyes would have been struck dead.

"Beware, father!" said the young man, in a trembling voice, and shaking his head.

"Sheathe your sword!" said Don Ruiz.

"First lower your cane, father!"

"First obey, unhappy boy! when I order you to obey."

"Father!" muttered Don Fernand, becoming pale as death once more, "do not keep your cane raised against me, or, by the living God! I shall go to some extremity."

He turned to Don Ramiro. "Oh, do not go, Don Ramiro," he said; "I can face an old man's cane and a coxcomb's sword at the same time."

"You hear, señores!" cried Don Ramiro. "What am I to do?"

"Do as your heart bids you; act according to the affront you have received, Señor Don Ramiro," said the gentlemen, stepping back and abandoning all thought of averting the results of the duel.

"Ungrateful, wicked youth!" cried Don Ruiz, still holding his cane over his son's head, "can you not learn from your opponent how a son should act before his father?"

"No," retorted Don Fernand; "for my opponent has given way from cowardice, and I do not class cowardice among the manly virtues."

"The man who thinks or says that I am a coward —"

"Lies, Don Ramiro," the old man interposed; "it is for me to say it, not you."

"Oh, let us have done with this!" cried Don Fernand, with one of the roars of rage with which he answered wild beasts when he fought with them.

"For the last time, villain! will you obey me? will you sheathe your sword?" persisted Don Ruiz, more threateningly than ever.

And it was evident that, if Don Fernand did not obey on the moment, on the second, the degrading cane would fall upon him.

But, with the swiftness of thought, he pushed Don Ruiz away with the back of his left hand, while with the right hand, making a clever feint, he ran his sword through his opponent's arm; Don Ramiro parried too late.

Don Ramiro remained on his feet; but the old man fell, so violent was the blow dealt him.

He had received it fairly in the face.

The spectators uttered a cry of horror; the son had struck his father.

"Room! room!" roared Don Fernand, pouncing upon the two flowers, which he picked up and hid in his breast.

"Oh, may Heaven crush you, infamous villain!" cried Don Ruiz, trying to rise; "yes, Heaven, in default of men, for the cause of an outraged father is the cause of Heaven!"

"Death to him! death to the sacrilegious son who has raised his hand against his father!" cried the by-standers. with one voice.

And one and all drew their swords and surrounded Don Fernand.

For an instant was heard the clashing of ten swords against one; then, as the maddened boar rushes through the helpless pack, so the *Salteador*, with inflamed eye and foaming at the mouth, rushed through the opposing circle.

He passed close to the prostrate Don Ruiz, darted at the old man a glance in which there was more hatred than repentance, and disappeared in one of the narrow streets leading to the Zacatin.

XXVI.

THE MALEDICTION.

THE spectators of this scene — wherein every spectator
had eventually become an actor — were struck dumb.

Don Ramiro alone, wrapping his cloak around his
bleeding right arm, walked toward the old man and
said, offering him his left hand, —

"Señor, will you do me the honor to accept this hand
to assist you to rise?"

Don Ruiz took the offered hand, and rose with difficulty.

"Oh, ungrateful, unnatural son!" he cried, extending his hand in the direction in which Don Fernand
had disappeared, "may God's vengeance pursue you
wherever you fly! May your hand, which has profaned
my white hair and covered my face with blood, be
powerless to defend or avenge you against these swords
drawn by the hands of strangers in my defence! and
may God, seeing your sacrilege, take from you the air
you breathe, the light that shines for you, and the earth
that bears you!"

"Señor," said one of the gentlemen, respectfully,
approaching Don Ruiz, "here is your hat."

"Señor," said a second, approaching with the same
respect, "shall I fasten the clasp of your cloak?"

"Señor," said a third, "here is your cane."

At that word Don Ruiz seemed to throw off his
torpor.

"A cane!" he repeated; "of what use is a cane to me? A sword is what I need! O Cid! O Cid Campeador! see how we are changed since you rendered up your great soul to God! In your days sons avenged the insults that strangers put upon their fathers; to-day strangers avenge the insults fathers receive from their sons."

He turned to the gentleman who handed him his cane.

"Yes, yes! give it me," he said; "an insult inflicted with the hand should be avenged with the cane. With this cane, therefore, I will wreak my vengeance on you, Don Fernand. But I deceived myself; how can this cane avenge me, when, as soon as I have it in my hand, I use it, not for purposes of attack, but to lean upon? How can I avenge myself if the instrument of my vengeance, powerless to strike the man I pursue, serves only to strike the ground, as if to say, 'Earth! earth! open the door of the tomb for the old man, my master!'"

"Señor, señor, be calm!" said one of the spectators. "Doña Mercedes, your wife, is hurrying hither, followed by a girl as beautiful as the angels."

Don Ruiz turned and met Doña Mercedes' eyes with such a look in his own that she stopped and clung trembling to the arm of Doña Flor, beautiful as the angels, as the gentleman had said, but pale as a statue.

"What is the matter, monseñor?" she asked Don Ruiz. "In Heaven's name, what has happened?"

"The matter, madame," cried Don Ruiz, whose wrath seemed to gather fresh strength in his wife's presence, — "the matter is that your son has struck me in the face; that the blood has flowed beneath the hand of him who calls me father, and that, when I had fallen under the blow I received, it was not he, but Don Ramiro, who put forth his hand to lift me up! Madame, thank Don Ramiro, who gave his hand to your husband when he lay prostrate beneath the hand of your son."

"Oh, calm yourself, calm yourself, señor!" implored Doña Mercedes; "see all these people standing about us."

"Let them come! let them draw near! for they come to defend me! Come, one and all!" cried Don Ruiz, "and know from my own mouth, learn by my own voice, that I am an infamous man, who has been struck in the face! Ay, men! look at me, and tremble to have sons! Ay, women! look at me, and tremble to give birth to children who, to reward you for twenty-five years of sacrifices, care, and suffering, beat your husbands! I have appealed for justice to the Supreme Master, and I appeal for justice to you; and if you do not promise me on the instant that you will take it upon yourselves to see that justice is done the outraged father, — why, I will appeal to the king!"

And, as the terror-stricken throng remained speechless in face of that crushing despair, he cried, —

"Ah! you, too, deny me justice! Then I appeal to King Don Carlos. King Don Carlos! King Don Carlos! justice! justice!"

"Who calls King Don Carlos?" said a voice. "Who seeks justice at his hands? He is here."

The crowd instantly parted; and through the path thus opened, a young man came forward, dressed in a simple gentleman's costume, — a young man, whose flashing eye and pale, fair face were hidden beneath a broad-brimmed felt hat, while a dark cloak enveloped and concealed his figure.

Behind him, dressed in a costume as simple as his own walked the grand justiciary.

"The king!" cried the crowd.

"The king!" stammered Doña Mercedes, turning pale.

"The king!" echoed Don Ruiz, with an accent of triumph.

A great circle was formed in a twinkling, with the king and Don Inigo, Don Ruiz, and Doña Mercedes leaning on Doña Flor's arm, in the centre.

"Who demanded justice?" the king asked.

"I, sire," said Don Ruiz.

The king looked at him.

"Aha! you again? Yesterday you asked for a pardon; to-day you ask for justice! Have you always something to ask?"

"Yes, sire; and this time I will not leave Your Majesty until you have granted what I ask."

"If what you ask is just," the king replied, "you will have no difficulty in obtaining it."

"Your Majesty shall be the judge," said Don Ruiz.

Don Inigo made a sign for the crowd to withdraw, so that the words of the complainant should reach the king's ear alone.

"No, no," said Don Ruiz; "I wish every one to hear what I have to say, so that, when I have finished, every one may bear witness that it is the truth."

"Remain, all, and listen," said the king.

"Sire," continued Don Ruiz, "is it true that you have forbidden duelling in your dominions?"

"It is true, and this very morning I ordered Don Inigo to prosecute duellists without truce or pity."

"Well, sire, a moment since, here, upon this square, beneath the windows of my house, two young men were fighting, surrounded by a circle of gentlemen."

"Oho!" said the king, "until this moment I have always supposed that they who chose to disobey a king's edicts selected some isolated spot, where the solitude would at least make it possible that the crime should remain unknown."

"Even so; but these young men, sire, had selected the most frequented square in Granada and the bright sunlight to settle their dispute."

"You hear, Don Inigo?" said the king, turning half around.

"My God! my God!" murmured Doña Mercedes.

"Can he intend to denounce his son, madame?" asked Doña Flor.

"The subject of their quarrel is of little consequence," continued Don Ruiz, with a glance at the grand justiciary, indicating that he kept the secret for the honor of his family. "I do not know nor do I care to know what it was; what I do know is that two young gentlemen were fighting fiercely, with drawn swords, before my door."

Don Carlos frowned.

"And you did not come out?" he said; "you did not cast the weight of your name and the authority of your gray hairs between the swords of those young madmen? In that case, you are as guilty as they; for whoever gives countenance to a duel or does not oppose it, is an accessory thereto."

"I came out, sire, and I approached the young men and bade them put up their swords; one of them obeyed me."

"It is well," said the king: "that one shall be less severely punished; but the other?"

"The other refused to obey me, sire; the other continued to provoke his opponent; the other, by his insults, forced his opponent, who had already sheathed his sword, to draw it anew, and the fight went on."

"You hear, Don Inigo? Despite Don Ruiz' remonstrances, the fight went on. What did you do then?" the king asked, turning to the old man once more.

"After imploring, sire, I threatened; after threatening, I raised my cane."

"And then?"

"He who had already withdrawn once, withdrew a second time."

"And the other?"

"The other, sire — the other struck me in the face!"

"A young man struck an old man, a *rico hombre*, Don Ruiz?"

And Don Carlos's eyes questioned the crowd, as if he expected that the spectators would contradict Don Ruiz.

But all mouths remained closed, and, in the silence, Doña Flor's stifled sighs and Mercedes' restrained sobs could be heard.

"Go on," said the king to Don Ruiz.

"Sire, what penalty does a young man incur who strikes an old man?"

"If he is a plebeian, the scourge on the public square, and a place in my galleys between a Turk from Algiers and a Moor from Tunis; if he is of noble birth, he is subject to imprisonment for life and public degradation."

"And suppose that he who dealt the blow was the son," continued Don Ruiz, with a sombre expression, "and he who received it the father?"

"What do you say, old man? I do not understand Spanish readily, and I cannot have heard aright."

Don Ruiz repeated slowly, and in a voice whose every syllable echoed painfully in the hearts of the two women, —

"Suppose that he who dealt the blow was the son, and that he who received it was the father?"

A murmur ran through the crowd.

The king recoiled a step, and gazed at the old man with an incredulous expression.

" Impossible! " he said.

" Sire," said Don Ruiz, with one knee on the ground, " I solicited at your hands the pardon of my son, a murderer and robber! Sire, I now solicit at your hands justice against the child who raised his hand against his father! "

" O Don Ruiz! Don Ruiz! " cried Don Carlos, laying aside for a moment the calm, cold serenity beneath which he concealed his real sentiments; " do you know that you are demanding your son's death? "

" I do not know, sire, what penalty is visited upon such a crime in Spain, for it has no prototype, and will be likely to have no imitators; but this is what I say to you, O my king: Disregarding the sacred command which comes first after those of the Church, my son Don Fernand has dared to raise his hand against me; and, as I cannot wreak vengeance for the crime with my own hand, I have come to you to lodge my complaint against the culprit; and if you deny me justice, why, then, sire, — listen to the threat an outraged father makes against his king, — if you deny me justice, I will appeal from Don Carlos to God! Sire," he added, rising from his knees, " you have heard me: now it is your affair, not mine."

And he withdrew, following the path that the silent throng opened before him, every man uncovering and bowing low before the outraged father.

Mercedes, seeing Don Ruiz pass without speaking to her or looking at her, fainted in Doña Flor's arms.

Don Carlos cast upon the afflicted group one of the sidelong glances which were peculiar to him, then turned

to Don Inigo, who was paler and more agitated than if
he had been the person accused.

"Don Inigo," said he.

"Sire," the grand justiciary replied.

"Is not yonder woman the mother?"

And he pointed, over his shoulder, to Doña Mercedes.

"Yes, sire," faltered Don Inigo.

"Very good. As you are my grand justiciary," continued Don Carlos, after a pause, "this affair is for you
to deal with. Make use of all the means that are at
your disposal, and do not appear before me until the
culprit is arrested."

"Sire," said Don Inigo, "rest assured that I will use
all possible diligence."

"Do so, and without delay, for this matter is of more
importance to me than you imagine."

"Why so, sire?" the grand justiciary asked in a
trembling voice.

"Because, as I reflect upon what has happened, I cannot think that such an accusation was ever brought
before any king known to history."

He walked away, deep in thought, muttering, —

"What is the meaning of this, O Lord? A son has
struck his father!"

The king sought from God the explanation of a mystery to which men could not give him the key.

Don Inigo meanwhile remained where he stood, as if
rooted to the spot.

XXVII.

RIVER AND MOUNTAIN TORRENT.

THERE are predestined existences: some roll on with the moderation and majesty of the vast rivers, like the Amazon and Mississippi, which flow through thousands of leagues of level fields between their headwaters and the sea, and carry vessels as large as cities, laden with passengers in sufficient number to found a colony.

Others, which take their sources on the highest mountain-tops, rush headlong down in cataracts, in foaming torrents, and after a course of only ten or fifteen leagues, plunge into some stream, or river, or lake, which absorbs them, and where all that is left for them to do is to agitate and disturb for some little time the waters with which they mingle.

For the traveller to follow the former in all their windings, to describe their banks and inspect their surroundings, weeks, months, ay, years are required; for the pedestrian to follow the irregular course of the latter requires only a few days: the spring becomes a cascade, the cascade becomes a cataract, the cataract becomes a mountain torrent, and all are born and die within a space of ten leagues and in the course of a week.

But during that week the pedestrian who has followed the banks of the rushing stream has experienced more emotion perhaps than he who has followed the banks of the great river for a whole year.

The tale that we have undertaken to tell our readers
belongs to the category of cascades, cataracts, and torrents; from the very first page the incidents rush headlong, foaming and roaring to the last.

For those who are carried onward by the hand of God,
all the rules of motion are transposed, and, when they
have reached their goal, it seems to them that they have
made the journey, not on foot, not on horseback, not
in a carriage, but in some fantastic machine, rolling
through cities, villages, and fields, like a locomotive
emitting smoke and flame, or in a balloon sailing so
rapidly through the air that plains, villages, cities, vanish like mere specks lost in space; so that the strongest
are attacked by vertigo and every breast is oppressed.

We have now accomplished two-thirds of the terrible
journey; and — except for the cool-headed pilot called
Don Carlos, who under the name of Charles V. is
destined to brood over public cataclysms as he is brood-
ing to-day over private disasters — every one had left or
was about to leave the square where the last events we
have described had taken place, with sorrowful heart
and bewildered brain.

We have seen Don Fernand take his leave first of all;
then Don Ruiz, cursing his son, threatening his king,
invoking his God; and lastly, the king, always calm, but
more sombre than usual, because of the terrible thought
that during his reign a son had committed the crime,
hitherto unknown, of dealing a blow at his father,
ascended at a slow, tranquil gait the slope leading to
the Alhambra, whither he was returning after visiting
the prisons with the grand justiciary.

The only actors interested in the scene just enacted,
who still remained standing, as if turned to stone in the
midst of the crowd, whose eyes were fixed upon them

with wonder and sorrow, were Mercedes, almost fainting
on Doña Flor's shoulder, and Don Inigo, stricken dumb,
as it were, by the king's words: " Do not appear before
me until the culprit is arrested."

So he must arrest the man for whom he had such a
profoundly sympathetic feeling; the man whose pardon
he had once so urgently solicited, to no effect, when he
was guilty only of crimes which offend man, and whose
punishment was far more inevitable now that he had
committed one of those sacrilegious acts which offend
God, — he must arrest him, or else, himself a rebellious
subject and accessory to one of the greatest crimes that
ever shocked human sensibility, he could never again
appear before his king.

And perhaps, in his heart, he was inclined to adopt
the latter alternative; for, postponing until later the
issuance of the necessary orders for Fernand's arrest, he
hurried, first of all, into the house to procure for Doña
Mercedes the assistance that her condition demanded.

The most essential thing was to take her to her room,
but, strangely enough! when Don Inigo, strong and
vigorous as a young man, had approached Don Fernand's
mother with the purpose of carrying her into the house,
Doña Mercedes, starting at the sound of his steps, had
opened her eyes with an expression almost resembling
terror.

" No, no! " she said, " no, not you! not you! "

And Don Inigo bowed to that strange manifestation
of repugnance, and went to summon Don Fernand's
nurse and Vicente, the old retainer, who had been Ruiz'
squire during the war with the Moors, while Doña
Flor, overwhelmed with surprise, murmured in an
undertone, —

" Why not my father, señora? "

But Mercedes, closing her eyes and summoning all her strength, although she still acted as if she were in a swoon, attempted, with Doña Flor's assistance, to walk slowly toward the house; so that she had almost reached the door when the two servants came out to help her.

Doña Flor would have entered the house with Mercedes, but her father stopped her at the door.

"We have entered this house for the last time," said Don Inigo; "say farewell to Doña Mercedes, and join me here."

"Say farewell to her! entered the house for the last time! Why so, father?"

"Can I remain beneath the roof of the mother whose son I am to doom to death?"

"To death! Don Fernand!" cried the girl, turning pale; "you think that the king will sentence Don Fernand to death?"

"If there were a punishment worse than death Don Fernand would have to undergo that."

"Father, could you not go to your friend, Don Ruiz, and move him?"

"I cannot."

"Cannot Doña Mercedes go to her husband and induce him to withdraw his complaint?"

Don Inigo shook his head.

"She cannot."

"Oh, my God!" cried the girl, darting into the house, "oh, I will go and appeal to a mother's heart, and I hope that that heart will find a way to save her son."

Doña Mercedes was sitting in the same room on the ground-floor where she had stood before her son, an hour before, compressing with her hand the joyous beating of her heart; again her hand was pressed against her heart, but this time to prevent its bursting with agony.

"Mother, mother," said Doña Flor, "is there no way of saving Don Fernand?"

"Did your father give you any hope, my child?" she asked.

"No."

"Believe what your father says, my poor girl."

She began to sob bitterly.

"But, madame," urged Doña Flor, "it seems to me that if, after twenty years of married life, you should appeal to Don Ruiz —"

"He would refuse me."

"A father is always a father, madame."

"Yes, a father," said Mercedes.

And she dropped her head between her hands.

"No matter, madame, make the trial, I implore you!"

Mercedes sat for a moment lost in thought.

"It is not my right, but it is my duty," she said at last.

She called the old squire.

"Vicente, where is your master?" she said.

"He went to his room, madame, and locked himself in."

"You see," said Mercedes, grasping at the excuse offered her.

"Beg him, with your sweet voice, to open the door, madame, and he will open it."

Mercedes tried to rise, and fell back on her chair.

"I have n't the strength," she said; "you see."

"I will assist you, madame," said the young girl, putting her arm around Mercedes, and lifting her with a strength one would not have expected to find in that frail body.

16

Mercedes sighed, and allowed herself to be led.

Five minutes later the weeping mother and lover knocked at Don Ruiz' door.

"Who is there?" Don Ruiz demanded in a dull voice.

"I," replied Doña Mercedes, almost inaudibly.

"Who are you?"

"His mother."

They heard something like a groan inside the room; then slow, heavy steps approached, and the door opened.

Don Ruiz appeared, with haggard eye and dishevelled hair and beard. He seemed to have aged ten years in half an hour.

"You?" he said. "But you are not alone," he added, as he caught sight of Doña Flor; "I was surprised that you dared to come alone."

"To save my child I would dare do anything!" said Mercedes.

"Enter, then, but alone."

"Don Ruiz," murmured Doña Flor, "will you not permit your friend's daughter to add her prayers to those of a mother?"

"If Doña Mercedes is willing to say before you what she has to say to me, enter."

"Oh, no, no!" cried Mercedes, "I enter alone, or not at all!"

"Alone, then, madame," said Doña Flor, bowing to the unhappy mother's desire, and recoiling before the gesture of Don Ruiz, who waved her back.

The door closed upon Mercedes.

Doña Flor remained where she stood, bewildered by this domestic drama which was being enacted before her, but which she did not understand.

She seemed to be listening, but she was not listening.

The beating of her own heart atoned for the silence of her mouth.

And yet it seemed to her that she heard Mercedes' plaintive, hesitating tone succeed the hollow, threatening voice of Don Ruiz. Then she heard the sound of a fall that made the floor groan.

It occurred to her that the sound was occasioned by Doña Mercedes falling to the floor.

She ran to the door and opened it; Mercedes was, in truth, lying at full length on the floor.

She ran to her and tried to raise her; but Don Ruiz motioned to her. It was evident that Mercedes had fallen under the weight of an emotion she could not endure.

Don Ruiz was standing some ten feet away, and if the fall had been caused by any violence on his part, he would not have had time to walk so far. Moreover, with an expression in which affection was not altogether lacking, he took her in his arms and carried her into the dressing-room, where he laid her on a sort of divan.

"Poor woman! poor woman!" he muttered.

Then he returned to his bedroom and locked himself in once more, without a word to the young girl, and as indifferent to her presence as if he were alone.

After some five minutes Mercedes opened her eyes, collected her thoughts, tried to remember, with the help of external objects, recognized where she was, recalled the errand that had brought her there, and rose to her feet.

"Oh, I knew it! I knew it!" she murmured, shaking her head.

Still leaning upon Doña Flor, she returned to her room and fell upon a chair.

At that moment they heard Don Inigo's voice at the door, which he dared not pass, —

"My child, my child, we can remain here no longer."

"Yes, yes," said Mercedes, hastily, "go!"

The maiden fell upon her knees.

"Madame," said she, "give me your blessing, so that what I am about to try may meet with more success than what you have just tried."

Mercedes placed her hands lightly on the girl's head, and said in a dying voice, —

"May God bless you as I bless you!"

Whereupon Doña Flor rose, walked unsteadily to the door, took her father's arm, and went with him from the house.

But they had taken only a few steps in the street when she stopped.

"Where are you going, father?" she asked.

"To occupy the apartments the king ordered prepared for us at the Alhambra, to which I preferred those offered me by Don Ruiz."

"Very well, father; I would make no change in the route you propose to take; but let me call at the convent of the Annonciade, as we pass."

"Yes," said Don Inigo; "that is, in truth, a last resort."

Five minutes later the portress at the convent admitted Doña Flor, while her father stood against the wall, awaiting her exit.

XXVIII.

THE BOAR KEEPS THE DOGS AT BAY.

Don Inigo had been standing there but a few moments when it seemed to him as if the whole population was hurrying curiously toward the Granada gate.

He followed the crowd with his eyes, at first with the vague glance of the man whose mind is engrossed by more serious interests than those which move the mob; but finally, compelled by the uproar and bustle all about him to pay more serious attention to what was taking place, he made inquiries as to the causes of the excitement.

He then learned that a nobleman, against whom an order of arrest had been issued, had refused to give himself up, and, having taken refuge in the Vela Tower, was defending himself with desperation against the men who were trying to capture him.

The first thought that was likely to come to Don Inigo's mind, and that did in fact so come, was that the nobleman in question was Don Fernand. Without an instant's loss of time, he darted in the direction in which the people were going. As he ascended the slope leading to the Alhambra, the crowd became more dense and the uproar greater; at last, with great difficulty, Don Inigo forced his way to the square of Las Algives.

There the main action of the drama was taking place; like a raging, roaring sea, the mob was laying siege to the Vela Tower.

From time to time the crowd parted to make room for a wounded man who retreated with his hand upon his wound, or for a dead body that was being removed.

The grand justiciary made inquiries and learned what we are about to narrate.

A young gentleman, pursued by five or six of his own class, being tired of running, had taken refuge in the tower and awaited his pursuers there.

Thereupon the combat had begun with fatal fury. Perhaps, if he had had to do only with the five or six gentlemen who were pursuing him at first, the fugitive would have triumphed over them; but, at the cries of the assailants, the clashing of swords, the insults answered by threats, the soldiers on guard at the palace had hurried to the spot, and, having been informed that the gentleman was subject to an order of arrest signed by the king himself, they had joined the assailants.

A desperate struggle had ensued.

Don Fernand — for it was he — had taken up his position on the narrow winding stairway, which led to the platform two floors above; there he had found it an easy matter to defend himself; he had contested the ground step by step, and on every step a man had fallen.

The battle had lasted an hour when Don Inigo arrived. He approached the tower, trembling with apprehension, and yet retaining some slight hope that the fugitive was not Don Fernand; but that hope was of short duration.

He had hardly set foot inside the tower when he heard the young man's voice above the tumult.

"Come on! come on, cowards!" he shouted. "I am alone against you all! I shall leave my life here, I know that; but there are not enough of you yet to make up the price at which I propose to sell it!"

It was certainly he.

If things were left to follow their present course, it was impossible, as Don Fernand himself had said, that he should escape death. Death was inevitable and near at hand.

On the contrary, if Don Inigo should succeed in arresting him, there was still the one last chance of reprieve that always exists for the condemned man in a mother's love and the clemency of a king.

Therefore Don Inigo resolved to put an end to the combat.

"Stay!" he cried to the attacking party; "I am Don Inigo Velasco, grand justiciary of Andalusia, and I come from King Don Carlos."

But it was no easy matter thus to calm the wrath of a score of men held at bay by a single man.

"Death! death!" replied five or six voices, while a shriek of pain and the sound of a body rolling down the stairs indicated that Don Fernand's sword had found a new victim.

"Do you not hear me?" cried Don Inigo, in a loud voice. "I tell you that I am the grand justiciary, and that I come in the king's name."

"No!" said one of the assailants, "let the king allow us to do justice ourselves, and justice will be well done."

"Beware, my masters!" said Don Inigo, who asked nothing better than to turn his wrath from the fugitive to his pursuers.

"But what do you want?" asked several voices.

"That you should let me pass."

"What for?"

"To demand the rebel's sword."

"Indeed, that will be an interesting spectacle," said come; "let him pass."

"How now," cried Don Fernand, "do you hesitate? Do you recoil? O you wretches! O you cowards!"

And another shriek of pain indicated that the young man's sword was buried anew in living flesh.

The result was a fresh clamor, and again the clash of steel on steel was heard.

"Do not kill him! do not kill him!" cried Don Inigo, in despair. "I must take him alive."

"Alive!" shouted Don Fernand; "did I not hear one of you say that he would take me alive?"

"Yes, I!" cried the grand justiciary, from the foot of the stairs.

"You! Who are you?" demanded Fernand.

"I am Don Inigo."

Don Fernand felt a shudder run through every limb.

"Ah!" he muttered, "I recognized your voice before you told me your name. Well, what do you want with me?" he added aloud. "Come up, but come alone."

"Gentlemen," said Don Inigo, "allow me to pass."

Don Inigo spoke in such a commanding tone that every one made way for him, standing close against the wall of the narrow staircase.

Don Inigo began to ascend, step by step; but on every stair lay a dead or wounded man. He was obliged to step over ten bodies to reach the first landing, where Don Fernand awaited him.

The young man's left arm was wrapped in his cloak, of which he had made a buckler; his clothes were torn, and the blood was flowing from two or three wounds.

"What do you want with me," he demanded of Don Inigo, — "you who have caused me more fear with a single word than those fellows with their weapons?"

"What I want," said the grand justiciary, "is that you should give up your sword to me."

"My sword?" repeated Don Fernand, with a roar of laughter.

"What I want," continued Don Inigo, "is that you should cease to defend yourself and acknowledge yourself my prisoner."

"To whom did you promise to perform that miracle?"

"The king."

"Very good; return to the king and tell him that he intrusted you with an impossible mission."

"Why, what do you hope for? What do you expect, poor fool?"

"To die killing!"

"Then kill!" said the grand justiciary, walking toward him.

Don Fernand made a threatening gesture, then lowered his sword.

"Hark ye," he said, "do not interfere in this matter: let it go on to its end between myself and the men who have undertaken it; you will gain nothing by interfering, I swear to you! And yet, on my word as a gentleman, I should be in despair if any harm should befall you."

Don Inigo took a step forward.

"Your sword!" said he.

"I told you that it was useless to demand it, and you have had an opportunity to see that it is dangerous to try to take it."

"Your sword!" Don Inigo repeated, taking another step toward him.

"At least, draw yours!" cried the young man.

"God forbid that I should threaten you in any way, Don Fernand; no, I choose to owe everything to persuasion. Your sword, I beg you."

"Never!"

"I entreat you, Don Fernand."

"What a strange influence you exert over me!" exclaimed the young man. "But, no, no, I will not give you my sword."

Don Inigo put out his hand.

"Your sword!"

There was a moment's silence, during which Don Inigo put forth, to persuade Don Fernand, the strange power of fascination he had exerted over him from the day he first saw him.

"To think," he muttered, "that my own father could not make me return my sword to its scabbard; to think that twenty men have been unable to wrest it from my hands; to think that I feel as strong as a wounded bull, strong enough to cut a whole regiment in pieces, and that you, disarmed as you are, have but to say a word!"

"Give it to me!" said Don Inigo.

"Oh, but be sure of this, that it is to you alone that I surrender it; that you alone inspire fear and respect in my heart; and that it is at your feet, not at the king's, that I lay this sword, red with blood from the hilt to the point."

And he humbly laid his sword at Don Inigo's feet.

The grand justiciary picked it up.

"It is well," he said; "and Heaven is my witness that at this moment, Don Fernand, I, the judge, would most gladly change places with you, the accused, and that I should suffer less from the danger you incur than from the pain that rends my heart!"

"What do you propose to do with me?" demanded Don Fernand, frowning.

"You must give me your word not to attempt to escape, to go at once to prison, and there await the king's pleasure."

"You have my word."

"Follow me."

Don Inigo walked to the stairs.

"Give place!" he said, "and let no voice be raised to insult the prisoner; henceforth he is under the protection of my honor."

Every one drew aside. The grand justiciary, followed by Don Fernand, descended the blood-drenched stairs.

When they reached the door, the young man cast a disdainful glance about; whereupon, despite Don Inigo's command, shouts arose on all sides and fierce threats were heard. Don Fernand turned pale as death and rushed to pick up a sword that had fallen from a dead man's hand.

But Don Inigo had only to raise his hand.

"I have your word," he said.

"And you can rely upon it," said the prisoner, bowing.

He went down into the city to surrender himself at the prison, while the other crossed the square of Las Algives to join Don Carlos in the palace of the Alhambra.

The king was waiting, sombre and silent, walking back and forth in the hall of the Two Sisters, when the grand justiciary was announced.

He paused in his walk, raised his head, and fixed his eyes on the door.

Don Inigo appeared.

"Will Your Majesty permit me to kiss your hand?" he said.

"As you venture to appear in my presence, it must be that the culprit is arrested," said Don Carlos.

"Yes, sire."

"Where is he?"

"He should be in prison at this moment."

"You sent him thither under a strong escort?"

"Under the safest escort I could find. — his honor. sire."

"You trusted to his word?"

"Your Highness forgets that a gentleman's word is the strongest chain by which he can be bound."

"It is well," said Don Carlos; "this evening you will attend me to the prison. I have heard the father's complaint; it remains for me to hear the son's defence."

Don Inigo bowed.

"And yet," murmured the king, "what can a son who has struck his father say in his own defence?"

XXIX.

THE EVE OF THE DÉNOUEMENT.

THE day, already pregnant with the events it had under-taken to bring forth for the morrow, was destined to promise even more entertainment for the public curiosity before the sun, which had risen from behind the glisten-ing peaks of the Sierra Nevada, should sink behind the frowning summits of the Sierra Morena.

As we have said, while Don Inigo betook himself to the palace, Don Fernand, a prisoner on parole, betook himself to the prison, carrying his head proudly erect, not as one vanquished, but as a victor; for, in his own eyes, he had not succumbed: he had obeyed a sentiment which, while it ordered him to sacrifice his wrath and probably to yield up his life, was still not without a certain charm for him.

He went down, therefore, toward the city, followed by a part of those who had been present at the terrible battle he had fought; but as Don Inigo had given orders that no one should insult the prisoner, and as the admi-ration that courage always arouses in a courageous people spoke even louder than the grand justiciary's command to the noble Spanish heart, they who followed him — talking of the terrific blows they had seen him give and receive — seemed rather an honorable cortége than a degrading escort.

At the foot of the slope leading to the Alhambra, Don Fernand met two veiled women; both stopped suddenly with a double exclamation of surprise and joy. He too stopped, partly because of the exclamation, partly because of the magnetic sentiment that stirs within us, not only when we meet a person who is dear to us, but when we are destined to see her in the near future.

But, even before he had asked himself who the women were toward whom his heart instinctively flew out, one of them put her hand to her lips, and the other, with outstretched arms, faltered his name.

"Ginesta! Doña Flor!" he murmured; while, with the respect the multitude always exhibits for great sorrow, they who had followed the young man from the square of Las Algives, and who proposed to follow him to the prison, halted at some little distance, in order to allow the prisoner and the two young women to speak freely together.

The interview was a brief one; a few words only were exchanged between Don Fernand and Ginesta, a glance or two between Don Fernand and Doña Flor.

Then the two girls went on toward the Alhambra, and Don Fernand toward the prison.

The reader will understand the object of Ginesta's visit to the palace: warned by Doña Flor of Don Fernand's danger, she had come to make a second trial of her power over Don Carlos.

But this time she had not the parchment that proved her birth nor the million she had paid for her dowry.

Assuming the memory of the King of Spain to be as unreliable as a king's memory ordinarily is, she was henceforth to her brother, as to all the world, simply the poor little gypsy, Ginesta.

But she still had her heart, — her heart, wherein she hoped to find sufficient prayers and tears to move the heart of Don Carlos, however cold and inaccessible it might be.

She feared only one thing: that she might be unable to reach the king.

Great was her joy, therefore, when the door was opened to her as soon as she pronounced her name.

The trembling Doña Flor, whose only hope was in her, waited at the door.

Ginesta followed her guide. He softly opened the door of the room, which had been transformed into a sort of study, stood aside to let the girl pass, and closed the door without announcing her.

Don Carlos was striding back and forth, his head hanging forward on his breast, his eyes fixed on the floor.   You would have said that the weight of half the world was already pressing upon that Atlas of nineteen.

Ginesta knelt upon one knee, and remained in that posture for some moments before the king seemed even to perceive that she was there.   At last he raised his eyes, gazed at her with a distraught expression, that gradually became questioning, and asked, —

" Who are you ? "

" Do you not recognize me, sire ? " replied the gypsy. " In that case, I am indeed unfortunate."

Thereupon Don Carlos seemed to make an effort of memory ; his glance, at certain times, seemed to experience less difficulty in reading the future than fatigue in reading the past.

" Ginesta! " he said.

" Yes, yes, Ginesta," murmured the girl, overjoyed to be recognized.

" Do you know that the messenger from Frankfort will arrive to-day or to-morrow, if nothing happens to delay him ? " queried the king, halting in front of the gypsy.

" What messenger ? " said Ginesta.

"The messenger who will inform me whether the empire belongs to Francis I. or to me at this moment."

"God grant that it is yours, sire!" said Ginesta.

"Oh, if I am chosen emperor," cried Don Carlos, "how quickly I will begin by resuming possession of Naples, which I have promised to the pope; Italy, which I have yielded to France; Sardinia, which I have — "

. He realized that he was repeating aloud the thoughts with which his mind was filled, and that he was not alone.

He passed his hand across his brow.

Ginesta took advantage of the pause.

"If you are emperor, will you pardon him, sire?" she said.

"Pardon whom?"

"Fernand, the man I love, the man for whom I will pray to my dying day."

"The son who struck his father?" said Don Carlos, in a hoarse voice, as if the words stuck in his throat.

Ginesta bowed her head.

What could she do in face of such an accusation, above all, in face of such an accuser, poor child, except bow her head and weep?

She bowed her head and wept.

Don Carlos looked at her for a few moments, and perhaps it was unfortunate for her that she dared not raise her eyes to his; for she would certainly have surprised a gleam of compassion in his glance, fleeting though it may have been.

"To-morrow," he said, "you and all Granada will know my decision in that matter. Meanwhile remain. at the palace; it is useless for you to return to your convent, whether the culprit lives or dies."

Ginesta felt that any entreaty on her part would be thrown away, and she rose to her feet, murmuring, —

"Do not forget, O king, that, although I am a stranger to you in the sight of men, I am your sister in God's sight!"

Don Carlos waved his hand.

Ginesta left the room.

Doña Flor was still waiting at the door.

Ginesta narrated what had taken place between the king and herself.

At that moment an usher passed out, summoning the grand justiciary to attend upon the king.

The two girls followed the usher, hoping to learn something from Don Inigo.

Meanwhile Mercedes, praying on her knees in her bedroom, was waiting with no less anxiety than Ginesta and Doña Flor.

She had returned to her former apartments; was it not there that Don Fernand, in the days when he was an outlaw, but still free, used to visit her?

Happy days!

Poor mother! who had reached the point where she called those days of shuddering fear and anguish happy!

Ah! then she still had some doubt.

Now all doubt was removed, hope was almost extinct.

Beatrice and Vicente had been sent out by her for news. The news they brought became more alarming from moment to moment.

At first she had hoped that Fernand would escape to the mountains.

"Once in the mountains," she said to herself, "he will in good time go down to some seaport, and embark for Africa or Italy."

17

She would never see her son again, but he would be alive!

About one o'clock she learned that he had refused to fly farther before the shouting mob that pursued him, and had halted in the square of Las Algives.

At two o'clock she learned that he was fighting in the Vela Tower, and had already killed or wounded eight or ten men.

At three o'clock she learned that he had surrendered to Don Inigo, and had given himself up at the prison, without guards, in accordance with his word.

At four o'clock she learned that the king had promised the grand justiciary not to pronounce his judgment until he had questioned the accused.

At five o'clock she learned that the king had informed Ginesta that, on the morrow, she and all Granada would know what his judgment was.

On the morrow, therefore, the judgment would be pronounced.

What would that judgment be?

During the evening a vague but terrible rumor reached her ears.

They said in the city — in sooth, they were fain to content themselves with saying it, as there was no proof that it was really so — that the king had sent for the grand justiciary and had ordered him to have a scaffold erected on the square of Las Algives after nightfall.

For whom was that scaffold?

The king had visited the prisons with Don Inigo, and he had done nothing but grant pardons.

For whom was the scaffold, if not for Don Fernand?

But was it true that the order had been given?

Vicente undertook to obtain a positive answer to that question: he would watch all night, and nothing should take place on the square of Las Algives without his knowing it and reporting it to his mistress.

About nine o'clock in the evening he left the house; but an hour later he returned, saying that he had found it impossible to reach the square of Las Algives, as all the entrances were closed and guarded by sentinels.

There was nothing to do but to wait and pray.

Doña Mercedes resolved to pass the night in prayer.

She knelt, and heard the watchmen cry the hours one after another.

The dismal voice crying the hour of midnight and bidding the people of Granada sleep in peace had hardly died away in the distance, when it seemed to Doña Mercedes that she heard a key turning in the lock of the door through which Don Fernand was accustomed to enter.

She turned on her knees in the direction of that door, and saw it open and admit a man whose face was covered with a broad felt hat and his figure wrapped in a great cloak.

Her son alone had a key to that door.

"Fernand! Fernand!" she cried, rushing to meet the nocturnal visitor.

But she stopped abruptly when she noticed that the man who had entered the room and locked the door behind him was a head shorter than Fernand.

At the same time the stranger raised his hat and let fall his cloak.

"I am not Fernand," he said.

Mercedes recoiled a step.

"The king!" she faltered.

The stranger shook his head.

"Madame, I am not the king — not here, at least," he said.

"What are you, then, sire?" Mercedes asked.

"A confessor. To your knees, woman! and confess that you have been false to your husband. It is impossible that a son should strike his father."

Mercedes fell on her knees and exclaimed, holding out her trembling hands to the king, —

"O sire, sire! God has sent you! Listen, and I will tell you everything."

XXX.

THE CONFESSION.

At that exordium the king began to breathe more freely.

"I am listening," he said in a curt, imperious tone.

"Sire," murmured Mercedes, "I am about to tell you things of the sort that a woman finds it difficult to tell, although I am very far from being as guilty as I may seem at first glance to be; but, in speech at least, be indulgent to me, I entreat you, or I feel that I cannot go on."

"Speak with confidence, Doña Mercedes," replied Don Carlos, in a slightly softened tone, "and never was secret kept more religiously by the priest into whose ear it was whispered than the secret will be which you are about to confide to your king."

"I thank you humbly, sire!" said Mercedes.

And, after passing her hand across her forehead, not to collect or concentrate her memories, — it was easy to see that they were all at hand, — but to wipe away the sweat of anguish by which it was still bedewed, she began, —

"Sire, I had been brought up with the son of a friend of my father, as a brother and sister are brought up together, without suspecting for an instant that there was any other sentiment in the world than fraternal affection, when suddenly a dispute concerning money matters embroiled those two friends who were supposed to be inseparable.

"Nor was that all: the rupture was widened by an actual demand for money. Who was in the wrong? Who was in the right? I have no idea; but what I do know is that my father paid the sum demanded, and left Seville, where we lived, for Cordova, in order not to be in the same city with the man who had been his friend, but had become his mortal enemy.

" The rupture between the fathers separated the children.

"I was barely thirteen years old at that time; he whom I had always called my brother was seventeen; we had never said that we loved each other, perhaps we had never thought it, when that unexpected separation, decided upon and carried out with great suddenness, showed us clearly what was in our hearts.

"Something wept and bled profusely within us; it was that friendship, which had become love and was suddenly shattered by the hands of our parents.

" Was that a thing that they had in mind? Did they know the evil they were doing? I believe that they did not even suspect it; but, even if they had suspected it, I think that their mutual hatred had become too intense for them to disturb themselves in the least concerning the influence it might have upon our love.

" Thus our families were separated, both by hatred and by distance. But we swore to each other, in a last interview, that nothing should separate us.

" And, in truth, what share had we poor children, who were born side by side and had grown up together, in the animosities of our parents? And when they had said to us again and again, every day for ten years, ' Love each other!' were we not excusable for not obeying when they suddenly said to us, ' Hate each other! ' "

Mercedes seemed to await a word of encouragement from the king before continuing; but he replied, —

"I do not know what love is, madame, having never loved."

"In that case," said Mercedes, despondently, "I am very unfortunate, sire, for you will understand nothing of what I still have to tell you."

"Excuse me, señora, for I am a judge, having been king from childhood, and I know what justice is."

Mercedes continued: —

"We kept our word; our very separation favored our love, of which our parents knew nothing. My father's house, at Cordova, was close beside the Guadalquivir; my room, which was at the extreme rear of the house, had a window with a grating looking on the river. My lover purchased a boat, and, leaving his home at Seville thrice each month, on the pretext of hunting in the Sierra, came beneath my window, disguised as a fisherman, to tell me that he loved me still, and to hear from my mouth that I still loved him.

"Our hope at first was that the hatred between our families would be allayed; but it constantly increased.

"Every form of entreaty was resorted to by my lover to induce me to fly with him.

"I resisted.

"Thereupon he fell a prey to a sort of dull despair; those nocturnal interviews, which made him perfectly happy at first, were no longer sufficient for him.

"The war between the Christians and the Moors was fiercer than ever.

"One night he informed me that he was weary of life, and was going to take part in the war and be killed.

"I wept, but I did not yield. He went away.

"For a year I saw no more of him; but during that

year reports constantly came to my ears of such glorious exploits performed by him that, if I could have loved him more, my love would have been augmented by his gallantry and his renown.

"These reports were brought to us, most of the time, by a young man who was present with him in the battles he described, and had shared his dangers. That young man, his companion-in-arms, was the son of one of my father's friends, and his name was Don Ruiz de Torrillas."

The king listened, with a sombre look in his eyes, silent and impassive as a statue. Doña Mercedes ventured to look up at him to try to judge from his expression whether she had best abridge or prolong her narrative.

Don Carlos understood the mute question.

"Go on," he said.

"The close attention with which I listened to what Don Ruiz told me, the eagerness with which I ran to him when his presence was announced, made him think, I doubt not, that my sympathy was for himself, while in reality it related entirely to him who was absent; so his visits became more frequent, and, failing his voice, his eyes began to tell me the secrets of his heart.

"Thenceforth, although it cost me dear to hear no more of the man who filled my whole mind, and who had carried away all my joy with him, I ceased to go downstairs when Don Ruiz came.

"Indeed, he soon ceased to come; the army to which he belonged was engaged in the siege of Granada.

"One day we learned that Granada was taken.

"It was a great joy to us, as Christians, to know that the Moorish capital was in the hands of the Catholic king; but, in my own case, a long-standing sorrow drowned all joy, and the news found my father overwhelmed by fresh misfortunes.

"What remained of our fortune came from my father's first wife; that fortune belonged to a son, a sort of adventurer, who was supposed to be dead, and whom I hardly knew, although I was his sister.

"He appeared, and claimed his fortune.

"My father asked only the necessary time to settle his accounts; but he told me that, when the accounts were settled, we should be utterly ruined.

"I thought the moment a favorable one. I ventured to say a few words concerning the old friend with whom he had fallen out; but at the first word I uttered his eyes flashed fire.

"I held my peace.

"His hatred revived with every fresh grief.

"I had to make up my mind never to refer to the subject again.

"On the night following that day, being unable to sleep, I was sitting on the balcony that overlooked the stream; the grating of my window was open, for it seemed to me that I could not breathe freely through the iron bars.

"The melting snows had swollen the Guadalquivir, which flowed almost beneath my feet. I was looking up at the sky, following the floating clouds which a fitful breeze caused to change their shape and aspect twenty times in a quarter of an hour, when I saw, amid the shadows that overhung the river, a boat rowed by a single fisherman. I drew back in order not to be seen, and intending to resume my place when he had passed; but suddenly a dark form appeared in front of me, shutting out the stars; a man climbed over the balcony rail; I gave a shriek of terror, but a well-known voice answered the shriek, —

"'It is I, Mercedes. Silence!'

"It was he, in very truth. I should have fled; it did not occur to me to do so; I fell half fainting into his arms. When I came to myself — alas! I no longer belonged to myself, sire!

"The unhappy man had not come with the purpose of committing that crime; he had come to see me for the last time, and to bid me farewell; he was setting out with the Genoese, Columbus, on a voyage of discovery. In the distance he had seen me on the balcony; my retreat had left the way clear. He had never found the grating open before; it was the first time he had entered my room.

"Thereupon he renewed his instances to induce me to follow him; if I would accompany him on the adventurous journey he was about to undertake, he would obtain Columbus's consent to my going disguised as a man; if I preferred any other part of the world, all places were alike to him, provided that he lived there with me. He was rich and independent; we loved each other; we should be happy together anywhere.

"I refused.

"Before daybreak he left me. We said farewell forever, — at least we thought so; he was to join Columbus at Palos, and they were to sail the following month.

"Ere long I discovered that our misfortunes did not stop halfway: I was about to become a mother!

"I wrote the fatal news to him, hoping and yet fearing that he had already sailed, and waited, in solitude and tears, until God should decide my fate.

"One night, when I had been so long without a reply that I was certain that he was already sailing toward the unknown world which immortalized the name of Columbus, I heard beneath my window the signal that announced his presence.

"I believed that my ears had deceived me, and I waited, trembling with excitement.

"The signal was repeated.

"Oh, I confess that my joy was beyond words as I flew to the window and opened it.

"He was there, in a boat, holding out his arms; Columbus's departure was postponed, and he had travelled across a large part of Spain to see me for the last time, or to take me with him.

"Alas! our very misfortune gave him the hope that I would go with him.

"I resisted. I was the only remaining comfort, the only companion of my poor father, who was reduced to poverty. I was determined to confess everything to him, to run the risk of his wrath, but never to leave him.

"Oh, that was a terrible night, sire! and one that, at all events, could not be repeated.

"Columbus's departure was appointed for August 3. Only by a miracle of speed had he come, only by another miracle of speed could he return and arrive in time.

"Oh, sire, sire, I cannot tell you all the entreaties, prayers, supplications, he resorted to during that night. Twenty times he went down into his boat, and climbed back to the balcony again; the last time he took me in his arms and tried to carry me by force. I cried; I called. We heard the noise made by some person rising and coming to my help; he must fly or be discovered.

"He rushed off to his boat for the last time; and I, when I felt his heart leave mine, fell fainting on the floor! There Beatrice found me."

And poor Mercedes, almost as excited, almost as inanimate as she had been on that fatal night, wringing her hands and sobbing bitterly, fell back against a chair, although she was still on her knees.

"Take breath, madame," said Don Carlos, gravely and coldly; "I have the whole night to give you."

There was a brief silence, during which nothing but Doña Mercedes' sobs could be heard.   Don Carlos meanwhile was so entirely motionless that he might have been taken for a statue; so entirely self-controlled that not even his respiration was audible.

"He went away," faltered Mercedes.

And with those words her soul seemed to take flight.

"Three days later my father's friend, Don Francisco de Torrillas, called upon him.   He asked for a private interview, having, as he said, an affair of the utmost importance to discuss with him.

"The two old men were closeted together.

"Don Francisco came to ask my father for my hand in his own name and his son's.   His son loved me dearly, and had told him that he could not live without me.

"Nothing could have made my father happier than that proposition.   A single scruple withheld him from accepting it at once.

"'Do you know the state of my fortune?' he asked his friend.

"'No, but it is of little consequence.'

"'I am ruined,' said my father.

"'What then?'

"'Utterly ruined.'

"'So much the better!' his friend replied.

"'How so?'

'I am rich enough for both of us, and whatever price you put upon the treasure you give us, I can pay it.'

"My father gave Don Francisco his hand.

"'I authorize Don Ruiz to call upon my daughter,' he said; 'let him obtain Mercedes' consent, and Mercedes is his.'

"I had passed three terrible days. My father, who did not suspect the cause of my illness, had come each day to inquire for me.

"Ten minutes after Don Francisco's departure he was in my room, and told me all that had taken place. A quarter of an hour before I would not have believed that my unhappiness could increase: I found that I was mistaken.

"My father left me, after informing me that Don Ruiz would call the following day.

"I had not had the strength to answer him, and, when he had gone, I was completely crushed. Gradually, however, I emerged from my stupor and faced my situation, which appeared to me, not as the spectre of the past, but as the spectre of the future. By far the most terrible thing was the being compelled to lock up the fatal secret in my own breast. Oh, if I could have confided it to some one it seems to me that I should have suffered less!

"The night came. Notwithstanding Beatrice's entreaties to be allowed to remain with me, I sent her away. In solitude I could at least weep. O sire, the tears flowed freely, — the tears that would long ago have been exhausted, had not the Lord in his mercy decreed that the source of tears should be inexhaustible.

"As soon as night had descended upon the earth, as soon as silence reigned all about, I took my place on that balcony where I had been at once so happy and so wretched.

"It seemed to me that he would come.

"Oh, never had I longed for him so earnestly from the very bottom of my heart!

"If he had come, forgive me, father, but that time I could not have held out against him; wherever he had chosen to take me, I would have gone with him; wherever he had chosen to lead me, I would have followed.

"A boat appeared; a man was rowing up the Guadalquivir, singing.

"It was not his voice; he would have been silent. No matter, I hugged my delusion, and, with outstretched arms, I cried to the phantom I had created for myself, —

"'Come! come! come!'

"The boat passed. Probably the fisherman could not understand the voice that he heard in the darkness, or the woman who leaned toward him in the shadow.

"And yet he understood that there was sorrow of some sort afloat in the night; for before he reached my window he ceased his singing, and did not begin again until he had passed.

"The boat disappeared; I was left alone. All about me stretched the animate silence amid which you seem to hear the breathing of nature.

"The star-studded sky was reflected in the water; one would have said that I was suspended in mid-air; the void attracted me and gave me a sort of vertigo. I was so unhappy that I thought of dying. From the thought to its execution was only a step, — it was so easy; death opened his arms to me only three feet below.

"I felt my head bending forward, my body leaning over the balcony, my feet leaving the floor of their own accord.

" Suddenly I thought of my child.

" In killing myself I should be guilty not of suicide simply, but of murder.

" I grasped the balcony; I stepped back; I closed the grating; I threw the key into the river, so that I could not give way to the temptation of despair; and I walked backward to my bed and fell upon it.

" Slowly and painfully the hours passed. I saw the approach of dawn; I heard all the noises of the day begin one after another. Beatrice opened my door and entered the room.

" The daily life began once more.

" At eleven o'clock Beatrice announced Don Ruiz. He came with a message from my father.

" My mind was made up; I bade her admit him.

" He was at once shy and radiant.

" My father had told him that he had no doubt that his suit would be favorably received.

" But when he glanced at me, and saw how pale and cold I was, he too began to tremble and turn pale.

" I looked up at him and waited.

" His voice failed him; he tried ten times to tell me what his errand was.

" As he spoke, he felt that his words were shattered against the wall of adamant that encased my heart.

" At last he succeeded in telling me that he had loved me for a long time; that our marriage was agreed upon by his father and mine, and that only my consent was lacking to make him the happiest man on earth.

" ' Señor,' I replied in a firm voice, — for my reply had long been prepared, —' the honor you offer me cannot be accepted by me.'

" His face had been pale; it became livid.

" ' Why so, in God's name ? ' he asked.

" ' I love another man, and in seven months I shall be a mother! '

" He staggered, and almost fell.

" There was something so desperate in that confession — made to a man whom I had seen only five or six times, and whom I did not even bind to secrecy, as if, trusting in his honor, I considered that a useless formality — that it was impossible for him to persist in his suit.

" He bowed low before me, lifted the hem of my dress and kissed it, and left the room, saying only these three words, —

" ' God bless you!

" I was alone once more.

" Every moment I expected to see my father appear, and I trembled at the thought of being compelled to give him an explanation; but, to my great astonishment, I heard nothing from him.

" At the dinner hour I sent word to him that I was a little indisposed, and asked his permission to dine in my room.

" The permission was granted without remonstrance or comment.

" Three days passed.

" On the third day Beatrice once more announced Don Ruiz.

" As before, I ordered her to admit him. His manner of taking leave of me at our last interview had touched me deeply; there was something sublime in the respect he had shown a poor abandoned girl.

" He entered, and remained near the door.

" ' Approach, Señor Don Ruiz,' I said.

" ' My presence surprises and annoys you, does it not?' he asked me.

" ' It surprises me,' I answered, ' but does not annoy me, for I feel that I have a friend in you.'

" 'You are not mistaken,' he said; 'and yet I would have spared you the sight of me if it were not necessary to your tranquillity.'

" ' Explain your meaning, Señor Don Ruiz.'

" ' I could not tell your father that you had refused me for your husband, for he would have come and demanded an explanation, and you would not have given him the explanation you gave me, would you ? '

" ' I would rather die ! '

" ' You see that it was necessary to do as I did.'

" ' What did you do ? '

" ' I said that you had asked for a few days to make up your mind, and that you wished to be allowed to pass those few days in solitude.'

" ' It is to you, then, that I owe my tranquillity ? '

" He bowed.

" ' And now,' he said, ' it is important that you should believe me to be your sincere friend.'

" I offered him my hand.

" 'Ah, yes, my friend, my very sincere friend, I do believe it ! ' I said.

" ' Then, answer me with no more hesitation than before.'

" ' Question me.'

" ' Have you any hope of ever being able to marry the man you love ? '

" ' Impossible ! '

" ' Is he dead ? '

" ' He is alive.'

" A ray of joy that had gleamed in his eyes vanished.

" ' Ah ! ' he said, ' that is all I wanted to know.'

" Bowing once more to me, he left the room with a sigh.

18

"Three more days passed.

"During those three days I did not leave my room, and, with the exception of Beatrice, no one entered it, not even my father.

"On the fourth day Don Ruiz was announced once more.

"I almost expected him; I had ceased to dread the sight of him; he was my only confidant, and I was sure that he had told the truth when he told me that he was sincerely my friend.

"He entered respectfully, as usual, and did not approach me until I motioned to him to do so.

"I gave him my hand; he took it and touched it gently with his lips.

"Then, after a moment's silence, during which his eyes were fixed upon me with deep interest, he said, —

"' I have not ceased for one instant to think of your position; it is terrible! '

"I uttered a sigh.

"' We cannot, however much I may desire to assist you, postpone your reply forever.'

"' Alas! ' I exclaimed.

"' Of course I could say that I have withdrawn my suit; I would willingly incur the shame of allowing it to be thought that your father's ruin had cooled my affection for you; but how would that assist you? It would simply give you a reprieve for two or three months.'

"I burst into tears, for all that he said was exactly true.

"' Some day or other,' he continued, ' your father must learn your condition; everybody must know it; and then ' — he lowered his voice — ' then you will be dishonored! '

" ' But what can I do ? ' I cried.

" ' Marry a man who is devoted enough to you to be your husband in the eyes of the world, and no more than a brother in his relations with you.'

" I shook my head.

" ' Where can I find such a man ? ' I said.

" ' I have come to make you that offer, Mercedes; have I not said that I love you ? '

" ' You love me — but — '

" ' When I love, Mercedes, it is with all the great passions, not of the heart only, but of the soul, and among those passions is devotion.'

" I raised my head, and recoiled from him almost in dismay.

" I had not guessed that devotion could go so far.

" ' I will be your brother,' he repeated; ' but your child shall be my child, and never a word, I pledge you my honor as a gentleman, — never a word on that point shall be exchanged between us.'

" I looked at him, full of doubt and hesitation.

" ' Tell me,' he said, ' will that not be better than to throw yourself out of yonder window into the river that flows by the foot of your house ? '

" For a moment I stood speechless; then, falling at his knees, I exclaimed, —

" ' Brother, have pity on your wife, and save my father's honor ! '

" He raised me, kissed my hand, and left the room.

" A fortnight later I was Don Ruiz' wife.

" Don Ruiz kept his word like a loyal gentleman; but nature refused to lend a hand to the deceit, and, although Don Ruiz has always bestowed a father's care upon Don Fernand, Don Fernand has never had a filial feeling for him.

"Now, sire, you know all!"

"Except the name of the real father," said the king; "but you are going to tell me that."

"Don Inigo Velasco!" faltered Mercedes, casting down her eyes.

"It is well," said the king; "I know all that I wanted to know."

Thereupon he left the room, grave and stern, leaving the woman on her knees, and muttering as he went, —

"I knew that it was impossible for a son to strike his father!"

CONCLUSION.

THE next morning at daybreak a great multitude filled the square of Las Algives, crowding about a scaffold erected in the centre of the square.

The executioner stood, with folded arms, at the foot of the scaffold. An air of mystery prevailed throughout the city, and it was said that King Don Carlos was about to administer justice for the first time.

Many Moors could be recognized amid the throng, by their fiery eyes, even more readily than by their oriental costume. Those eyes were gleaming with joy at the prospect of seeing punishment meted out to a man of noble birth, a *rico hombre* and a Christian.

As the clock on the Vela Tower struck nine the gates of the Alhambra were thrown open; the guards formed in two lines, drove back the crowd, and compelled the people to form a great circle at some distance from the scaffold.

Then King Don Carlos appeared, casting a troubled glance on every side from beneath his restless eyelids. You would have said that he was looking about, as if from habit, for a long-expected messenger.

As the messenger did not arrive, the royal countenance resumed its customary immobility.

Beside the king walked a young woman whose face could not be seen because of the veil which covered it; but from her costume, which was at once rich and chaste, it was evident that she belonged to the noble caste.

Don Carlos passed through the crowd, and did not pause until he was within a few steps of the scaffold.

Behind him appeared the grand justiciary and Doña Flor. Doña Flor was leaning on her father's arm.

When their eyes fell upon the scaffold they both stopped, and it would have been impossible to say which was the paler of the two.

The king turned to see if the grand justiciary were following him; and when he saw that he had stopped, supporting his fainting daughter, and near fainting himself, he sent an officer to bid him come and join him.

At the same time two persons made their way through the crowd from the opposite direction. They were Don Ruiz and Doña Mercedes.

Both turned their eyes upon the scaffold, but with very different expressions.

Five minutes had not passed when Don Fernand and Don Ramiro, the two rivals, appeared, escorted by men-at-arms. Don Fernand had been arrested the day before, as we have described; Don Ramiro had surrendered himself voluntarily, in accordance with the order he had received.

All the actors in the drama, the first four acts of which had been played, were assembled for the last act. Silence fell upon the throng, and all awaited the unknown catastrophe, to which the executioner's presence lent a mysterious but awful significance.

Don Carlos raised his head, glanced for the last time toward the Moorish gate, and, seeing that nobody came, he fixed his eyes upon Don Inigo, who felt a shudder run over his whole body under that icy glance.

"Don Inigo Velasco de Haro," he said, in such a vibrating voice that, although it did not rise above the ordinary pitch, it was clearly heard by all, "on two occasions, without offering any reasons in support of your request, you have solicited the life of a man who has twice merited death. You are no longer grand justiciary of Andalusia."

A murmur arose among the actors in this scene, and was taken up by the crowd; Don Inigo stepped forward, doubtless to justify himself.

"You are no longer grand justiciary of Andalusia," continued King Don Carlos, "but you are constable of the kingdom; the man who holds the scales of justice unsteadily may gallantly wield the sword of war."

"Sire!" murmured Don Inigo.

"Silence, constable," interposed Don Carlos; "I have not done. — Don Ruiz," he continued, "for a long time I have known you to be one of the noblest gentlemen in my Spanish dominions; since yesterday I have known you to be one of the noblest hearts in the whole world."

Don Ruiz bowed.

"You are appointed grand justiciary of Andalusia in Don Inigo's place; you came to me yesterday to demand justice for the insult that had been put upon you: mete out justice yourself."

Don Ruiz trembled.

Doña Mercedes became pale as death.

"Don Fernand," the king continued, "you are twice guilty: once you rebelled against the laws of society, and that time I pardoned you; another time you rebelled against the laws of nature, and, deeming myself powerless to punish so great a crime, I leave it for the person outraged to pardon or punish at his will. But, in any event, from this moment your name is stricken from the roll of noblemen; I take away your title of

rico hombre, and I make you, not as pure, unfortunately, but as poor, as solitary, as naked as on the day
you came into the world! — Ginesta," continued the
king, " you are no longer the gypsy of the Moorish King
Inn or the novice of the convent of the Annonciade:
you are Duchess of Carmona, Marchioness of Montefrio,
Countess of Pulgar; you are made a grandee of the first
class, and that grandeeship you can confer, with your
name, on your husband, though you should take him
from the ranks of the people, from a Moorish tribe, or
at the gallows' foot."

He turned to Don Ramiro.

"Don Ramiro," he said, " you are free; you were
insulted and could not have done otherwise than answer
the insult; but, while fighting, you honored old age,
which is of all things the most worthy of respect after
the Lord God. I cannot make you richer than you are,
but, in memory of me, you will add the name of Carlos
to the names you bear, and place the Lion of Burgundy
in Chief in your crest. — And now let punishment or
reward be meted out to all! Begin, Don Ruiz, grand
justiciary of the realm."

Profound silence ensued. All eyes were turned upon
Don Ruiz, all ears were opened, and this is what they
saw and heard: —

Doña Mercedes, who up to that time had been motionless as a statue, seemed to lift her feet from
the ground with difficulty, and, walking slowly and
solemnly across the space between herself and her husband, who was standing with folded arms, she said to
him, —

" My lord, in the name of everything most sacred in
heaven and earth, the mother implores pardon for her
son! "

For a moment there was a silent conflict in Don Ruiz' heart and upon his features.

Then he placed one of his hands on Doña Mercedes' head, and with an expression and accent of infinite sweetness, he said, —

"I pardon!"

A loud murmur ran through the crowd. Don Fernand turned frightfully pale. He looked down at his side for a weapon; and, if he could have found his Basque dagger, perhaps he would have stabbed himself rather than accept that pardon from the old man.

But Don Fernand was disarmed, and in the hands of his guards.

"It is your turn, Duchess of Carmona!" said Don Carlos.

Ginesta came forward and knelt at Don Fernand's feet, raising her veil as she did so.

"Don Fernand, I love you!" she said.

The young man uttered a cry, stood for a moment like one bewildered, cast a long glance at Doña Flor, and held out his arms to Ginesta, who clung to him, joyous with a joy that she had never known before.

"Duchess of Carmona, Marchioness of Montefrio, and Countess of Pulgar, do you take for your husband the condemned felon Fernand, who has neither name, nor rank, nor fortune?" asked Don Carlos.

"I love him, sire! I love him!" Ginesta repeated.

And, compelling Don Fernand to kneel, she fell on her knees with him before the king.

"It is well," said Don Carlos; "a king has only his word. Rise, Duke of Carmona, Marquis of Montefrio, Count of Pulgar, grandee of Spain of the first class in right of your wife, — the sister of a king and daughter of a king!"

Then, giving the actors and spectators no time to recover from their astonishment, he turned to Don Ramiro.

" It is your turn, Don Ramiro," he said.

Don Ramiro walked unsteadily from where he stood to Doña Flor. There was a sort of gold and purple cloud before his eyes, while the voices of all the angels in heaven seemed to be singing in his ears.

He knelt upon one knee before her.

" For two years I have loved you, señora," he said. " Don Ramiro d'Avila dared not tell you so; but in the presence of the king, his godfather, Don Carlos d'Avila humbly asks for your hand."

" Señor," faltered Doña Flor, " ask my father."

" I am your father for to-day, Doña Flor," said Don Carlos, " and I give your hand to your love courier."

The three groups were still in the positions we have indicated, when suddenly a great clamor was heard in the direction of the gate of the Judgment; a moment later, a horseman, covered with dust, whom Don Carlos recognized by his costume as a German nobleman, appeared upon the scene, waving a parchment in the air, and shouting, —

" The king? Where is the king? "

Don Carlos in his turn became pale as death; you would have said that he who had just pronounced judgment was about to be judged himself.

" The king? Where is the king?" the horseman repeated.

The crowd made way for him.

Don Carlos stepped forward and said, in a firm voice, although his almost livid face betrayed the anguish of his heart, —

" He is here! "

The horse stopped short, trembling in every limb, and throwing himself back upon his haunches.

Everybody waited in breathless suspense.

The horseman stood up in his stirrups.

" Give ear all who are here present ! " he cried; " listen, Granada ! listen, Burgos ! listen, Valladolid ! listen, Spain ! listen, Europe ! listen, the whole world ! Hail to Charles V., Emperor elect ! honor to his reign ! glory to his sons and his sons' sons ! "

Leaping from his horse, and falling on his knees, he presented the document that declared the election of King Don Carlos to the imperial throne of Germany.

Don Carlos took it with a trembling hand; but it was impossible to detect the slightest trace of emotion in his voice, as he said, —

" Thanks, my Lord Duke of Bavaria; I shall not forget that I am indebted to you for my first knowledge of this great news."

And then, as all the spectators repeated with joyous shouts the words of the messenger, " Glory to Charles V. ! glory to his sons and his sons' sons ! " the emperor raised his hand.

" Gentlemen," said he, " to God alone be glory, for God alone is great ! "

BLANCHE DE BEAULIEU

LIST OF CHARACTERS.

Period, 1793-1794.

———◆———

GENERAL ALEXANDRE DUMAS, the author's father.
GENERAL MARCEAU, a young republican leader.
MAXIMILIEN ROBESPIERRE,
SAINT-JUST,
COLLOT D'HERBOIS,
BILLAUD-VARENNES,
ROBERT LINDET,   } revolutionists.
COUTHON,
CAMBON,
CARNOT,
BARRÈRE,
DANTON, leader of the Mountain.
CAMILLE DESMOULINS,
PHILIPPAUX,   } adherents of Danton.
HÉRAULT DE SÉCHELLES,
LACROIX,
HÉBERT, of the Commune.
DELMAR, representative of the people.
CARRIER, proconsul at Nantes.
BLANCHE DE BEAULIEU, daughter of the Marquis de Beaulieu, a
    Vendean.
TINGUY, in the service of Marquis de Beaulieu.
THE CURÉ OF SAINTE-MARIE DE RHÉ, a Vendean priest.

GENERAL ALEXANDRE DUMAS.

The Brigand, 287.

BLANCHE DE BEAULIEU.

I.

WHOEVER, during the evening of December 15, 1793, had started from the little town of Clisson to go to the village of Saint-Crépin, and had halted on the crest of the mountain at whose foot flows the river La Moine, would have seen a curious spectacle on the other side of the valley.

In the first place, at the spot where his eyes would have sought the village among the trees, against an horizon already darkened by the twilight, he would have noticed three or four columns of smoke, which, isolated at their bases, joined as they spread out, swayed a moment like a bronzed dome, then, yielding gracefully to a damp, westerly breeze, floated to the eastward, confounded with the low-lying, hazy clouds. He would have seen the smoke redden slowly, then disappear altogether, while from the roofs of the houses sharp tongues of flame darted in its place with a dull roar, now twisting about in spiral columns, now bending and rising again like the mast of a ship. It would have seemed to him as if all the windows would open soon to vomit fire. From time to time, as a roof fell in, he would have heard a smothered crash, he would have distinguished a more vivid flame, accompanied by myriads of sparks, and would have seen, in the blood-red light of the conflagration, arms glistening and a circle of soldiers extending around the village. He would have heard cries and laughter, and he would have said to himself in dismay, " God forgive me, an army is warming itself with a village! "

In fact, a republican brigade of twelve or fifteen hundred men had found the village of Saint-Crépin abandoned and had set fire to it.

It was not cruelty, it was one method of carrying on war, — a plan of campaign, like any other; experience proved that it was the only judicious one.

There was one isolated cottage, however, that was not burned; it seemed, indeed, as if all necessary precautions had been taken to prevent the fire reaching it. Two sentinels were on guard at the door, and every moment orderlies and aides-de-camp entered, coming out again almost immediately with orders.

He who issued the orders was a young man, apparently of some twenty to twenty-two years of age. Long, fair hair, parted on the forehead, fell in wavy locks on either side of his thin white cheeks; his whole face bore the imprint of that fatal melancholy that is stamped upon the brow of those who are destined to die young. The blue cloak in which he was enveloped did not conceal his person so thoroughly that you could not see the insignia of his rank, the epaulets of a general; but the epaulets were of wool, the republican officers having patriotically offered the Convention all the gold on their coats. He was leaning over a table on which a map was spread; he was marking thereon with a pencil, by the light of a lamp which paled in the glare of the conflagration, the road his troops were to follow. It was

General Marceau, who was destined to be killed three years later at Altenkirchen.

"Alexandre!" he said, half rising. "Alexandre! you everlasting sleeper, are you dreaming of Santo Domingo that you sleep so soundly?"

"What is it?" said the person thus apostrophized, springing to his feet with a start, his head almost touching the ceiling of the cabin; "what is it? is the enemy upon us?"

The words were uttered with a slight Creole accent, which preserved their sweetness despite their menacing tone.

"No; an order from General-in-Chief Westermann has arrived."

And while his colleague was reading the order, — for the person he addressed was his colleague, — Marceau gazed with childish curiosity at the muscular form of the herculean mulatto who stood before him.

He was a man of twenty-eight, with short, curly hair, dark complexion, open forehead, and white teeth, whose almost superhuman strength was known throughout the army, which had seen him, on a day of battle, cut through a helmet to the cuirass, and on a day of parade smother between his legs a horse that was running away with him. He also had not long to live; but, less fortunate than Marceau, he was fated to die far from the field of battle, poisoned by order of a king. It was General Alexandre Dumas; it was my father.

"Who brought you this order?" he asked.

"Delmar, the representative of the people."

"Very good. Where are the poor devils to assemble?"

"In a forest a league and a half from here. Look at the map! there's the place."

"True; but on the map we don't see the ravines, the mountains, the felled trees, the thousand and one roads that run into and out of the right road, so that you can hardly tell where you are, even by daylight. Infernal country! And with it all it's always so cold!"

"Look!" said Marceau, pushing the door open with his foot, and pointing to the burning village. "Go out and warm yourself! Well, what have you there, citizens?"

The last words were addressed to a group of soldiers, who, while searching for supplies, had discovered, in a sort of dog kennel adjoining the cottage, a Vendean peasant, who seemed to be so drunk that it was probable that he had not been able to accompany the people of the village when they abandoned it.

Let the reader imagine a farm laborer with a stupid face, long hair, a broad-brimmed hat, and a gray jacket; a creature made in man's image, but a degree below the beasts, — for it was evident that the mass lacked instinct. Marceau asked him a few questions; patois and wine made his replies unintelligible. He was about to turn him over as a plaything to the soldiers, when General Dumas suddenly ordered the cottage to be cleared, and the prisoner locked in there. He was still at the door; a soldier pushed him inside; he stumbled across the room and leaned against the wall, swayed unsteadily a moment on his half-bent legs, then fell heavily at full length, and lay motionless on the floor. A sentry was posted at the door, and they did not even take the trouble to close the window.

"In an hour we can march," said General Dumas to Marceau; "we have a guide."

"Who is he?"

"That man."

" Very good, if we want to start to-morrow. There's twenty-four hours' sleep in what that rascal has drunk."

Dumas smiled.

" Come," he said. And he led his colleague to the shed where the peasant had been discovered. A thin partition separated it from the interior of the cabin, and the partition was plentifully supplied with cracks, which enabled one to see what was going on there, and must have made it possible to hear every word spoken by the two generals who had been there a moment before.

" And now," he added, lowering his voice, " look ! "

Marceau obeyed, yielding to the ascendency his friend exerted over him, even in the ordinary affairs of life. He had some difficulty in distinguishing the prisoner, who, by accident, had fallen in the darkest corner of the cabin. He was still lying in the same place, absolutely motionless. Marceau turned to look for his colleague; he had disappeared.

When he looked back into the cabin it seemed to him that the man who occupied it had made a slight movement; his head was now in a position which enabled him to embrace the whole interior at a glance. Soon he opened his eyes, with the prolonged yawn of one just waking from sleep, and saw that he was alone.

A singular expression of satisfaction and intelligence passed over his face.

From that moment it became evident to Marceau that he would have been the man's dupe had not a keener glance than his divined the truth. He examined him, therefore, with renewed attention: his face had resumed its former expression, his eyes were closed, his movements were those of a man about to fall asleep again; in one of those movements he kicked the fragile table on

which lay the map and the order from General Westermann which Marceau had thrown down there; everything fell to the floor; one of the sentries opened the
door and put his head in at the noise, saw what had
caused it, and said to his companion, with a laugh, —

"It's the citizen, dreaming."

The citizen heard the words, his eyes opened anew,
and a threatening glance followed the soldier for an
instant; then, with a swift movement, he seized the
paper on which the order was written, and hid it in his
breast.

Marceau held his breath; his right hand seemed glued
to his sword hilt; his left hand and his forehead sustained the weight of his whole body as he leaned against
the partition.

The object of his attention was then lying on his side;
soon he began to move slowly, helping himself along
with his elbow and knee, but still in a recumbent position, toward the door of the cabin. The space between
the threshold and the lower part of the door enabled
him to see the legs of a group of soldiers standing outside; thereupon he began, slowly and patiently, to
crawl toward the open window. When he arrived within
three feet of it, he felt in his breast for a weapon which
was hidden there, gathered his body for a spring, and
with a single leap — the leap of a jaguar — sprang out of
the cabin. Marceau uttered a cry; he had had no time
to foresee or prevent that manœuvre. Another cry
answered his; it was a malediction. The Vendean, on
landing outside the window, had found himself face to
face with General Dumas. He had tried to strike him
with his knife; but the general, seizing his wrist, had
turned the knife against his breast, so that he had only
to push to make the Vendean stab himself.

"I promised you a guide, Marceau; here's one, and an intelligent one, too, I fancy. I might order you shot, knave," he said to the peasant, "but it suits my purpose better to allow you to live. You overheard our conversation, but you won't report it to them who sent you. — Citizens," — he addressed the soldiers whom the curious scene had attracted, — "do two of you take a hand each of this man, and take your places with him at the head of the column: he will be our guide; if you see that he's leading you astray, or if he makes a motion to run away, blow his brains out, and toss him over the hedge."

An order or two, issued in a low voice, set in motion the broken line of soldiers encircling the ashes that had been a village. The groups lengthened out, each platoon seemed welded to the next. A black line formed and marched down the long, sunken road that runs from Saint-Crépin to Montfaucon like a wheel in a rut; and when, a few moments later, the moon looked out from between two clouds, and shone for a moment on that line of bayonets gleaming noiselessly, you would have fancied that you were looking upon an immense black serpent with steel scales crawling through the darkness.

II.

A NIGHT march is a melancholy thing for an army. War is a fine thing on a fine day, when the blue sky looks down on the *mêlée*, and crowds of people, standing around the battlefield as on the benches at a circus, applaud the victors; when the quivering tones of the brass instruments make the heart's courageous fibres vibrate, when the smoke from a thousand cannon covers you with its shroud, when friends and enemies are there to see how nobly you meet death: it is sublime. But at night! To have no idea how you will be attacked or how you are to defend yourself; to fall without seeing who strikes you or where the blow comes from; to feel those who are still on their feet stumble over you without knowing who you are, and walk upon you! Ah! then you do not pose as a gladiator; you roll, and twist, and bite the earth, and tear it with your nails: it is horrible!

That is why the army marched in gloom and silence; the soldiers knew that on either side of the road were high hedges, fields filled with furze and broom, and that at the end of the march there was to be a battle, — a night battle.

They marched for about half an hour. From time to time, as I have already said, a moonbeam filtered between two clouds, and revealed the peasant who acted as guide walking at the head of the column, his ear open to the slightest sound, and still watched by the two soldiers beside him. Sometimes they heard a rustling among the leaves at the side of the road. The head of the column would suddenly halt; several voices would shout, "Qui vive ?" There would be no reply, and the peasant would say, with a laugh, —

"It's a hare leaving his form."

Sometimes the two soldiers imagined that they saw something they could not clearly distinguish moving in front of them; they would say to each other, —

"Look!"

And the Vendean would reply, —

"It's your shadow: march on!"

Suddenly, at a turn in the road, they saw the figures of two men start up in front of them. They tried to cry out. One of them fell before he could utter a sound; the other staggered a moment, and had only time to cry, —

"Help!"

Twenty musket shots rang out on the instant; by the light of the explosion they could distinguish three men running away: one of them staggered along the bank beside the road, hoping to reach the other side of the hedge. They ran to him, — he was not the guide; they questioned him, but he did not reply; a soldier ran his bayonet through his arm to see if he was dead, — he was.

Thereupon Marceau became the guide. The study he had made of the localities gave him hope that he would not lose his way. In fact, after a quarter of an hour's march they discovered the dark mass of the forest. There it was that, according to the notice the republicans had received, the inhabitants of several villages, the remnants of several armies, some eighteen hundred men all told, were to assemble to hear mass.

The two generals divided their little force into several columns, with orders to surround the forest and march toward the centre by all the paths leading in that direc-

tion; they calculated that half an hour would be sufficient to enable them to reach their respective positions.
One platoon halted at the road that entered the forest
where they approached it; the others stretched out in
both directions to form a circle. For a moment or two
their measured tread could be heard; it grew fainter and
fainter, then died away altogether, and everything was
silent. The half-hour before a battle passes quickly.
The soldier hardly has time to see if his musket is well
primed, and to say to his neighbor, —

"I have twenty or thirty francs in the corner of my
knapsack; if I die, send them to my mother."

The word "Forward!" rang out, and every one jumped
as if he were not expecting it.

As they advanced, it seemed to them that the cross-
roads which formed the centre of the forest was lighted;
as they drew near they could see the flaming torches;
soon objects became more distinct, and a spectacle that
no one of them had conceived was offered to their
gaze.

Upon an altar, roughly made of stones piled together,
the curé of Sainte-Marie de Rhé was saying mass; old
men stood around the altar, torch in hand, and all about
them knelt women and children praying. Between the
republicans and that group a wall of men was stationed,
and presented the same plan of battle for defence, on a
narrower base, as that adopted for the attack. It would
have been evident enough that they had been warned,
even if the guide who had fled had not been a prominent figure in the front rank; now he was a Vendean
soldier in full uniform, wearing on the left breast the
red cloth heart which was used as a rallying-sign, and
on the hat the white handkerchief which took the place
of a plume.

The Vendeans did not wait to be attacked; they had stationed sharp-shooters in the woods, and began the firing. The republicans marched on, with their muskets ready, but without firing a shot, without replying to the constant fire of their enemies, without speaking, except to say, after each discharge, —

"Close up! close up!"

The priest had not finished his mass, and he kept on; his flock seemed unconscious of what was taking place, and remained on their knees. The republican troops continued to advance. When they were within thirty paces of the enemy, the front rank knelt on one knee; three lines of muskets were lowered like grain bent by the wind. The word to fire was given: they saw the light through the Vendean ranks, and some bullets, passing through, struck down women and children at the foot of the altar. For a moment there was a great outcry and confusion in the assemblage. The priest raised the host, all heads were bowed to the earth, and all was silence once more.

The republicans discharged a second volley at ten paces, as calmly as at a review, with as much precision as if they were firing at a target. The Vendeans replied, and after that neither side had time to reload; it was the bayonet's turn, and here all the advantage lay with the republicans, who were regularly armed. The priest continued to say mass.

The Vendeans fell back; whole ranks fell, with no sound save muttered maledictions. The priest saw what was happening; he made a sign, — the torches were extinguished, and the battle was continued in the darkness. Thereafter it was simply a scene of disorder and carnage, in which every one struck without seeing where he struck, savagely, and died without asking

quarter, which is seldom given when the request is
made and answered in the same tongue.

But the words, "Mercy! mercy!" were uttered in a
heartrending tone at Marceau's knees, as his sword was
raised to strike.

It was a young Vendean, a mere child, unarmed, who
was trying to escape from the horrible *mêlée*. "Mercy!
mercy!" he exclaimed; "in Heaven's name, in the name
of your mother!"

The general led him a few yards away from the battlefield, to remove him from the glances of his soldiers;
but he was soon compelled to stop: the young man had
fainted. Such excessive terror on the part of a soldier
astonished the general; he was none the less zealous in
his efforts to assist him; he opened his coat to give him
air: it was a woman.

There was not an instant to lose; the Convention's
orders were precise. Every Vendean taken under arms,
or present at a meeting, whatever his or her sex or age,
was to perish on the scaffold. He seated the girl at the
foot of a tree and hurried back to the field of battle.
Among the dead he noticed a young republican officer
whose figure seemed to him to be almost the same as
the stranger's; he speedily removed his coat and his
hat, and returned to the Vendean.

The cool night air soon restored her to conscious-
ness.

"Father! father!" were her first words.

Then she rose and pressed her hands against her forehead as if to collect her thoughts.

"Oh! it is terrible! I was with him, and I deserted
him. Father, father! He must be dead!"

"Mademoiselle Blanche, young mistress," said a man
whose head suddenly appeared behind the tree, "the

Marquis de Beaulieu lives; he is saved. *Vive le roi* and the good cause!"

The man who said these words disappeared like a ghost, but not so quickly that Marceau had not time to recognize the peasant of Saint-Crépin.

"Tinguy, Tinguy!" cried the girl, putting out her arms to the farmer.

"Silence!" said the general; "a single word will betray you. I could not save you then, and I wish to save you. Put on this hat and coat and wait here."

He returned to the battlefield, gave orders for the troops to fall back upon Cholet, left his colleague in command, and returned to the young Vendean.

He found her ready to go with him. They walked together toward a sort of high-road, where Marceau's servant was waiting with horses, which could not go into the heart of the country where the roads are naught but ravines and bogs. There his embarrassment redoubled. He feared that his young companion would not know how to ride, and had not the strength to walk; but she soon reassured him by the way in which she managed her mount, with less strength, to be sure, but with as much grace and address as the best horseman.[1]

She saw Marceau's surprise and smiled.

"You will be less astonished," said she, "when you know me. You will see by what chain of circumstances

[1] Even if what follows should not explain this skill, which is rare among us in a woman, the custom of the province would justify it. Even the ladies of the *châteaux* ride, literally speaking, like a Longchamps dandy; but they wear under their dresses, which the saddle raises, trousers like those worn by children. The women of the lower classes do not take even that precaution, although the color of their skin led me for a long time to think the contrary. — (*Author's note*)

manly exercises have become familiar to me; you seem so kind that I will tell you the whole story of my life, which has been so full of trouble, young as I am."

"Yes, yes, but later," said Marceau; "we shall have time enough, for you are my prisoner, and for your own sake I do not propose to restore your liberty. What we have to do now is to get to Cholet as fast as we can. So sit firmly in your saddle, and put your horse to the gallop, my cavalier!"

"Gallop it is!" rejoined the Vendean.

Three quarters of an hour later they arrived at Cholet. The commanding general was at the mayor's office. Marceau went up, leaving his servant and his prisoner at the door. He made a report of his expedition in a few words, and went with his little party to seek quarters at the Hôtel des Sans-Culottes, a name which had replaced on the sign the words, "Au Grand Saint Nicolas."

Marceau took two rooms. He escorted the young woman to one of them, urged her to lie down without undressing and snatch a few moments' rest, which she must sadly need after the horrible night she had passed, and then shut himself into his own room; for now he had the responsibility of another life on his hands, and he must needs think of the means of preserving it.

Blanche, too, had food for thought in plenty: in the first place her father, and secondly this young republican with the sweet face and voice. It all seemed like a dream to her. She walked about her room to make sure that she was really awake, pausing in front of a mirror to convince herself that it was really she. Then she wept as she thought of her desolate position. The idea of death — of death on the scaffold — did not occur to her; Marceau had said, in his gentle voice, —

"I will save you."

And, after all, why should she, born only yesterday, be put to death? Lovely, inoffensive creature that she was, why should men demand her head and her blood? She could hardly believe that she was in any danger. Her father, on the contrary, a Vendean leader, killed others, and might be killed; but she, a poor girl, whose hand had but just quitted the grasp of childhood! Ah! far from being disturbed by evil omens, life seemed joyous and fair to her, the future boundless; the war would come to an end, the empty château would be filled with guests once more. Some day a young man, worn by fatigue, would seek hospitality there; he would be twenty-four or twenty-five years old, have a sweet voice, fair hair, and a general's uniform, and he would remain there a long while.— Dream on, dream on, poor Blanche!

There is a period of youth when misfortune seems so incongruous with life that it seems that it can never gain a footing there; however melancholy a thought may be, it ends with a smile. It is because we see life from only one side of the horizon; the past has not yet had time to make us doubt the future.

Marceau also was dreaming; but he already knew something of life. He was familiar with the political antipathies of the moment; he knew the exigencies of a revolution; he was trying to devise a means of saving Blanche, who was sleeping. A single expedient suggested itself to him: that was to escort her himself to Nantes, where his family lived. He had not seen his mother or sister in three years, and being within a few leagues of the town, it seemed quite natural that he should apply to the commanding general for leave of absence. He resolved to act upon that idea. The day

was just breaking; he repaired to General Westermann's
quarters, and his request was granted without hesitation.
He asked that the necessary papers be given him at
once, thinking that Blanche could not start too soon; it
was essential that the furlough should bear a second
signature, that of the representative of the people, —
Delmar. He had arrived only a half-hour before with
despatches; he was taking a few moments' sleep in the
adjoining room, and the general promised to send
Marceau the document as soon as he awoke.

On entering the inn, he met General Dumas, for
whom he was looking. The two friends had no secrets
from each other; the elder was soon made acquainted
with the whole adventure. While breakfast was being
prepared, Marceau went up to his prisoner's room, learning that she had already asked for him; he announced a
visit from his colleague, who was not slow to present
himself. His first words reassured Blanche, and, after
a moment's conversation, she felt nothing more than the
inevitable embarrassment of a young girl with two men
whom she hardly knows.

They were about to take their seats at the table, when
the door opened. Delmar, the representative of the
people, appeared on the threshold.

We had no time, at the beginning of the narrative, to
say a word concerning this new personage.

He was one of those men whom Robespierre used
like an arm at the end of his own to enable him to
reach into the provinces; who believed that they understood his system of regeneration because he said to them,
"We must regenerate;" and in whose hands the guillotine was more active than intelligent.

The sinister apparition made Blanche tremble, even
before she knew who he was.

"Aha!" said he to Marceau, "so you want to leave us already, citizen-general? But you behaved so well last night that I can refuse you nothing. I am a little inclined to find fault with you, however, for having allowed the Marquis de Beaulieu to escape; I had promised the Convention to send them his head."

Blanche was standing, pale and cold as a statue of Terror. Marceau unconcernedly stood in front of her.

"But a thing postponed is not abandoned," continued Delmar. · "The republican greyhounds have a good nose and good teeth, and we are on his trail. Here is your furlough," he added. "It is all right, and you can start when you choose. But I have come to ask you to invite me to breakfast first; I could not bear to part with such a gallant fellow as you are without drinking to the health of the Republic and the extermination of the brigands."

In the position then occupied by the two generals this mark of esteem was anything but agreeable to them. Blanche had taken her seat and recovered her courage in some degree. They took their places, and the young girl, in order not to sit opposite Delmar, was obliged to sit beside him. She sat far enough away from him not to touch him, and gradually became more at ease as she noticed that the representative of the people paid more attention to the meal than to those who partook of it with him. From time to time, however, a sanguinary word or two fell from his lips, and sent a shudder through the girl's veins. But, after all, there seemed to be no real danger for her; the generals hoped that he would leave them without addressing her a word directly. The desire to start afforded Marceau a pretext for hurrying through the meal. It was drawing to a close, and they were all beginning to breathe more at ease, when

a discharge of musketry was heard on the public square
in front of the inn; the generals jumped for their
weapons, which they had laid aside. Delmar stopped
them.

"Good, my brave fellows!" he said, laughing, and
balancing himself on the legs of his chair, — "good!
I like to see that you are on your guard; but come back
to the table, — there's nothing for you to do out there."

"What is the noise?" Marceau asked.

"Nothing," said Delmar; "last night's prisoners
being shot."

Blanche uttered a cry of horror.

"Oh, the wretches!" she cried.

Delmar put down his glass, which he was about to
put to his lips, and slowly turned toward her.

"Ah! this is a fine state of things," he said; "if
soldiers tremble like women, we must make the women
soldiers. To be sure, you're very young," he added,
taking both her hands and looking her in the face; "but
you will get used to it."

"Oh, never! never!" cried Blanche, without reflecting how dangerous it was for her to manifest her feelings before such a witness. "I shall never get used to
such horrors."

"My child," rejoined Delmar, releasing her hands,
"do you think that a nation can be regenerated without
some blood-letting, that factions can be put down without erecting scaffolds? Did you ever see a revolution
pass the level of equality over a people without taking
off some heads? Woe to the great at such times, for
the staff of Tarquin has marked them out!"

He paused for a moment, then continued, —

"After all, what is death? A dreamless sleep, without an awakening. What is blood? A red liquor

almost like that contained in this bottle, which produces no effect on our minds except because of the idea we attach to it. Sombreuil drank it. Well, have you nothing to say? Come, haven't you any philanthropic argument at your tongue's end? A Girondin in your place wouldn't lack an abundance of them."

Blanche was compelled, therefore, to continue the conversation.

"Oh," she said, trembling, "are you quite sure that God has given you the right to strike thus?"

"Does not God himself strike?"

"Yes, but He looks beyond life, while man, when he kills, knows neither what he gives nor what he takes away."

"Very good. The soul is immortal or it is not; if the body is only dust, is it a crime to restore to dust a little sooner what God borrowed of it? If a soul inhabits it, and that soul is immortal, I cannot kill it; the body is only a garment which I remove from it, or, rather, a prison from which I set it free. Now, listen to my advice, for I propose to give you some advice: keep your philosophical reflections and your schoolboy arguments to defend your own life, if ever you fall into Charette's hands or Bernard de Marigny's, for they would show you no more mercy than I have shown their men. As for myself, you might possibly have reason to repent repeating them in my presence: remember."

He went out.

There was a moment's silence. Marceau laid aside his pistols, which he had cocked during this conversation.

"By my soul!" he said, pointing after him with his finger, "never was man so near death without suspecting it as you were just now! — Do you know, Blanche,

20

that if a word or a gesture had escaped him, indicating that he recognized you, I would have blown out his brains?"

She was not listening. A single thought had possession of her mind: that that man was under instructions to pursue the remnant of the army commanded by the Marquis de Beaulieu.

"O my God!" she said, hiding her face in her hands. "O my God! when I think that my father may fall into that tiger's hands; that, if he had been taken prisoner last night, it is possible that he might now be — It is execrable, it is atrocious! is there no longer any pity in the world?—Oh, forgive me, forgive me!" she said to Marceau. "Who has more reason than I to know the contrary? My God! my God!"

At that moment the servant entered, and announced that the horses were ready.

"Let us go, in Heaven's name! there is blood in the air we breathe here."

"Let us go," echoed Marceau.

And all three went down the stairs together.

III.

MARCEAU found at the door a detachment of thirty horse, whom the commanding general had ordered under arms to escort him to Nantes. Dumas accompanied them for some distance; but about a league from Cholet his friend insisted that he should return; if he should go farther it would be dangerous for him to return alone. So he took leave of them and galloped back, soon passing out of sight at a turn in the road.

Then, too, Marceau wished to be left alone with the young Vendean. She had the story of her life to tell him, and it seemed to him that the story must be a deeply interesting one. He therefore rode up beside Blanche.

"Well," he said, "now that we are left to ourselves, and have a long ride before us, let us talk. Let us talk of you. I know who you are, but that is all. How came you to be at that meeting? How did you acquire the habit of wearing man's clothes? Speak! we soldiers are accustomed to hear only sharp, stern words. Talk to me a long while of yourself, of your childhood, I beg you."

Marceau, without knowing why, could not accustom himself to use the republican form of speech of the time in addressing Blanche.

Thereupon Blanche told him of her life: how her mother had died young, and left her, a mere child, to the care of the Marquis de Beaulieu; how her education, guided by a man, had made her familiar with

exercises which, when the insurrection broke out in La
Vendée, had proved so useful to her, and had enabled
her to accompany her father. She described all the
events of the war, from the *émeute* at Saint-Florent
down to the combat in which Marceau had saved her
life. She talked a long while, as he had asked her, for
she saw that it gave him pleasure to listen. Just as
she finished her narrative, Nantes appeared on the
horizon, its lights trembling in the haze. The little
party crossed the Loire, and a few moments later Marceau
was in his mother's arms.

After the first greetings he presented to his family his
young travelling companion; a few words sufficed to
arouse the lively interest of his mother and sisters.
Blanche had no sooner expressed a wish to resume the
garments of her sex than the two girls led her away,
and disputed with each other the pleasure of acting as
her lady's maid.

This conduct, simple as it may appear at first sight,
acquired a great value by reason of the existing circumstances. Nantes was writhing under the proconsulate
of Carrier.

It was a strange spectacle for the mind as well as for
the eyes, — the spectacle of a whole city bleeding from
the bites of a single man. We wonder what can be the
source of the power that one will exerts over eighty
thousand individuals whom it dominates, and how it is
that, when a single man says: "I wish it!" all the
others do not rise and say: "Very good! but we do not
wish it!" The fact is that servility becomes a fixed
habit in the mind of the masses, and that only individuals sometimes have a burning desire to be free. As
Shakespeare says, the people know no other way of
rewarding Cæsar's assassin than by making him Cæsar.

That is why there are tyrants of liberty as there are tyrants of monarchy.

And so blood was flowing in the streets of Nantes, and Carrier, who was to Robespierre what the hyena is to the tiger and the jackal to the lion, gorged himself with the purest of that blood, pending the time when he should give it back, mingled with his own.

There were new methods of massacre. The guillotine became notched and blunted so quickly! He conceived the idea of the *noyades*, whose name has become inseparable from his; boats were built for the purpose in the harbor, — people knew for what purpose and went to look at them on the ways. It was a novel and interesting thing to see the airholes twenty feet long, which opened so as to drop into the sea the wretched creatures set apart for that form of punishment; and, on the fatal day, when they were tried, there were almost as many people on the bank as when a vessel is launched with a wreath about its mainmast, and flags on every yard.

Oh! woe thrice over to the men who, like Carrier, have exerted their imaginations in inventing variations upon death; for every method of destroying man comes easily to man! Woe to those who, acting upon no theory, have committed useless murders! They are the ones who cause our mothers to tremble at the words *revolution* and *republic*, inseparable in their minds from *massacre* and *destruction;* and our mothers make us men, and who among us, as he went forth from his mother's hands at fifteen, did not shudder, too, at the words *revolution* and *republic?* which of us has not had to make over his whole political education before he dared look coolly upon that date which he had long looked upon as fatal, — 93? which of us has not re-

quired to put forth all his strength as a man of twenty-
five to look in the face the three colossi of the Revolution, — Mirabeau, Danton, Robespierre ? But at last
we have become accustomed to the sight of them; we
have studied the ground on which they walked, the
principles on which they acted, and involuntarily we
have recalled these awful words of another time: *Each
of them fell because he sought to put a drag on the
executioner's tumbril, which still had work to do.* They
did not outstrip the Revolution; the Revolution out-
stripped them.

Let us not complain, however; rehabilitation is
quickly accomplished in these days, for now the people
write the history of the people. It was not so in the
time of Messieurs the historiographers of the crown;
did I not hear it said when I was a child, that Louis XI.
was a bad king, and Louis XIV. a great prince ?

Let us return to Marceau and a family whom his
name protected even against Carrier. The young general's reputation for republicanism was so pure that
suspicion had not dared attack his mother and sisters.
That is why one of them, a girl of sixteen, as if she
were entirely ignorant of what was taking place about
her, loved and was loved, and Marceau's mother, timid
as a mother, seeing in a husband an additional protector,
hurried on as much as she could a marriage which was
on the point of being celebrated when Marceau and the
young Vendean arrived at Nantes. The general's return
at such a moment was a twofold joy.

Blanche was turned over to the two girls, who became
her friends as they kissed her; for there is an age when
every girl imagines that she has found a friend forever
in the friend she has known but an hour. They left
the room together; a matter almost as important as the

marriage itself filled their minds: the furnishing one of
their number with clothes, for Blanche did not choose
to continue to wear her masculine garments.

Soon they brought her back, arrayed in the clothes of
both; she had had to put on a dress belonging to one,
and the other's shawl. Foolish girls! to be sure, their
combined ages did not equal that of Marceau's mother,
who was still beautiful.

When Blanche returned, the young general stepped
toward her, and halted in amazement. In the costume
she had worn before, he had hardly noticed her celestial
beauty and her charms, which she had resumed with
her woman's garb. She had done her utmost, it is
true, to appear pretty: for a moment, before her mirror,
she had forgotten war, Vendée, and carnage. The most
artless soul has a coquetry of her own when she begins
to love and seeks to please the person she loves.

Marceau tried to speak, but could not utter a word.
Blanche smiled, and held out her hand, overjoyed, for
she saw that she appeared to him as beautiful as she
wished to appear.

That evening the young fiancé of Marceau's sister
came to the house, and as all love is selfish, from self-
love to maternal love, there was one house in the city
of Nantes where all was happiness and joy, when round
about it all was tears and sorrow.

Ah! how Blanche and Marceau abandoned themselves
to the delight of their new life! how far behind them
the other life seemed! It was almost a dream. But
from time to time Blanche's heart grew heavy and tears
gushed from her eyes; it was when the thought of her
father came suddenly to her mind. Marceau consoled
her; then, to divert her thoughts, told her of his first
campaigns; how the schoolboy had become a soldier at

fifteen, an officer at seventeen, colonel at nineteen, general at twenty-one. Blanche made him repeat the story often; for in all that he said there was no word of another love.

And yet Marceau had loved, — loved with all the strength of his heart, at least so he thought. Then he had been deceived, betrayed; contempt had with great difficulty found a resting-place in a heart so young that it contained nothing but passions. The blood that boiled in his veins had slowly cooled, — a melancholy coldness had taken the place of exaltation; in fact, Marceau, before he knew Blanche, was nothing more than a sick man, deprived, by the sudden cessation of fever, of the strength and energy which he owed to its presence alone.

And now all the dreams of happiness, all the elements of a new life, all the joyous impulses of youth, which Marceau thought had vanished forever so far as he was concerned, appeared again, still undefined in the distance, but where he might hope to reach them some day. He himself was astonished to find that a smile came sometimes to his lips without apparent cause; he breathed with the full force of his lungs, and no longer felt the tedium of living, which, only the day before, sapped his strength and made him long for speedy death as the only barrier that grief cannot pass.

Blanche, for her part, being drawn toward Marceau at first by a natural feeling of gratitude, attributed to that feeling the varying emotions that agitated her. Was it not a simple thing that she should desire the constant presence of the man who had saved her life? The words that fell from her preserver's lips could hardly be indifferent to her? Could his face, stamped with such profound melancholy, fail to awaken her compas-

sion? And when she saw him sigh as he gazed at her,
was she not always ready to say to him: "What can I
do for you, my friend, who have done so much for
me?"

Under the sway of these varying sentiments, which
gained fresh strength every day, Blanche and Marceau
passed the first part of their stay at Nantes; at last the
time for the marriage of the young general's sister
arrived.

From among the jewels he had ordered for her,
Marceau selected a beautiful and valuable set, which
he offered to Blanche. She gazed at it, at first, with
girlish coquetry, but soon she closed the case.

"Are jewels in harmony with my situation?" she
said sadly. "Jewels for me! while my father is flying,
perhaps, from farm to farm, begging for a crust of bread
to keep him alive, and for leave to seek shelter in a
barn; while I, myself proscribed — No; let my simple
dress screen me from observation; remember that I may
be recognized."

Marceau urged her in vain; she would consent to
accept nothing but an artificial red rose, which she saw
among the ornaments.

The churches were closed, so that the marriage ceremony was performed at the Hôtel de Ville. It was short
and melancholy; the young girls regretted the choir
decorated with candles and flowers, the canopy held
over the heads of the young couple, beneath which the
laughter of those who hold it is mingled with the benediction of the priest, who says: "Go hence, my children,
and be happy!"

At the door of the Hôtel de Ville a deputation of
watermen awaited the bride and groom. Marceau's
rank was responsible for that mark of respect to his

sister; one of the men, whose face seemed familiar to
the general, held two bouquets: he gave one to the
bride, then walked up to Blanche, who gazed fixedly
at him, and presented her with the other.

"Tinguy, where is my father?" she asked, turning
pale.

"At Saint-Florent," replied the waterman. "Take
this bouquet; there's a letter among the flowers. *Vive
le roi* and the good cause, Mademoiselle Blanche!"

Blanche tried to stop him, to speak to him, to question him; he had disappeared. Marceau recognized the
guide, and, in spite of himself, admired the peasant's
devotion, adroitness and audacity.

Blanche read the letter with an anxious heart. The
Vendeans were meeting with defeat after defeat; a whole
population was leaving the country, recoiling before fire
and famine. The rest of the letter was devoted to acknowledgments to Marceau. The marquis had learned
everything through Tinguy's watchfulness. Blanche
was depressed; the letter cast her back into the midst
of the horrors of war; she leaned on Marceau's arm
more heavily than usual, she spoke to him more inti-
mately and in a softer voice. Marceau would have
liked her to be even more depressed; for the deeper the
melancholy, the more completely reserve is cast aside;
and, as I have already said, there is much selfishness in
love.

During the ceremony, a stranger, who had, he said,
intelligence of the utmost importance to communicate to
Marceau, was ushered into the salon. Marceau, leaning toward Blanche, who had his arm, did not notice
him when he entered; but suddenly he felt her arm
tremble, and raised his head: they were face to face
with Delmar.

The representative of the people approached slowly, with his eyes fixed on Blanche and a smile playing about his lips; Marceau, his brow bathed in sweat, watched him come forward as Don Juan watches the statue of the Commander.

" Have you a brother, citizeness ? "

Blanche stammered something, and was on the point of throwing herself into Marceau's arms.   Delmar continued : —

" If my memory and your resemblance to him do not lead me astray, we breakfasted together at Cholet.   How does it happen that I have not seen him in the ranks of the republican army since that time ? "

Blanche felt that her strength was deserting her. Delmar's piercing eye watched the progress of her confusion, and she was about to quail beneath it, when it turned from her and fastened upon Marceau.

Then it was Delmar's turn to tremble.   The young general had his hand on the hilt of his sword, which he grasped convulsively.   The face of the representative of the people soon resumed its habitual expression.   He seemed to have entirely forgotten what he had come to say, and, taking Marceau by the arm, he led him into a window recess, talked with him for some minutes concerning the situation of affairs in La Vendée, and informed him that he had come to Nantes to agree with Carrier as to the new and stricter measures to be adopted with regard to the insurgents.   He told him that General Dumas had been recalled to Paris; and, taking leave of him before long, he passed with a bow and a smile the chair upon which Blanche had fallen when she released Marceau's arm, and on which she had remained, pale and cold.

Two hours later Marceau received orders to start

instantly to rejoin the army of the West and resume command of his brigade.

This sudden and unexpected order astonished him; he fancied that he could detect some connection between it and the scene that had taken place just before. His furlough did not expire for a fortnight. He hurried to Delmar's lodgings to obtain some explanation from him; Delmar had left Nantes immediately after his interview with Carrier.

It was necessary to obey; to hesitate was to court destruction. At that period the generals were subject to the authority of the representatives of the people sent by the Convention, and, if some reverses were caused by their bungling, more than one victory was due to the alternative constantly presented to the leaders, of winning battles or losing their heads on the scaffold.

Marceau was with Blanche when he received the order. Dazed by a blow so entirely unexpected, he had not the courage to inform her of his departure, which would leave her alone and defenceless in the midst of a city whose streets were watered every day by the blood of her compatriots. She noticed his embarrassment, and, as her anxiety conquered her bashfulness, she drew near him with the unquiet glance of a woman who knows that she is beloved and has the right to ask questions. Marceau handed her the order he had received. Blanche had no sooner cast her eyes upon it than she realized the peril to which her protector would be exposed by failure to obey; her heart sank within her, and yet she summoned courage to urge him to go without delay. Women have more of that sort of courage than men, because, in their case, it is connected with modesty.

Marceau gazed sadly at her.

"And do you bid me go, Blanche, — you? Indeed," he said, rising, and as if speaking to himself, "what reason have I to expect anything else? Madman that I was! When I have thought of going away, it has occurred to me, sometimes, that it might cost her some regret and a few tears."

He strode up and down the room.

"Madman! regret! tears! As if I were not perfectly indifferent to her!"

As he turned he found himself face to face with Blanche. Two tears were rolling down the girl's cheeks; she did not speak, but her breast rose and fell with her spasmodic sobs. Marceau felt the tears in his eyes, too.

"Oh! forgive me," he said; "forgive me, Blanche, but I am very unhappy, and unhappiness makes me suspicious. Living thus, beside you, my life seemed to be mingled with yours; how separate your hours from my hours, my days from your days? I had forgotten everything; I believed that this would last forever. Oh! misery! misery! I have been dreaming, and now I am awake. Blanche," he added, more calmly, but in a more melancholy tone, "the war we are engaged in is a cruel and murderous one; it is possible that we may not meet again."

He took Blanche's hand; she was sobbing.

"Promise me that if I fall far away from you — I have always had a presentiment, Blanche, that my life would be a short one — promise me that you will think of me sometimes; that my name will sometimes come to your lips, even if it be only in a dream; and I, Blanche, promise you that, if there is time between life and death for me to pronounce a name, a single one, it shall be yours."

Blanche was choked by her tears; but there were in her eyes a thousand promises more tender than those Marceau demanded. With one hand she pressed Marceau's, who was at her feet, and with the other pointed to the red rose, which she wore in her hair.

"Forever! forever!" she faltered.

And she fell in a swoon.

Marceau's cries summoned his mother and sisters. He thought that Blanche was dead; he was writhing on the floor at her feet. In love everything is exaggerated, — hopes and fears. The soldier was only a child.

Blanche opened her eyes, and blushed when she saw Marceau at her feet and his family around him.

"He is going away," she said; "perhaps to fight against my father. Oh! spare my father if he should fall into your hands; remember that his death would kill me. What more can you ask?" she added, lowering her eyes. "I did not think of my father until after I thought of you."

Thereupon, summoning all her courage, she begged Marceau to go. He himself realized the necessity of doing so, and no longer resisted her entreaties and his mother's. The necessary orders were given, and, an hour later, he had said farewell to Blanche and his family.

Marceau left Nantes by the same road he and Blanche had ridden over together; he allowed his horse to take his own gait, for at every step he was reminded of some passage in the young Vendean's narrative. He reviewed, so to speak, the story she had told him; and the danger to which she was exposed, of which he had not thought while he was with her, seemed to him much greater now that he had left her. Every word Delmar had spoken rang in his ears; every moment he was on the point of stopping his horse and returning to Nantes; and it required all his good sense to prevent his yielding to his craving to see her again.

If Marceau had been able to think of aught beside the subject that filled his whole mind, he would have noticed a horseman, in the distance, coming toward him, who, after drawing rein a moment to make sure that he was not mistaken, urged his horse to a gallop to join him; and he would have recognized General Dumas as promptly as he himself was recognized by him.

The friends leaped from their horses and threw themselves into each other's arms.

At the same instant a man, with perspiration dripping from his hair, his face and clothes scratched and torn, leaped over a hedge, rolled, rather than ran, down the bank, and fell, exhausted, almost voiceless, at the feet of the two friends, uttering the one word: —

"Arrested!"

It was Tinguy.

"Arrested? who? Blanche?" cried Marceau.

The peasant made an affirmative gesture; the poor fellow could not speak. He had made five leagues, running across fields and hedges, through furze and broom; he might perhaps have run one league, two leagues more, to overtake Marceau; but, having overtaken him, he collapsed.

Marceau gazed at him with open mouth and staring eyes.

"Arrested! Blanche arrested!" he kept repeating, while his friend put his flask of wine to the peasant's clinched teeth. "Blanche arrested! That was why they sent me away. Alexandre," he cried, taking his friend's hand, and forcing him to rise, — "Alexandre, I

am going back to Nantes; you must go with me, for my
life, my future, my happiness, all are there."

His teeth chattered violently; his whole body was
shaken by a convulsive trembling.

" Let the man tremble who has dared to lay his hand
on Blanche! Do you know that I love her with all the
strength of my soul; that life is not possible for me
without her, that I must save her or die? Oh! fool,
madman that I was to leave her! — Blanche arrested!
where has she been taken?"

Tinguy, to whom that question was put, was beginning to come to himself. The veins in his forehead
swelled as if they were about to burst; his eyes were
injected with blood; and his chest was so oppressed, his
breathing so labored, that he could hardly reply when
the question was put to him a second time.

" To the Bouffays prison."

The words were no sooner out of his mouth than the
two friends started back toward Nantes at a gallop.

IV.

THERE was not a moment to lose; therefore the friends rode straight to the house occupied by Carrier on Place du Cours. When they arrived, Marceau leaped from his horse, mechanically took his pistols, which were in the holsters, concealed them beneath his coat, and rushed to the apartments of the man who held Blanche's destiny in his hands. His friend followed him more calmly, although fully prepared to defend him if he needed his assistance, and to risk his life as recklessly as upon the battlefield. But the deputy of the Mountain knew too well how universally abhorred he was not to be suspicious, and neither entreaties nor threats could procure the two generals an interview.

Marceau returned to the street more tranquilly than his friend expected. In the last moment or two he seemed to have adopted a new plan, which he matured in haste, and there was no further doubt as to his purpose when he begged General Dumas to go at once to the post house and wait for him at the Bouffays gate with a carriage and post horses.

Marceau's name and rank opened the prison doors to him; he ordered the jailer to show him to the cell in which Blanche was confined. The jailer hesitated a moment. Marceau repeated the command in a more imperative tone, and the man obeyed, motioning to him to follow.

" She is not alone," said his guide, opening the low arched door of a dungeon so dark that it made Marceau

21

shudder; "but she 'll soon be rid of her companion, for
he 's to be guillotined to-day."

With those words he closed the door on Marceau,
urging him to abridge as much as possible an interview
which might compromise him.

Still dazzled by the sudden transition from light to
darkness, Marceau put out his arms like a man walking
in his sleep, trying to pronounce the word "Blanche,"
which his mouth refused to form, and unable to pierce
with his eyes the shadows that surrounded him. He
heard a stifled cry. The girl threw herself into his
arms; she had recognized him at once, for her eyes were
already accustomed to the darkness.

She threw herself into his arms, for there was a
moment when terror caused her to forget her age and
sex; she thought of nothing but the question of life or
death. She clung to him as a shipwrecked sailor clings
to a rock, with inarticulate sobs and a convulsive pressure of her arms.

"Ah! ah! you have not abandoned me!" she cried
at last. "They arrested me, dragged me here; I saw
Tinguy in the crowd that followed me; I cried: ' Marceau! Marceau!' and he disappeared. Oh! I was far
from hoping to see you again — even here. But you
have come — you have come — you won't leave me.
You will take me away; you won't leave me here!"

"I would willingly, at the price of all my blood, take
you away instantly; but — "

"Oh, pray look about you; feel of these dripping
walls, this filthy straw! You are a general, can you
not — "

"This is what I can do, Blanche: knock at yonder
door, blow out the brains of the turnkey who opens it,
take you out into the courtyard, let you breathe the

fresh air and see the sky once more, and die in your defence; but when I am dead, Blanche, they will bring you back to this dungeon, and there will not be a single man left on earth who can save you."

" But can you save me ? "

" Perhaps."

" Soon ? "

" In two days, Blanche; I ask you for two days. But you must first answer a question on which your life and mine depend. Answer as you would answer God. Blanche, do you love me ? "

" Is this the time and place when such a question should be asked, or when one can answer it ? Do you think that these walls are used to hearing declarations of love ? "

" Yes, this is the proper time; for we are between life and the grave, between existence and eternity. Blanche, answer me quickly. Every moment robs us of a day, every hour of a year. Do you love me, Blanche ? "

" Oh ! yes, yes — "

The words escaped from the young girl's heart, and, forgetting that no one could see her blushes, she hid her face on Marceau's arm.

" Very well, Blanche, you must accept me on the spot as your husband."

The girl quivered from head to foot.

" What can be your purpose ? "

" My purpose is to snatch you from the jaws of death; we will see if they dare send the wife of a republican general to the scaffold."

Blanche understood his whole thought; she shuddered at the danger to which he would expose himself to save her. Her love gathered new strength; but, summoning all her courage, she said firmly, —

" It is impossible."

" Impossible?" echoed Marceau, " impossible? Why, this is madness! What obstacle can there be between us and happiness, since you have just confessed that you love me? Do you think this is all child's play? Listen to me; listen, in God's name: this means death to you! Do you hear? death on the scaffold, the headsman, the tumbril, the knife!"

" Oh! pity, pity! it is terrible! But think of yourself. When I am once your wife, if that title does not save me, it destroys you with me!"

" So that is your reason for rejecting the only means of safety that is left open to you! Ah! well, listen to me, Blanche, for I have a confession to make to you. When I first saw you, I loved you; my love has become a passion; I live upon it as a part of my life. My life is yours ; my fate will be the same as yours; happiness or the scaffold, I will share everything with you; I will not leave you ; no human power can part us; or, if I do leave you, I have only to shout *Vive le roi!* Those words will throw your dungeon open to me again, and we will never leave it except together. Oh! well, let it be so: a night in the same dungeon, a ride in the same tumbril, death on the same scaffold, that will be something."

" Oh! no, no! go! leave me, in Heaven's name, leave me!"

" You bid me go! Beware what you say and what you mean; for, if I go from here without having you for my own, without your giving me the right to defend you, I will go to your father — your father, whom you have forgotten, who is weeping for you — and I will say to him: ' Old man, your daughter might have been saved, but she did not choose; she preferred that your last days should be passed in mourning, and that her blood should be spattered on your gray hairs. Weep, old man, weep, — not because your daughter is dead, but because she did not love you enough to live.' "

Marceau pushed Blanche away; she fell on her knees a few steps from him, and he walked back and forth, with clinched teeth, his arms folded across his breast, and the laughter of a madman, or one of the damned. He heard Blanche's sobs, tears gushed from his eyes, his arms fell nervelessly at his sides, and he grovelled at her feet.

"Oh! in pity's name, by all that you hold most sacred in this world, by your mother's grave, Blanche, Blanche, consent to become my wife. You must; it is your duty."

"Yes, it is your duty, young maiden," said a strange voice, which made them both start and rise from the floor; "it is your duty, for it is the only way of preserving a life that is hardly beginning; religion commands you to do it, and I am ready to bless your union."

Marceau turned in amazement, and recognized the curé of Sainte-Marie-de-Rhé, who was present at the assemblage he had attacked on the night Blanche became his prisoner.

"O father!" he cried, seizing his hand, and pulling him toward Blanche, "obtain her consent to live."

"Blanche de Beaulieu," said the priest, in a solemn tone, "in the name of your father, whom my years and the friendship between us entitle me to represent, I adjure you to yield to the entreaties of this young man, for your father himself, if he were here, would do as I do."

Blanche seemed to be torn by a thousand conflicting

sentiments; but at last she threw herself into Marceau's arms.

"O my love," she said, "I have not the strength to resist you longer. I love you, Marceau! I love you, and I am your wife."

Their lips met; Marceau's joy was beyond bounds; he seemed to have forgotten everything. The priest's voice soon roused him from his trance.

"Make haste, my children," he said; "for my moments here on earth are numbered; and if you delay I can only give you my blessing from on high."

The lovers shuddered. That voice called them back to earth! Blanche looked about her with fearful eyes.

"O my love," she said, "what a moment to unite our destinies! what a temple for a marriage! Do you think that a union consecrated beneath these gloomy, depressing arches can be a happy and lasting one?"

Marceau started; for he himself was assailed by superstitious terror. He led Blanche toward a part of the dungeon where the light, creeping between the crossed bars of a narrow air-hole, made the darkness less dense; there they both fell on their knees, awaiting the priest's blessing.

He put forth his hand, and pronounced the sacred words. At the same moment there was the clashing of weapons and the measured tread of soldiers in the corridor; Blanche, in deadly terror, threw herself into Marceau's arms.

"Can it be that they have come for me already?" she cried. "O my love, my love, how horrible death would be at this moment!"

The young general had jumped in front of the door, a pistol in either hand. The soldiers fell back in amazement.

"Be not alarmed," said the priest, coming forward. "I am the one for whom they have come; I am the one who is to die."

The soldiers surrounded him.

"My children," he exclaimed, in a firm voice, addressing the newly-made husband and wife, — "to your knees, my children; with one foot in the grave I give you my last blessing, and a dying man's blessing is sacred."

The soldiers stood in awed silence; the priest took from his breast a crucifix, which he had succeeded in concealing from all eyes; he stretched it out toward them; being prepared for death himself, he prayed for them. There was a moment of solemn silence, during which everybody believed in God.

"Forward!" said the priest.

The soldiers surrounded him; the door closed, and the party disappeared like a nocturnal vision.

Blanche threw herself into Marceau's arms.

"Oh! if you leave me, and they come for me in that way, if I have not you to help me pass through that door, oh! Marceau! think of it, — the scaffold! I on the scaffold, far from you, weeping and calling you, and having no reply! Oh! do not go away, do not go away! I will throw myself at their feet, I will tell them I am not guilty, and if they will leave me in prison with you all my life I will bless them. But if you leave me — Oh! do not leave me!"

"Blanche, I am sure of saving you; I will answer for your life. In less than two days I will be here with your pardon, and then it will not be a lifetime in a dungeon, but a lifetime of fresh air and happiness, of liberty and love!"

The door opened, and the jailer appeared. Blanche

held Marceau more tightly in her arms; she would not
let him go, and yet every moment was precious. He
gently unclasped her hands, whose grasp detained him,
and promised her that he would return before the close
of the second day.

"Love me always," he said, rushing from the cell.

"Always!" said Blanche, staggering back and pointing to the red rose he had given her, which she wore in
her hair; and the door closed upon her like the door of
hell.

V.

MARCEAU found General Dumas waiting in the jailer's house; he called for pen and ink and paper.

"What are you going to do?" his friend asked, alarmed by his excitement.

"Write to Carrier, ask him for two days' respite, and tell him that he will answer to me for Blanche's life with his own."

"Madman!" rejoined his friend, snatching away the letter he had begun. "You threaten, and you are in his power; have you not disobeyed the order you received to rejoin the army? Do you think that, when he is already afraid of you, his fears would pause even to find a plausible pretext? Within an hour you would be arrested; and then, what could you do, either for her or for yourself. Take my advice, and by your silence give him a chance to forget, for nothing but his forgetting can save her."

Marceau's head had fallen between his hands; he seemed to be reflecting deeply.

"You are right," he suddenly cried, springing to his feet. And he drew his friend into the street.

A few people were assembled about a post-chaise.

"If it should be foggy to-night," said a voice, "I don't know what should prevent a score of good fellows from coming into the town and carrying off the prisoners. It 's shameful how poorly Nantes is guarded."

Marceau started, turned, recognized Tinguy, exchanged a meaning glance with him, and leaped into the vehicle.

"To Paris!" he said to the postilion, giving him money.

The horses set off with the swiftness of lightning.
Everywhere there was the same diligence; everywhere,
by the lavish use of money, Marceau obtained a promise
that horses should be ready for him on the following
day, and that no obstacle should delay his return.

During the journey he learned that General Dumas
had handed in his resignation, asking as a favor to be
employed as a private in another army; he had, consequently, been placed at the disposal of the Committee
of Public Safety, and was on his way to Nantes when
Marceau met him on the Clisson road.

At eight o'clock in the evening, the carriage containing the two generals entered Paris.

Marceau and his friend parted on Place du Palais-
Égalité.

Marceau walked down Rue Saint-Honoré toward
Saint-Roch, stopped at number 366, and asked for
Citizen Robespierre.

"He is at the Théâtre de la Nation," replied a girl
of sixteen or eighteen; "but if you will come again in
two hours he will have returned."

"Robespierre at the Théâtre de la Nation! Aren't
you mistaken?"

"No, citizen."

"Very well, I will look for him there, and if I don't
find him I will return and wait for him here. This is
my name: Citizen General Marceau."

The Théâtre-Français had separated into two troupes:
Talma, accompanied by the patriot actors, had emigrated
to the Odéon. It was to that theatre, therefore, that
Marceau found his way, amazed to have to seek the
austere member of the Committee of Public Safety at a
place of amusement.

They were playing "The Death of Cæsar." He entered the balcony; a young man offered him a seat beside him in the front row. Marceau accepted it, hoping to see from there the man he sought.

The play had not begun; the audience seemed to be in a strange state of effervescence; laughter and signals were freely exchanged, and started, as from a sort of headquarters, from a group seated in the orchestra; that group dominated the theatre, and was itself dominated by a single man: that man was Danton.

Beside him, speaking when he was silent, holding their peace when he spoke, were Camille-Desmoulins, his fanatical worshipper, Philippaux, Hérault de Séchelles, and Lacroix, his apostles.

It was the first time that Marceau had found himself in the presence of that Mirabeau of the people. He would have recognized him by his loud voice, his imperious gestures, his lordly brow, even if his name had not been pronounced several times by his friends.

We ask indulgence while we say a few words as to the state of the different factions into which the Convention was divided. They are essential to a proper understanding of the scene which follows.

The Commune and Mountain had joined forces to bring about the revolution of the 31st of May. The Girondins, after having tried in vain to effect a federation of the provinces, had fallen, almost undefended, in the midst of those who had chosen them and who simply did not dare to shelter them in the days of their proscription. Before the 31st of May, the power was nowhere; after the 31st of May they felt the necessity of joining forces in order to make prompt action possible. The Assembly possessed the most extensive power; a faction had taken possession of the Assembly; a few men swayed that faction; naturally, the power was in the hands of those men. The Committee of Public Safety, up to the 31st of May, had been made up of neutral members of the Convention; the time for its renewal arrived, and the extreme *Montagnards* made places for themselves upon it. Barrère remained as a representative of the former committee, but Robespierre was chosen a member; Saint-Just, Collot d'Herbois, and Billaud-Varennes, supported by him, put down their colleagues, Hérault de Séchelles and Robert Lindet; Saint-Just undertook the duty of surveillance, Couthon that of softening down propositions that were too violent in tone; Billaud-Varennes and Collot d'Herbois managed the proconsulates of the departments; Carnot attended to the department of war, Cambon to the finances, Prieur (de la Côte-d'Or) and Prieur (de la Marne) to internal and administrative affairs; and Barrère, who soon joined them, became the daily orator of the party. As for Robespierre, he had no defined functions, but exercised a general oversight of the whole, commanding that political body as the head commands the material body and makes every member act in obedience to its will.

In that party the Revolution was incarnate; it was bent upon carrying out the Revolution with all its consequences, so that the people might some day enjoy all its results.

That party had to contend against two others: one wished to outdo it, the other to hold it back. Those two parties were: —

The Commune, represented by Hébert.

The Mountain, represented by Danton.

In "Père Duchesne" Hébert popularized obscenity of speech; insult followed the victims and laughter the exe-

cutions. In a short time it made tremendous progress.
The Bishop of Paris and his vicars abjured Christianity;
the Catholic worship was replaced by the worship of
Reason, the churches were closed; Anacharsis Clootz
became the apostle of the new goddess. The Committee
of Public Safety took fright at the power of this ultra-
revolutionary faction, which they thought had fallen
with Marat, and which rested on immorality and atheism; Robespierre undertook to attack it single-handed.
On December 5, 1793, he defied it from the tribune;
and the Convention, which had perforce applauded the
abjurations at the demand of the Commune, decreed, at
the demand of Robespierre, who also had a religion of
his own to establish, that *all violence and all measures
contrary to liberty of worship were forbidden.*

Danton, in the name of the moderate portion of the
Mountain, demanded the overthrow of the revolutionary
government; the "Vieux Cordelier," edited by Camille
Desmoulins, was the organ of the party. The Committee of Public Safety, that is to say, the dictatorship,
was created, in its view, only to repress within and conquer without; and as the committee had been repressed
within and beaten on the frontier, it — that is, the party
led by Danton — demanded that a power which had
become useless should be shattered in order that it
might not subsequently become dangerous; the Revolution had pulled down, the Dantonists wished to rebuild
on ground that had not been cleared.

These were the three factions by which the Convention was torn in the early days of 1794, when the action
of our narrative takes place. Robespierre accused Hébert
of atheism and Danton of corruption; he was accused by
them of ambition, and the word *dictator* began to be
whispered.

Such, then, was the condition of affairs when Marceau, as we have said, saw Danton for the first time, as he was using the orchestra for a tribune, and tossing words of weighty import to those who surrounded him. The play was "The Death of Cæsar;" the word had been passed to the Dantonists; they were all present at the perform- ance, and, at a signal from their leader, they were to signify the application of these lines to Robespierre:

> Oui, que César soit grand, mais que Rome soit libre.
> Dieux! maîtresse de l'Inde, esclave aux bords du Tibre,
> Qu'importe que son nom commande à l'univers,
> Et qu'on l'appelle reine alors qu'elle est aux fers !
> Qu'importe à ma patrie, aux Romains que tu braves,
> D'apprendre que César a de nouveaux esclaves !
> Les Persans ne sont pas·nos plus fiers ennemis;
> Il en est de plus grands.   Je n'ai pas d'autre avis.[1]

And that is why Robespierre, who had been warned by Saint-Just, was at the Théâtre de la Nation that evening; for he realized what a weapon in the hands of his enemies the charge they made against him would be, if they succeeded in popularizing it.

But Marceau looked in vain for him in that bril- liantly lighted hall, where the line of the boxes alone remained in a sort of half-darkness, because of the pro- truding of the galleries above them; and his eyes, fatigued by the vain search, returned constantly to the

---

[1] Ay, let Cæsar, if you will, be great, but let Rome be free.
Ye gods! of all the Indies mistress, but on Tiber's banks a slave,
What boots it that her name doth sway the universe,
And that she 's called a queen, when she with chains is laden ?
What boots it to my country, to the Romans whom you defy,
To learn that Cæsar hath new slaves ?
The Persians are not our most arrogant foes;
There are greater than they.   I say no more.

group in the orchestra, whose noisy conversation attracted
the attention of the whole audience.

"I saw our dictator to-day," said Danton. "They
undertook to make peace between us."

"Where did you meet?"

"At his rooms; I had to climb the Incorruptible's
three flights."

"What did you say to each other?"

"I said that I was fully aware of the Committee's
hatred of me, but that I did not fear it. He answered
that I was wrong, that they had no evil intentions with
respect to me, but that we must have an understanding."

"An understanding! an understanding! that would
be very well with people who act in good faith."

"That is just the answer I made him; at that he drew
in his lips and wrinkled his forehead. I continued:
'Of course the royalists must be put down; but we must
strike no blows except such as will do some good, and
not confound the innocent with the guilty.'—'Why,
who told you,' retorted Robespierre, sharply, 'that any
innocent man has been put to death?'—'What do
you say to that? no innocent men put to death!' I
cried, turning to Hérault de Séchelles, who was with
me; and I came away."

"Was Saint-Just there?"

"Yes."

"What did he say?"

"He ran his hand through his fine black hair, and
from time to time arranged the knot of his cravat like
Robespierre's."

Marceau's neighbor, whose head was resting on his
hands, started and uttered the sort of hissing noise that
comes from between the clinched teeth of a man who is
holding himself back; Marceau paid little heed to him,

and turned his attention once more to Danton and his friends.

"The coxcomb!" said Camille Desmoulins, referring to Saint-Just; "he has so high an opinion of himself that he carries his head respectfully on his shoulders, like the blessed sacrament."

Marceau's neighbor removed his hands, and Marceau recognized the gentle, beautiful face of Saint-Just, pale with anger.

He rose and drew himself up to his full height.

"I will make you carry yours like a Saint Denis, Desmoulins!" he exclaimed.

Thereupon he turned and left the balcony, the people standing aside to let him pass.

"Well, well! who would have supposed he was so near?" laughed Danton. "Faith, the package reached its address."

"By the way, Danton," said Philippaux, "have you seen Laya's pamphlet against you?"

"What say you? Laya writes pamphlets? Let him rewrite the 'Friend of the Laws.' I should like right well to read it, — the pamphlet, I mean."

"Here it is."

Philippaux handed him a pamphlet.

"And he signed it, *pardieu!* Why, he does n't know, it seems, that if he does n't hide in my cellar they 'll cut off his head."

"Hush! hush! the curtain is rising."

The word *hush!* passed from mouth to mouth through the hall; but a young man who was not in the plot continued to carry on a private conversation, although the actors were on the stage. Danton put out his hand, touched him with his finger, and said, with courtesy, in which there was a slight admixture of irony: —

"Citizen Arnault, let me listen as if they were playing 'Marius at Minturnæ.'"

The young author knew too much not to respect a
request conveyed in those terms; he held his peace, and
the most absolute silence made it possible for every one
to listen to one of the worst plays that ever was put
upon the stage, — "The Death of Cæsar."

But notwithstanding that silence, it was evident that
no particularity in the little conspiracy we have described
had forgotten the purpose for which he had come.
Glances were exchanged, signals became more frequent
as the actors approached the passage which was to call
forth the explosion.

"It 's in Scene III.," Danton whispered to Camille.

And he was repeating the lines with the actors, as if
to hasten their delivery, when this passage occurred,
immediately preceding that for which they were
waiting: —

> César, nous attendions de ta clémence auguste
> Un don plus précieux, une faveur plus juste,
> Au-dessus des États donnés par ta bonté.
>
> CÉSAR.
> Qu'oses-tu demander, Cimber?
>
> CIMBER.
> La liberté! [1]

Three salvoes of applause greeted the words.

[1] Cæsar, we look to thy great clemency
For a more precious gift, a juster favor,
Above the States bestowed by thy kind heart.

CÆSAR.
What dar'st thou ask, O Cimber!

CIMBER.
Liberty!

22

"All goes well," said Danton.

He half rose from his seat.

Talma began: —

"Oui, que César soit grand, mais que Rome soit libre — "

Danton stood erect, casting about him the glance that a general casts over his army, assuring himself that every man is at his post, when suddenly his eyes rested on a certain point in the hall. The front of a box was raised; Robespierre protruded his sharp-featured, livid face. The eyes of the two enemies met, and could not look away from each other; there was in Robespierre's eyes all the irony of triumph, all the insolence of security. For the first time Danton felt a cold perspiration start out all over his body. He forgot the signal he was to give; the lines passed without applause or murmurs; he fell back beaten; the front of the box was raised, and all was said. The *guillotineurs* carried the day over the *Septembriseurs:* 93 imposed a spell upon 92.

Marceau, whose mind was engrossed by something very different from the tragedy, was perhaps the only one who witnessed, without understanding it, the scene we have described, which lasted only a few seconds. He had time, however, to recognize Robespierre; he rushed from the balcony, and arrived in the corridor in time to meet him.

He was as calm and cool as if nothing had happened. Marceau accosted him, and mentioned his name. Robespierre offered him his hand; Marceau, yielding to his first impulse, withheld his own. A bitter smile passed over Robespierre's lips.

"What do you want of me?" he asked.

"An interview of a few moments."

" Here, or at my house ? "

" At your house. "

" Come, then. "

And the two men, agitated by such widely different emotions, walked away, side by side: Robespierre, calm and indifferent; Marceau, excited and curious.

So this was the man who held Blanche's destiny in his hands; the man of whom he had heard so much, whose incorruptibility alone was evident, but whose popularity could not but seem a problem. In truth, he had made use of none of the methods employed by his predecessors to gain popularity. He had neither the enthralling eloquence of Mirabeau, nor the paternal firmness of Bailly, nor the sublime impetuosity of Danton, nor the obscene arts of Hébert; if he worked for the people, he did it secretly, and without rendering an account of his work to the people. Amid the general levelling of language and costume, he had retained his polished speech and his fashionable dress;[1] in fact, he seemed to take as much pains to hold himself above the common herd as others took to mingle with it; and one would readily understand, at first sight, that that singular being must be either an idol or a victim of the multitude: he was both.

They reached the house. A narrow staircase led them to a room on the third floor; Robespierre opened the door. A bust of Rousseau, a table on which the " Con-

---

[1] Robespierre's usual attire is so well known that it has become almost proverbial. On the 20th Prairial, the day of the Feast of the Supreme Being, whose pontiff he was, he was dressed in a blue coat, a waistcoat of embroidered muslin over pink; black satin breeches, white silk stockings, and shoes with buckles completed the costume. He wore the same coat when he was carried to the scaffold.

trat Social " and " Émile " lay open, a commode and a few chairs were the only furniture of the room. But the greatest neatness prevailed everywhere.

Robespierre saw the effect produced on Marceau by the sight.

" This is Cæsar's palace," he said, with a smile; " what have you to ask the dictator ? "

" The pardon of my wife, condemned to death by Carrier."

" Your wife, condemned by Carrier ! the wife of Marceau, the republican of the days of antiquity ! the Spartan soldier ! What is Carrier doing at Nantes, pray ? "

" Atrocious things."

Marceau thereupon drew an outline of the picture we have placed before the reader's eyes. Robespierre, during his recital, twisted about on his chair without interrupting; at last Marceau came to an end.

" So that is how I am always to be understood," said Robespierre, in a hoarse voice, — for his emotion was so great as to effect that change in his tone, — " wherever my eyes are not present to see and my hand to check useless carnage ! There is enough blood that it is abso- lutely necessary to shed, and we are not at the end of it yet."

" But about my wife's pardon, Robespierre ? "

Robespierre took a sheet of white paper.

" Her maiden name ? "

" Why ? "

" It is necessary for me to establish her identity."

" Blanche de Beaulieu."

Robespierre dropped the pen he held.

" The daughter of the Marquis de Beaulieu, the leader of the brigands ? "

"Blanche de Beaulieu, the Marquis de Beaulieu's daughter."

"How does it happen that she is your wife?"

Marceau told him the whole story.

"Young fool! young madman!" he exclaimed; "do you know — ?"

Marceau interrupted him.

"I did not come to ask for insults or advice; I ask you for her pardon. Will you give it me?"

"Marceau, will family ties, the influence of love, ever induce you to betray the Republic?"

"Never."

"Suppose you should find yourself face to face with the Marquis de Beaulieu, sword in hand?"

"I should fight him as I have already done."

"And suppose he should fall into your hands?"

Marceau reflected a moment.

"I would send him to you, and you yourself should be his judge."

"Do you swear to that?"

"On my honor."

Robespierre took up the pen once more.

"Marceau," he said, "you have had the good fortune to keep yourself pure in everybody's sight; I have known of you for a long time; I have long desired to see you."

Noticing Marceau's impatience, he wrote the first three letters of his name, then stopped.

"Listen: I ask you to give me five minutes now," he said, gazing earnestly at Marceau. "I give you a whole life in return for five minutes; they will be well paid for."

Marceau made a motion to signify that he would listen. Robespierre continued: —

"Some one has slandered me to you, Marceau; and yet you are one of the few men by whom I wish to be really known; for what care I for the judgment of men whom I do not esteem? Listen, then: three assemblies have in turn sought to guide the destiny of France, have been each represented by one man, and have accomplished the mission with which the age intrusted them: the Constituent, represented by Mirabeau, shook the foundations of the throne; the Legislative, incarnate in Danton, overthrew it. The work of the Convention is immense, for it is called upon to finish the work of tearing down and to begin that of rebuilding. I have in my mind a lofty aspiration, — to become the type of this period, as Mirabeau and Danton, respectively, were the types of theirs. In the history of the French people there will be three men, represented by the figures 91, 92, 93. If the Supreme Being gives me time to finish my work, my name will be above all names; I shall have done more than Lycurgus among the Greeks, than Numa at Rome, than Washington in America; for each of them had only a people just born to pacify, while I have an ancient, outworn society to regenerate. If I fall — spare me from uttering a blasphemy against you in my last hour, O my God! — if I fall before the allotted time, my name, which will have accomplished only the half of what it had to do, will retain the stain of blood that the other part would have wiped out; the Revolution will fall with it, and both will be calumniated. — That is what I had to say to you, Marceau; for I wish that certain men should, in any event, keep my name living and pure in their hearts, like the flame of the lamp in the tabernacle, and you are one of those men."

He finished writing his name.

" And now, here is your wife's pardon. You can go without even giving me your hand."

Marceau took his hand and wrung it; he tried to speak, but there were so many tears in his voice that he could not articulate a word, and Robespierre spoke first.

" Come, you must go; there is not a moment to lose. *Au revoir !* "

Marceau rushed downstairs; General Dumas was coming up as he went down.

" I have her pardon! " he cried, throwing himself into his arms; " I have her pardon. Blanche is saved! "

" Congratulate me too," his friend replied. " I have just been appointed commander-in-chief of the army of the Alps, and I have come to thank Robespierre."

They embraced. Marceau rushed into the street, hurried to Place du Palais-Égalité, where his carriage awaited him, ready to depart with the same speed with which it had brought him thither.

What a burden was lifted from his heart! what happiness awaited him! what joy after so much sorrow! His imagination plunged into the future; he anticipated the moment when, from the threshold of the dungeon, he should cry to his wife: " Blanche! you are free through my efforts; come, Blanche, and let your love and your kisses pay the debt of your life."

From time to time, however, a vague feeling of uneasiness passed through his mind, a sudden chill struck his heart. At such times he urged on the postilions, promised them money, gave it them lavishly and promised more; the wheels flew along the pavement; the horses devoured the road, and yet it seemed to him that they were hardly moving! Everywhere the relays were ready, there was no delay; everything seemed to partake of the excitement by which he was possessed. In a few hours he had left Versailles, Chartres, Le Mans, and La Flèche behind him; he saw Angers in the distance. Suddenly he felt a terrible, appalling shock: the carriage was overturned and broken. He rose, bruised and bleeding, cut the traces of one of the horses with his sword, leaped quickly upon him, galloped to the first posting station, hired a race-horse, and continued his journey even more swiftly than before.

At last he has passed Angers, espies Ingrande, rides through Varades and Ancenis. His horse is dripping with foam and blood; he passes Saint-Donatien, and Nantes is in sight, — Nantes! which contains his soul, his life, his future! A few moments more and he will be in the city. He reaches the gate; his horse falls exhausted in front of the Bouffays prison; he has arrived, so what matters it!

"Blanche! Blanche!"

"Two tumbrils just left the prison yard," said the turnkey; "she was on the first."

"Malediction!"

And Marceau darts away on foot, amid the people who are hurrying in vast throngs toward the public square. He overtakes the last of the two tumbrils; one of the condemned men recognizes him.

"Save her, general. I couldn't do it, and I was taken. *Vive le roi* and the good cause!"

It was Tinguy.

"Yes, yes!"

Marceau opens a path for himself; the crowd jostles and crushes him, but carries him on; he arrives on the square in the midst of the crowd; he is facing the scaffold, he waves his paper, shouting: —

"Pardon! pardon!"

At that moment the executioner, holding up a young girl's head by its long, fair hair, presented the hideous spectacle to the people; the horrified crowd turned away, for they fancied that it was vomiting torrents of blood! — Suddenly, from the midst of that silent multitude, a frenzied cry arose, in which all the human forces seemed to be concentrated.   Marceau had recognized, between the teeth of that head, the red rose he had given the young Vendean.

THE END.

www.ingramcontent.com/pod-product-compliance
Lightning Source LLC
Chambersburg PA
CBHW010854090426
42737CB00019B/3367